Together for a season:

All-age seasonal resources for Lent, Holy Week and Easter

Gill Ambrose, Peter Craig-Wild,
Diane Craven, Peter Moger

Edited by Gill Ambrose

 CHURCH HOUSE
PUBLISHING

Church House Publishing
Church House
Great Smith Street
London SW1P 3NZ
Tel: 020 7898 1451
Fax: 020 7898 1449

ISBN 978-0-7151-4063-5

Published 2007 by Church House Publishing.

Cover design by blue pig design ltd

Printed in England by The Cromwell Press Ltd, Trowbridge, Wiltshire

Contents

Easter

Foreword

Common Worship and other new forms of worship – with adults and children all giving praise together – have brought about little less than a revolution. *Together for a Season* is an exciting series of books that will transform things still further. There is something for everyone here. This material takes all ages seriously and uses all the senses – movement, sound, space and light – to provide an enriching experience for children who worship together with the whole community.

This pattern of worship and celebration builds on the wealth of the Christian tradition. A brief visit to Assisi at St Francistide or to Santiago da Compostela at the Feast of St James dramatically shows the visitor how these places have been shaped by centuries of Christian life and worship, shared by adults and children alike. It is not only the worship, but the sense of carnival and celebration, which touches every part of life. All this makes clear how the story of Jesus, as focused in the saints and those who have been touched by them, has fashioned the life of the wider community. It was something similar that St Francis captured when he pioneered the making of cribs for Christmastide.

The Church of England, showing a characteristic reticence, once treated its 'red letter days' and great seasonal feasts with much modesty. The arrival of *Lent, Holy Week and Easter* and *The Promise of his Glory* transformed this. *Common Worship: Times and Seasons* brings together material from these two classic volumes and new resources for the Christian Year. The new series *Together for a Season* will complement these riches, allowing parishes and other local Christian congregations to take this material into both homes and communities. These volumes indicate that Christian worship and life, adults and children are all entirely 'of a piece'. They form part of the seamless garment of Christ himself, which is his Church.

The 'pathways' through the seasons and sample services included in these volumes offer an opportunity to make connections between worship and living the gospel within every aspect of our lives. This will not displace the quiet celebration of our great feasts; it will complement that. It may, however, allow our own communities to echo some of the carnival already celebrated in other parts of the world.

And it will be a carnival where all worship together and celebrate together – at home, in church and in the community.

✠ Stephen Wakefield

Acknowledgements

The Scripture quotations contained herein are from The New Revised Standard Version of the Bible, Anglicized Edition, copyright © 1989, 1995 by the Division of Christian Education of the National Council of the Churches of Christ in the United States of America and are used by permission. All rights reserved.

The meditative Eucharist was developed by the Revd Paul Cudby. This service uses material from *Common Worship* which is copyright © The Archbishops' Council 2000.

The Liturgy around the Cross was developed by Diane Craven and Paul Howlett and uses material from *Common Worship* which is copyright © The Archbishops' Council 2000. Meditations in this liturgy are © Diane Craven 2005.

Prayers used on pages 62–3 are taken from *Easter Garden* by Nicola M. Slee, copyright © 1990. Used by permission of Zondervan.

'At the sepulchre' is taken from *The Passion of our Lord according to St John* by J. S. Bach, in a translation made by T. A. Lacey which is copyright © Novello & Co. Ltd, 1929, renewed 1957.

Prayers at the Easter Garden and prayers in the group materials for adults and children are copyright © Diane Craven 2005, 2006.

The quotation on page 124 is taken from *The Sorrowful Way: The mind of Christ, the path of discipleship and the Christian year* by Michael Perham, copyright © SPCK 1998, p.101.

'Now the green blade riseth': words by J. M. C. Crum, copyright © Oxford University Press 1928 from *The Oxford Book of Carols* and reproduced by permission.

Eight all-age worship ideas for Good Friday were created and developed by Ian Birkinshaw, St Michael-le-Belfrey, York and are copyright © Ian Birkinshaw. Used by permission.

The authors also wish to express their gratitude to the Parish of St Mildred, Addiscombe in Croydon, Diocese of Southwark, especially to Marie King and Meg Simmons for their inspiration and hard work in developing materials with the children in the parish.

Ideas for The Liturgy of Palm Sunday were supplied by Dr Anthony White and people of the parish of Cheveley, Diocese of Ely.

A Eucharist for Pentecost and the other Pentecost materials were written by Rachel Nicholls.

The authors wish to express their thanks to Alistair Daniel and Anna Ambrose for their contributions to the opening essay, 'Continuing to help the liturgy to live'. They are also grateful to Tracey Messenger, Commissioning Editor at Church House Publishing, for advice, encouragement and support throughout the writing process.

In addition, Peter Craig-Wild would like to thank:
- My wife, Dhoe, who lost days off and even holidays as I tried creatively to make time to get on with it!
- My sister Jacki and brother-in-law Dave, for the loan of their 'getaway' on Morecambe Bay where most of my part was written;
- John Marsh, who so willingly helped with the Lenten tree group material;
- Peter Moger, who contributed so willingly and so quickly on the Easter schedule and the essays on the Eucharistic Prayer;
- the people and worship leaders of St Mary's, Mirfield, so often the guinea pigs for half formed ideas.

Gill Ambrose wishes to thank her husband Tom for a great deal of time spent exploring and evaluating ideas, for unfailing encouragement, and for not complaining when she spent far too long sitting at the computer.

To them and many more …

THANK YOU

How to use this book

A companion to *Common Worship: Times and Seasons*

This is the second of a three-volume series of books created as a companion to *Common Worship: Times and Seasons* (T&S), the Church of England Liturgical Commission's directory of liturgical material for the seasons of the Christian year. If you have read and used the first volume, which provides material for Advent, Christmas and Epiphany, you can probably skip through this introduction quite quickly. If this is your first encounter with this material, however, you might want to take a bit of time to read on quite carefully.

The books in this three-volume companion provide ideas and suggestions for bringing to life the liturgical texts provided in *Times and Seasons*, both in formal worship and in groups for adults and children alike, as well as in the home and in outreach in the local community. The authors have taken as their starting point the assumption that worship and the Christian life are inclusive. There are times when it is appropriate for different groups of people to do things separately, and provision is made for this. There is material for groups of children and adults to use separately. But basically we belong together: we learn and teach one another, young and old, experienced and inexperienced, academic and practical alike. Each of the worked-out services provided ensures that there is something for everyone. Use is made of space, light and symbol as well as word and text. The rich tradition of Christian worship is drawn upon fully. Much of the material provided for use at home and in outreach is suitable for anyone to use and is specifically designed to work with mixed age groups.

Three seasons, one big idea

This second volume again explores three seasons: Lent, Holy Week and Easter. It is often said that Lent and Holy Week belong together and are in fact one season. While not wishing to dispute this, the change of pace that Holy Week marks as the season moves onwards is acknowledged in this book by giving it a section of its own. The intensity of observations during Holy Week is helpfully acknowledged by grouping these resources together. Nevertheless, it is important to emphasize that Lent, Holy Week and Easter are one big idea and form an enormously important cycle of experience for a three-month period of the year.

Three pathways

LENTEN TREE   HEAD, HANDS   STATIONS
               AND HEART   OF THE CROSS

Like the first volume, this book offers three pathways based on three ideas to help us explore different aspects of the suffering, death and resurrection of Jesus. The Stations of the Cross have been known for many centuries and will be quite familiar to some people. The Lenten tree mirrors the use of the Jesse tree, which constitutes one of the pathways through Advent, Christmas and Epiphany in the first volume. The Head, hands and heart theme emerges as a very potent way to explore the suffering of Christ and its message for us in the sufferings we do and will encounter in our lifetime as well as for exploring the triumph and glory of the risen Christ.

The Lenten tree

The use of the Lenten tree, like the Jesse tree in Advent, provides the possibility of an integrated pathway through Lent. Adding symbols on the key days throughout the season provides for a coherent, cumulative journey. The origins of the Lenten tree are not very clear: classic books tend to deal exclusively with its meaning rather than to explore its origins. Its use seems to have become popular in free church circles in the early 1990s, but Augustine of Hippo wrote about the Lenten cross as far back as the fourth century.

Head, hands and heart

This pathway seeks to provide opportunities to bring into harmony what we say with our lips, what we believe in our hearts and what we show forth in our lives. The Lenten journey and its disciplines are concerned with this work of integration. Through the practice of self-denial and prayer, through study and the opportunity to consider again God's call, we are making space for God to transform us and to write the law on our hearts.

Stations

A recognition of the importance of art and movement in worship has led in recent years to a new flourishing of the practice of the stations of the cross, and the extension of this practice to a broad range of Christian traditions. The themes of journey and pilgrimage emerge very strongly in the Lent and Easter seasons. *Times and Seasons* offers a set of stations of the cross drawn solely from biblical texts. It also offers a series of Stations of the Resurrection. This book offers an extension of this to the creation of more stations throughout Lent, with the opportunity of exploring the whole idea with some thoroughness.

Choose your pathway

The suggestion in the pages that follow is that churches might choose one of these pathways (the Lenten tree; Head, hands and heart or the Stations) as a visual liturgical focus for a particular year, using it from Ash Wednesday through to Pentecost as a centrepiece for visual aspects of the liturgy and exploring the word. This will require some imagination and a willingness to explore the potential of the symbols to the full.

The book therefore offers a choice of three pathways through the seasons. *This is a choice: no one should try to follow all three at once!* Each pathway provides material for worship, study, outreach and exploration at home from Ash Wednesday to Pentecost.

Sample services

In addition there are several services for significant occasions, using texts and suggestions from *Times and Seasons*. Each service uses the texts from the Liturgical Commission's book and is laid out in full in tabular form, to demonstrate the different layers to which we need to be sensitive in building a liturgy. The column headings, following the observations made in the introductory essay in the first volume, 'Living liturgy', by Peter Craig-Wild, are these:

Structure, movement and flow	Words/ text of the service	Multisensory aspects	Participation of the congregation

The services offered in this way for the period from Ash Wednesday to Pentecost are:

- A service for the beginning of Lent
- The Liturgy of Palm Sunday: Commemoration of the Lord's entry into Jerusalem
- The Easter Vigil: A service for Saturday evening
- The Easter Vigil: An all-night service with sleepover
- The Easter Liturgy from the Service of the Word onwards
- The Eucharist on Easter Day
- A service for Ascension Day
- A Eucharist for Pentecost

The structure

Following the introductory sections, the book divides into material for each of the three seasons: Lent, Holy Week and Easter. Each seasonal section is further subdivided into five:

1. **A seasonal introduction,** which describes for us the 'feel' of the season and provides some background to the way in which we celebrate.
2. **Stand-alone material,** which includes the fully laid out services, with their words and the suggestions for multisensory provision and participation by the congregation.
3. **The Lenten tree pathway,** with material to use in inclusive worship; material for use by groups of adults and groups for children; material to use at home and suggestions for outreach into the local community.

4. **The Head, hands and heart pathway,** with material to use in inclusive worship; material for use by groups of adults and groups for children; material to use at home and suggestions for outreach into the local community.

5. **The Stations pathway,** with material to use in inclusive worship; material for use by groups of adults and groups for children, material to use at home and suggestions for outreach into the local community.

How to use the material

The services

The worked-out services provide a model for the way in which material from *Times and Seasons* might be used. However, they are also designed to be used as they are by readers of this book. A warning, though – don't pick up the book on Saturday night and expect to be able to present these services the following morning! Each service has been planned to be as interactive and multisensory as possible. All the ideas are provided, but you will need to determine how to make them fit your circumstances. All the services can be used with large and small congregations alike, and in any sort of building, but you will need to think about how you do this, and who will be involved. Once you have used one or two of them, you will get the feel of how they work and you will then be able to take the material from *Times and Seasons* and build more services yourself on this model.

New Patterns for Worship

In preparing to plan worship in this way, it would also be helpful to read (or reread) the beginning of the book *New Patterns for Worship*. The first 50 pages of that book provide much helpful background and advice about planning services in this way, and might be regarded as a companion to the material we offer here.[1]

The pathways

You will need to choose just one pathway for any particular year. The pathway you choose will then determine a route through the three seasons, with ideas for use of the main symbol of the pathway as a focus around which worship is built for much of the season. Material for worship is complemented by group study material, things to do at home, ideas for children's groups and for outreach.

The choice of one particular pathway does not mean that other symbols may not be used at all. In particular, some of the stand-alone worship ideas associated with a particular pathway might work well in some other context.

Music, hymns and songs

Music is important in worship, and a section at the beginning of the book provides ideas about how music can be used to enhance the way in which we celebrate the Eucharistic Prayer in particular. It might also be helpful to read the introductory essay 'Living liturgy' (see page 1 in Volume 1) for further valuable ideas on the importance of music in the enhancement of the liturgy. Throughout the books, suggestions are made for appropriate hymns and songs for acts of worship, and sometimes to sing in groups. Except where they are difficult to find, or they are only in one particular book, this book does not provide an indication of where they are to be found. There are now so many Christian hymn and song books that this would be an almost impossible task: it is certainly beyond the scope of this book. If you are familiar with your own collection of books, you will probably know where to find most of them in any case. If you need help in locating them, then the RSCM publication, *Sunday by Sunday*, which provides suggestions for music for worship for every Sunday and festival day of the year, might be helpful. It is published quarterly by RSCM, so it is very accurate. The address from which it can be ordered can be found in the Resources section at the back of the book. A publication that does the same kind job, but in a single volume rather than being published each quarter, is *Sing God's Glory: Hymns for Sundays and Holy Days, Years A, B and C.*[2]

In the sample services throughout the book, the title of a particular hymn or song is given only where that particular hymn contributes to the shape and flow of the service. Quite often the worship planner is simply advised that a hymn or song may be sung. It is assumed then that you will choose your own. Even the prepared services in the book therefore provide plenty of scope for music to reflect your own tradition. It also ought to go without saying that, where a hymn is suggested and you know it would be impossible to sing in your situation, then the sensible thing to do will be to change it. But do replace it with something appropriate! And don't just cut it out because you don't know it. Many new hymns and songs are not very difficult to learn, and it does us all good to learn something new from time to time.

Collects

In the sample services throughout the book, where a collect for the day is used, it has been drawn from the *Common Worship: Additional Collects* (see Resources). This is a new collection of contemporary collects written to provide modern prayers for worship in the Church of England. The new prayers offer an alternative to, and complement, the original collects in *Common Worship*. If you wish to substitute what is suggested with one of the original *Common Worship* collects, then of course you should do so.

The material for groups

Material is provided for groups of adults and children. The material provided is intended to be enough for about an hour for children's groups, and slightly longer, perhaps approaching an hour and a half, for adult groups. However, all the material is designed to be used flexibly so you can add to or subtract from the given material if that is what your situation demands. The children's material is not banded by age and is almost all suitable to use in mixed age groups or by any age group.

Schools

There is a good deal of material in this book that is equally well suited to use in a school as in a church. A great deal of the material for use at home would be equally at home in the community that is a primary school classroom! Some of the worship resources would also be useful in school collective worship.

Resources

There is a resources section at the end of the book on page 240. This includes full details of all the books and other resources mentioned throughout the text.

Note on abbreviations

Material has been used from these main sources, which have been abbreviated as follows:
- CW: *Common Worship: Services and Prayers for the Church of England*, Church House Publishing, 2000;
- DP: *Common Worship: Daily Prayer*, Church House Publishing, 2005;
- CI: *Common Worship: Christian Initiation*, Church House Publishing, 2006;
- NP: *New Patterns for Worship*, Church House Publishing, 2002;
- T&S: *Common Worship: Times and Seasons*, Church House Publishing, 2006.

Icons used in the book

 The CD-ROM icon appears wherever text is also available to be downloaded from the CD-ROM.

CD-ROM contents

A Concluding Rite for the Sunday before Lent

A service for the beginning of Lent

A near-silent Eucharist

List of the Stations of the Cross

The Liturgy of Palm Sunday

Dramatized Palm Gospels

Dramatized readings for Good Friday

D-I-Y Stations of the Cross instructions sheet

A liturgy around the cross

A Good Friday Stations activity and service

The Easter Vigil: A service for Saturday evening

The Easter Vigil: An all-night service with sleepover

The Easter Liturgy from the Liturgy of the Word
   onwards

The Eucharist on Easter Day

A service for Ascension Day

A Eucharist for Pentecost

A Gathering Rite and a fully worked-out Service of
   the Word: The risen Jesus meets us in the waters
   of baptism

A Gathering Rite for the Second Sunday of Easter:
   The risen Jesus meets us in the joy of the
   resurrection

A Gathering Rite for a Eucharist or a Service of the
   Word: The risen Jesus meets us in the light of the
   resurrection

The risen Jesus meets us in the breaking of the bread

A Gathering Rite and fully worked-out Eucharist
   that might be used on Easter 6 (Years A & B) and
   Easter 5 (Year C): The risen Jesus meets us in the
   Word

A Gathering Rite for the Seventh Sunday of Easter:
   The risen Jesus meets us in each other

Photographs and illustrations

Continuing to help the liturgy live

Introduction

The first volume of *Together for a Season* began with an piece entitled 'Living liturgy' in which we were reminded that:

Just as a symphony is far more than a collection of notes on the stave, so liturgy is far more than texts. The conductor of the orchestra has to interpret the score and draw the best from the musicians in order to bring it to life. Worship planners too have to take the texts and, using whatever resources are available, construct a symphony of worship where the words jump off the page and resonate with our experience, bringing liturgy into life and life into liturgy.[1]

In that essay we noted that, within the liturgy, there are several strands and opportunities not just for words to speak to us, but for multisensory aspects of worship to communicate also. We proposed a fourfold approach to liturgical planning. Given the structure and the texts in the published service books, we proposed that, in service planning, we give attention also to the inclusion of multisensory experiences within the act of worship, and to the participation of the congregation. It was proposed therefore that a sheet for planning a service might have the following columns.

Structure, movement and flow	Words/ text of the service	Multisensory aspects	Participation of the congregation

Liturgy and drama

In this second volume, we develop these ideas further by looking at the relationship between liturgy and drama. We consider how, in some ways, liturgy is drama. In the first section, 'Learning from medieval drama', Anna Ambrose describes some of the dramatic celebrations that marked Holy Week and Easter in the early centuries of the Christian Church. She goes on to explore the close relationship between drama and liturgy in the early Middle Ages and the ways in which liturgical drama contributed to the development of the Holy Week and Easter liturgies we know today. There are those who dismiss the use of drama in the liturgy as an unwelcome modern invention, but we have here a testimony to its ancient place within the liturgy and as part of the development of liturgy.

In the second section, 'The drama of the Eucharistic Prayer', we explore how leaders of liturgies can learn from drama and from performance techniques, and use multisensory elements and music to enhance the drama of the prayer itself.

1: Learning from medieval liturgical drama

Anna Ambrose

Angels	Whom do you seek in the sepulchre, followers of Christ?	*Quem queritis in sepulchro christicolae?*
The Marys	**Jesus of Nazareth who was crucified, oh inhabitants of heaven**	***Ihesum nazarenum crucifixum o celocolae.***
Angels	He is not here, he has risen as he predicted; go and say that he has risen.	*Non est hic, surrexit sicut predixerat; Ite nunciate quia surrexit dicentes.*
The Marys	**Alleluia, the Lord is risen today; Christ the strong lion, the Son of God has risen**	***Alleluia, resurrexit dominus hodie; resurrexit leo fortis christus filius dei.***
Angels	Thank the Lord, say eia.	*Deo gracias, dicite eia.*

This dialogue between the Marys and the angels at Christ's tomb, was sung before the Introit to Mass on Easter Sunday in early tenth-century France. Even as a simple exchange between members of the clergy, the liturgical purpose of this dialogue, known as the *Quem queritis*, can be understood. The term *christicolae* refers not just to the biblical Marys or those speaking their words: its implied meaning is '*all* followers of Christ'. Humankind's collective culpability for the crucifixion is highlighted, and the direction to go and announce the resurrection applies to all.

By the late tenth century in England, the place of this dialogue has moved to the end of the service of Matins on Easter Sunday – at dawn. If we think in terms of the Gospel account of the visit of the Marys to the tomb, a new parallel emerges:

After the sabbath, as the first day of the week was dawning, Mary Magdalene and the other Mary went to see the tomb (Matthew 28.1).

This is a wonderful example of the belief in the here and now (*hic et nunc*) of liturgy, and its representative power. Of course, this is best known in terms of the Eucharist. Medieval theologians and philosophers such as Amalarius of Metz and Honorius of Autun, writing about the Eucharist, take the starting point of St Gregory's description that, in the Eucharist, 'one thing is made of visible and invisible'. They and their followers interpret the Eucharist as an elaborate representation of the life of Christ with multiple layers of meaning and, or course, real presence. These same beliefs about the potential significance of the liturgy also clearly underpin that Easter morning dialogue *Quem queritis*.

The dialogue is to be seen as an actual representation of past events in the present, for the purpose of future salvation – the announcement of the resurrection is here and now. In the dialogue, we therefore see something far more than a dramatic interruption to the Easter liturgy. This is a 'real-time' recreation of the moment when the Marys learn of the resurrection. It is intended to involve and inspire the congregation. The 'performance directions' contained in two English manuscripts (The *Regularis Concordia*, English monastic guidelines, and an early eleventh-century liturgical manuscript from Winchester) describing symbolic clothing and a physical display of empty grave-cloths to the congregation, only reinforce this interpretation.

Throughout the following centuries, the various additions and alterations that were made to the dialogue continue to illustrate the spiritual intentions and theological beliefs of the liturgists. The addition of new material, be it the lamenting of the Marys before the central dialogue or the Easter sequence after it, heightened the impact of the resurrection on the congregation. The same can be said for the two further biblical episodes that were added in some cases, the race of Peter and John to the tomb and Mary Magdalene's encounter with Christ in the garden.

Such cases of 'dramatic liturgy' are far from limited to the Easter *Quem queritis* dialogue. Perhaps the most similar are representations of the shepherds' arrival at the manger. Taking place early on Christmas morning, the timing of the representation again seems to mirror the biblical account of the episode and indicate a sense of liturgical here and now – *hic et nunc*. In many cases, as the birth of Christ is announced, a crib is uncovered – physical evidence of the nativity is presented to the congregation just as the resurrection is demonstrated by the display of empty grave-cloths at Easter. And in some instances, the representation is integrated into the surrounding liturgy to the extent that the text of the *Venite*, which follows, becomes a direction to the congregation to 'come and praise the Lord'.

Other ritual dramas can be found across Europe that recreate the events of the festivals on which they took place. The most common is the visit of the Magi to the Christ-child at Epiphany (*Officium Stellae* – the Star Service) but other examples range from the Flight into Egypt on Holy Innocents' Day (complete with live donkeys and spears being thrown indoors) to the meeting of Christ and the apostles on the road to Emmaus. All demonstrate a concern to transform the congregation into active participants in the recreation of the biblical episode.

These festive extensions to the 'normal' liturgy tell us a great deal about the medieval liturgists' theological beliefs. But what light can they shed on the development of the services in which many still participate today? There is no reason to suppose that the concern for the effect of the liturgy on the congregation, ordained or lay, was limited to these festive occasions; we must, surely, assume that it is demonstrated to such an extent that it was fundamental to the medieval liturgy. The same can be said for the representational or allegorical potential of liturgy. Similarly, the liturgies that take place in our churches shouldn't be, and hopefully aren't, seen as something the clergy do to an audience or perform in front of their passive congregations. We can use the knowledge of *Quem queritis* to suggest an approach to liturgy that looks for meaning beyond words in the present and seeks moments that involve, transport and transform.

Anna Ambrose studied medieval music and liturgy in the University of Cambridge

2: The drama of the Eucharistic Prayer

With every wave of liturgical revision there have been cries for a 'Eucharistic Prayer that can be used with children present'. During a discussion about how to engage children more effectively during the Eucharistic Prayer, conversation moved on to how we can actually engage anyone at all during what was termed the 'long, boring bit'. It seems a tragedy that the Eucharistic Prayer, so central to worship in so many churches each week, has come to be seen as 'that long, boring bit'. It ought to be a climax of the service rather than a let-down. So what might we do to remedy the situation?

Here we offer three different suggestions of ways to help this prayer to become the live offering of a congregation of all ages.

In the first piece, professional actor and storyteller, Alastair Daniel, shows how performance skills and techniques can help the President. In the second piece, Peter Craig-Wild encourages us to be aware of the multisensory aspects of the prayer and then Peter Moger suggests ways of using music to involve the congregation.

Performance

Alastair Daniel

As I have worked with young people over the years I have sought ways to engage the audience as co-performers with the storyteller. In this piece the liturgy will be seen as a performance act in which the president takes on the role of storyteller and the people gathered are the co-performers. Although, when the request has sometimes been made for a Eucharistic Prayer 'when children are present', it may be helpful to remind ourselves that *presence* does not necessarily imply *participation*. Yet *Common*

Worship tells us that in the Eucharist the whole congregation is the celebrant, though they are led by the president: this celebration is essentially a community activity.

So I look at how the president might try to engage the whole congregation in active worship by:

- developing confidence (both in children's participation and in the liturgy itself);
- making contact with the congregation;
- making the narrative clear.

Developing confidence in relationships and in the liturgical community

We are constantly told that young people have a short attention span, closer to three minutes than to ten. Yet those of us who regularly tell stories to children frequently experience a different reality. Such experiences have convinced me that the greatest enemy of maintaining the attention of young people is the assumption that it will be lost. Of course, there will be occasions when this is difficult; times when perhaps in the normal course of events we might choose not to tell them a story because they are tired or distressed. Nevertheless, if they are present in a church service, the action will proceed whether they are ready or not: it is at these times that children should simply be allowed to 'be' and busy bags or liturgy boxes, which are gaining in popularity, may provide the parent with a useful ally here.

However, the lesson from storytelling is that the teller knows that the story is for the whole group gathered together, and the group knows it too. Where the congregation is characterized by a sense of community that embraces all, focused on worship led by a president who is sensitive to the whole gathering, children will often be captured by this relationship. There is no style of worship, no Eucharistic Prayer, that is 'child friendly' in and of itself; rather, liturgy will be accessible to children of all ages through the way the leader relates to the community. If what is offered is a true reflection of the whole community (including its youngest members) and its desire and need to approach the living God, then it should engage the children. The role here is not just for the president but for the whole community.

Establishing contact with the gathered community

Making contact begins with where people sit or gather as they enter church. In the case of children, this may be at the beginning of the service or later if any children's groups enter partway through the liturgy. Sight is the principal sense through which we communicate and yet time and again those with young children are directed towards the back of the worship space where visibility is worst and connection between the president and the people is most distant. If children are to be engaged, they need to be able to see and be seen. Young children and those caring for them should be encouraged to be in places where they feel part of what is happening and adults should not feel inhibited from allowing young ones to stand on their laps or on the pew in order to see, or from taking a child into the aisle so that they can better see.

However, making contact is not simply an issue of being able to see. We make sense of encounters through clues in people's non-verbal communication. We know that we are approved of when someone smiles and we know we are receiving disapproval when we are frowned at. In order to participate in the worship of God, children need non-verbal cues that this story is theirs to hear and participate in. While it is true that the eucharistic president should avoid putting too much of his or her own personality into the work of presiding, we must remember that the president is the principal storyteller, enabling the liturgy to speak for people of all ages. In this context the words and actions of the president are not exempt from the general norms of human communication, which are non-verbal. For those familiar with Godly Play (see Resources, pp. 240–41) there may be much to learn from the role of the storyteller in this medium. While there is no eye contact as the story is told, nevertheless the storyteller is fully in touch with the 'congregation', drawing them into the action through words and gesture.

And at points in the action when the president invites people to respond verbally, when the arms are held in an open gesture 'embracing' the congregation, the president needs to make contact with those with whom he or she is sharing this story. Perhaps it is because we have become too wedded to the words of the text that this can be a problem. Here the adults in the congregation have a role to play. If we all managed without our books, we would not notice when the odd word was out of place and we would

all listen much more intently, thereby drawing in the non-readers with us, and working together in a more balanced partnership.

One prayer with different parts

The president of the Eucharist has a difficult role. The House of Bishops' report on eucharistic presidency suggests that

The Eucharistic president is to be a sign and focus of the unity, holiness, catholicity and apostolicity of the Church, and the one who has primary responsibility that the Church's four marks are expressed, actualised and made visible in the eucharistic celebration.[2]

As a storyteller I have to make the narrative as clear as possible, distinguishing between plot, characterization and my own comments on the story. This is achieved through changes in posture, movement, gaze and voice. In order that the marks of the Church are 'expressed, actualized and made visible' in the Eucharist, there must be distinguishing marks that make clear the different elements of the rite. During the Ministry of the Sacrament this responsibility falls almost exclusively upon the president and his/her skills as the 'teller' of our story at the holy table.

Within the Ministry of the Sacrament the president will need to differentiate between:
- dialogue with the congregation;
- acclamation and praise to God;
- the institution narrative (which can be further broken down to third and first person narrative) spoken before God on behalf of the people;
- invocation of the Holy Spirit;
- petition to God.

It is only during dialogue with the congregation, when there is direct address to the people, that the president should allow his/her eyes to scan. In this way the opening dialogue with the congregation and the invitation to communion create clear markers of inclusion either side of the Eucharistic Prayer itself. During the opening dialogue, the president has open arms, moving these down (the *orans* or praying position) as he or she addresses God in praise – the eyes should correspondingly move away from making contact with the people gathered; even if the president is to look away from the text, there should be clear visual cues that these words are a prayer addressed to God, not an exchange with the people.

If it is local practice to lift the bread and the wine during the dominical words and the president focuses on the elements, this associates this bread and this wine with that of the narrated past events; indeed, it connects those events with the material stuff of 'the here and the now' (this necessitates the learning of the dominical words, but this is not a large piece of text). The same principle may apply to the prayer for God's Spirit over the gifts, if they are elevated.

Acclamations

The acclamations need particular consideration. The president's introduction is itself acclamatory: these are opening words that are completed by the people and directed towards God. Eucharistic Prayer D has acclamations throughout the prayer (*V: This is his/our story; R: This is our song, Hosanna in the highest*) and this repeated refrain certainly makes it a prayer for young children to participate in verbally. They will do so, however, only if they are led enthusiastically and spontaneously by the rest of the congregation and the president needs to beware of addressing the congregation in the opening versicle, thereby encouraging them to respond to him/her rather than to God.

President as principal storyteller

The principle is simple: in telling our story, the president as principal storyteller must make the various elements of the narrative clear so that the rhythms of participation and contemplation are felt by even those too young to read the words. We are not concerned with a 'perfect' performance but in drawing everyone into a liturgy that communicates through both word and action.

Ritual movements

It is often the case that clergy learn a set of ritual movements (in whatever tradition) from their first incumbent: priest to priest. These can include small gestures that have personal significance to the individual in his/her role as the president of the Eucharist. However, when these gestures are in the view of the people, they cease to be private and those who preside at the holy table should give serious thought as to whether these actions really draw the congregation in to the action or simply

obscure the central actions of taking, blessing, breaking and sharing.

The use of the term 'performance' to describe worship can lead to the impression that this is a search for ritual perfection – such thoughts ignore the nature of the performance and the performers themselves. The whole community, youngest to oldest, performs this story together and, until we as people achieve perfection in ourselves, the liturgy will always be less than perfect. But this performance analogy does draw attention to how things are said and done, and the need for the president to connect with every one of his or her co-performers – the rhythms of this story that together we tell will then speak to all of what has been, what is, and what is to come.

Alastair Daniel is an actor and storyteller.

Multisensory aspects

Peter Craig-Wild

Because of our particular place in the history of the western Church, the main point of interest in the Eucharistic Prayer has been the textual content and, consequently, on how that text is performed. However, as Alastair Daniel points out, it is the non-verbal elements that are often the most notable and memorable, not just by children but by the whole congregation. In his work on multiple intelligences,[3] Howard Gardiner pointed out that fewer than a quarter of us have a predominantly auditory way of receiving and giving information: over three-quarters of us acquire information predominantly in other ways. Given these figures, it is astonishing that so much emphasis is placed upon spoken and written text in worship and so I want to explore ways in which the Eucharistic Prayer might be made more sensually interesting, not by creating unnecessary complex ritual, staging or movement, but by taking the meaning of the text and realities to which it points, and communicating them in an appropriate multisensory way.

- Let's begin with **movement**. So much of our worship is in a fixed place. We arrive at church – we sit in our pews – and we are fixed there. But why not move the whole congregation to gather around the holy table for the Eucharistic Prayer, reminding us that, regardless of age, we are all celebrants just as much as the president?

- The first real act in the Liturgy of the Sacrament is the **Preparation of the Table**. St Augustine reminded his congregations that, when the bread and wine were placed on the altar, it was they themselves who were being put there. Having the table prepared by different members of the congregation each week deepens the stake that each participant has in what follows. One might bring the white cloth, another the corporal, others candles, others the vessels, etc.
- **Lighting** is a cheap and easy way to enhance atmosphere. This could relate to movement if there has been some; switching lights on as we gather around the table or using (coloured?) lights to highlight the bread and wine (rather than the president).
- **Posture**, or more accurately change in posture, can affect mood and is also worth considering. While the rubrics of the Eucharistic Prayers all suggest that the same posture should be maintained by the congregation throughout the prayer, there is no reason why the congregation should not bow when the president bows. This also encourages the congregation to watch the president and the action rather than having their heads in books.
- **Symbols** needs rescuing from the emasculating prisons of churchmanship. Rather than having incense swung in a thurible, it could be placed in a bowl on the hot charcoal during the Sanctus and again during the sung doxology ('Blessing and honour…'); sanctuary bells could be rung as the congregation sings and so on.

The key principle is that whatever is done should enhance rather than distract from the meaning of the prayer and enable its truth to be embraced in a non-verbal way.

The classic fourfold actions in the Liturgy of the Sacrament are the taking/blessing/breaking/giving. In traditional ritual practice, these have all been the preserve of the president. Why not explore appropriate ways in which these can be more readily owned by the whole worshipping assembly?

And then there is the receiving of communion, a subversive act in itself. This all-inclusive action has the power to undermine the ageism of our culture in which the Church still so happily colludes.

Music

Peter Moger

Augustine of Hippo wrote that 'the one who sings prays twice'. There is little doubt that, when we sing something, the words are transformed and taken onto another plane. Singing, therefore, has always had a crucial part to play within worship.

With this in mind, it is sad that (even in some churches that boast a 'Sung Eucharist') the high point of eucharistic liturgy – the Eucharistic Prayer – can so often be devoid of music. In some cases this is due to a perceived lack of skill (or nerve!) on the part of the president, but, there is often little music for the Eucharistic Prayer itself – apart from perhaps the opening Dialogue and (more probably) the *Sanctus* and *Benedictus*, often sung to a well-worn 'congregational setting'. What should be an exciting moment in the liturgy that draws us closer into God's presence can turn out to be lack-lustre and predictable.

There are, though, other options in the use of music during the Eucharistic Prayer.

Singing the whole prayer

This is certainly not for the faint-hearted but, with a musically able president, can be a wonderfully uplifting experience. The time-honoured traditional plainchant tones are readily available (e.g. in *Common Worship: President's Book*), but there are published settings in other styles, too. A valuable resource for these is *Music for Common Worship II: Music for the President* (see Resources, p. 241).

Using refrains

Among the eight Eucharistic Prayers in *Common Worship* are four (A, D, F and H) with optional congregational refrains. The use of refrains reinforces the understanding that it is the gathered assembly that celebrates the Eucharist. Whilst these refrains can work well in spoken dialogue with the president, to sing them will heighten the text and involve the congregation to a greater degree.

This might be done as part of a totally sung prayer (see above). *Music for the President* (see above) includes a number of possible approaches. There is, though, a real need for more local churches to experiment with these texts and produce 'locally-grown' settings.

Using chants

A highly effective way of praying the Eucharistic Prayer is for the president to say (or sing) the words over the background of a repeated chant, sung by a choir, music group or the congregation. An example might be, say, a Eucharist at Pentecost, at which the Taizé chant 'Veni, sancte Spiritus' might be sung throughout the prayer (see below).

Instrumental music

One of my best ever liturgical memories was during one of the Duke Ellington 'Jazz Masses' held in the 1990s at Durham and Ely Cathedrals. During a spoken Eucharistic Prayer, a solo bass guitar player improvised an accompaniment. This is a reworking of an older tradition, still to be found in some French cathedrals, in which organists improvise under the words of the president. It has much to commend it, though we must acknowledge that it depends on local musicians having both skill and liturgical sensitivity.

A combination of approaches

A possible approach to the use of music during the Eucharistic Prayer is to use a combination of all the above. The worked example below suggests how this might be done, using *Common Worship* Eucharistic Prayer A, and an extended Preface for the Feast of Pentecost.

Prayer at the Preparation of the Table Father, by your Holy Spirit, you keep the Church in unity and truth. As we break bread together, may we be one with Christ in faith and hope and love, now and for ever. Amen. [T&S 486]	*After the hymn/song during the Preparation of the Table, instrumental music continues under the (spoken) Prayer at the Preparation of the Table, using the following pattern of chords:*  *This leads into quiet singing of the chant 'Veni, sancte Spiritus':*  Ve - ni San - cte Spi - ri - tus. © *Les Presses de Taizé*
The Lord is here. **His Spirit is with us.** Lift up your hearts. **We lift them to the Lord.** Let us give thanks to the Lord our God. **It is right to give thanks and praise.**	*When the singing of the chant has become established, the president begins the Eucharistic Prayer, either speaking the words, or singing them to the following simple tone:* 

It is indeed right, it is our duty and
   our joy,
always and everywhere to give you
   thanks,
holy Father, almighty and everlasting
   God,
through Jesus Christ, your only Son
   our Lord.
This day we give you thanks
because in fulfilment of your promise
you pour out your Spirit upon us,
filling us with your gifts, leading us
   into all truth,
and uniting peoples of many tongues
   in the confession of one faith.
Your Spirit gives us grace to call you
   Father,
to proclaim your gospel to all nations
and to serve you as a royal
   priesthood.
Therefore we join our voices with
   angels and archangels,
and with all those in whom the Spirit
   dwells,
to proclaim the glory of your name,
for ever praising you and singing:

[T&S 499]

[Holy, holy, holy Lord,
God of power and might,
heaven and earth are full of your
   glory.
Hosanna in the highest.]

A small group of singers continues singing the chant, over which, the
congregation sings:

Ho - ly, ho - ly Lord, God of pow'r and might, heav'n and earth are
full of your glo - ry. Ho - san-na in the high-est.__ Bless-ed is he_ who-comes,
comes in the name of the Lord.__ Ho - san - na in the
high - est, ho - san - na in the high - est.__

© 2006 Peter Moger

The president continues the Eucharistic Prayer, while the small group
of singers continues to sing the chant

Accept our praises, heavenly Father,
through your Son our Saviour Jesus
Christ,
and as we follow his example and
obey his command,
grant that by the power of your Holy
Spirit
these gifts of bread and wine
may be to us his body and his blood;

who, in the same night that he was
betrayed,
took bread and gave you thanks;
he broke it and gave it to his
disciples, saying:
Take, eat; this is my body which is
given for you;
do this in remembrance of me.

[To you be glory and praise for ever.]

In the same way, after supper
he took the cup and gave you thanks;
he gave it to them, saying:
Drink this, all of you;
this is my blood of the new covenant,
which is shed for you and for many
for the forgiveness of sins.
Do this, as often as you drink it,
in remembrance of me.

[To you be glory and praise for ever.]

Therefore, heavenly Father,
we remember his offering of himself
made once for all upon the cross;
we proclaim his mighty resurrection
and glorious ascension;
we look for the coming of your
kingdom,
and with this bread and this cup
we make the memorial of Christ your
Son our Lord.

[Great is the mystery of faith;]

[Christ has died:
Christ is risen:
Christ will come again.]

The congregation sings the refrain:

© *2006 Peter Moger*

(the chant continues)

© *2006 Peter Moger*

(the chant continues)

© *2006 Peter Moger*

Accept through him, our great high
  priest,
this our sacrifice of thanks and praise,
and as we eat and drink these holy
  gifts
in the presence of your divine
  majesty,
renew us by your Spirit,
inspire us with your love
and unite us in the body of your Son,
Jesus Christ our Lord.

[To you be glory and praise for ever.]

Through him, and with him, and in
  him,
in the unity of the Holy Spirit,
with all who stand before you in
  earth and heaven,
we worship you, Father almighty,
in songs of everlasting praise:

**[Blessing and honour and glory and
  power
be yours for ever and ever.
Amen.]**

[CW 185–7]

(the chant continues)

© *2006 Peter Moger*

(the chant continues)

© *2006 Peter Moger*

*After several repeats of the final doxology, the chant is sung several
times, getting progressively quieter.*

Lent, Holy Week and Easter:
mapping the journey

The hand of the Lord came upon me, and he brought me out by the spirit of the Lord and set me down in the middle of a valley; it was full of bones. He led me all round them; there were very many lying in the valley, and they were very dry. He said to me, 'Mortal, can these bones live?' I answered. 'O Lord God, you know.' Ezekiel 37.1-3 (Lent 5 Year A)

The miracle of new life

It is winter in Antarctica. No sun brightens the sky; a bitter wind blasts across the frozen wasteland and temperatures can plummet to –70 °C. It is surely one of the most inhospitable places in the world. A crowd of Emperor penguins can be seen, hardly visible in the drifting blizzard and huddled together for protection in this harsh landscape. Between their feet they carry an egg, tucked under their overhanging stomachs to shelter the new life from the bitter cold. And they wait for spring.

In London in 2006, it is snowing in March. The snowdrops are out, wishing they had brought overcoats and the crocuses are struggling through the hard soil. Spring seems some way off and yet the supermarkets are already full of gaudy displays of Easter eggs and the clothes shops are full to bursting with thin dresses and trousers that won't keep out the keen frost. And Lent has only just begun.

Underneath the soil in the garden, something is stirring. It is not yet visible but it is moving. It is the slow burning rise of the sap that will uncurl the leaves and the pulse of life that will in the end burst from the bulbs underground. Up here, we see nothing but bare earth. Perhaps those bulbs were dead. Perhaps this year those dead onions that the packet proclaimed to be daffodils actually were dead onions after all. But just maybe it will be true that those dried-up brown stumps will be transformed into wildly waving golden hosts. Or maybe not …

The lamp casts a glistening light on the crunchy snow in the winter that has lasted for a hundred years. Those who remember the land as it was in the past long for a return to the days of warmth and freedom. Now, all that has gone and Narnia and its inhabitants are in thrall to the spell of the white witch and the magic that has trapped them all in a winter that has no end. And they struggle to keep the memory alive.

Can these bones live?

Is it possible for life to come again to these dead places – to the harsh winter cold and the frozen earth; to the shrivelled-up stumps and the dead bulbs; to the empty fields, to the places that have forgotten what life looks like and to our own hearts? Can these bones live? That is perhaps above all the question that this part of our journey through the church year poses to us as individuals and to us as the Church. Can these bones – the dried-up parts of our lives, the disappointments and the failures, the wrecked relationships, the hard inflexibility of hearts and structures, the petty preoccupations that distract us all from the thrust of the gospel – can these bones live? If it were possible, if it could be true, what a message we would then have to share with our neighbours, our communities, our world. 'I am going to … bring you up from your graves, O my people … I will put my spirit within you, and you shall live … ' (Ezekiel 37.12-14).

The garden metaphor

Gardens are significant in this journey from death to life. For a start, tending a garden is in itself an act of faith. Gardeners witness daily miracles as new life asserts itself and barren wastelands are transformed with water and sun and care into flowering oases – they are indeed witnesses of transformation in the most unpromising of circumstances. If you have ever watched one of the many garden makeover programmes on the television you will immediately have a mental picture of the kinds of possibility that lurk beneath weed-infested patches of ground and in overgrown or just plain barren earth. Our journey in this part of the church year also begins in a garden. This garden is well tended and beautiful. In the centre stands a tree on which are the most delicious apples. This is the garden of innocence and plenty, of discovery and wonder that Eucharistic Prayer F speaks of:

You fashioned us in your image
and placed us in the garden of your delight.

[CW 198]

All is well then, but wait … there was a serpent in the garden, danger in the bushes, the choice and the loss, for this is also the garden from which Adam and Eve were cast out. So this season starts in Lent 1 Year A with this sombre reminder of opportunity, wrong choices, waste and rebellion that take such a long time and so much pain to right. And yet, in spite of Adam and Eve's being cast out of the garden, Genesis makes it clear that, though they are cast out, they are not left alone, just as Eucharistic Prayer F goes on to tell us:

Though we chose the path of rebellion
you would not abandon your own.
Again and again you drew us into your covenant of
grace.

[CW 198]

Ambiguity

It is worth recognizing for a start the ambiguities that this season contains. The Orthodox Church refers to this time of year as a time of 'bright sadness', capturing the mood of emptiness and hope. From a secular seasonal perspective, as the Anglo-Saxon word *lencten* that forms the origin of our word Lent suggests, we look forward to the lengthening of the daytime at the spring equinox – but just at the very time that the bleak February chill seems to make spring light and growth as distant as ever. The paradise garden with a serpent at its centre; life in death, life from death, dying in order that we might live; running away in order to find our way home (as the parable of the Prodigal Son teaches us); the king who is our servant; the messiah who saves us by dying; dead men that walk; sealed tombs that open; bones that live; men speaking in tongues when they are not drunk; a church built out of a group of terrified disciples … we are taken into the heart of some great mystery here where nothing is as it seems.

The very colours that we see from Lent to Pentecost contain and express ambiguity. White – the colour of innocence and purity, of spiritual things beyond the concerns of the earthly and the colour of 'not colour' – of *tabula rasa*, of absence. Red – the colour of lifeblood, of essential organs, of passion and of love but also the colour of danger and of fire. It is also interesting to note in this context that the Latin word *passio* contains within it two aspects of the passion of Christ: both love and suffering are present (he loved us to the end/he gave himself up). Purple – also an ambiguous colour since it is the colour of both kingship and of suffering. Black – the colour associated the most with death but also a colour of mystery. Gold or yellow – the colour of the sun, of life and of light but also of sickness (bile) and decay (yellowing leaves).

Joy and woe are woven fine

One of the persistent themes in the preaching of the late David Watson (paraphrasing Blake) was that 'joy and woe are woven fine' – that our relationships in the community of the Church are marked by costly self-giving and by pain as much as they are by joy. In this he taught us that they mirror both the death and the resurrection of Christ and one is incomplete without the other. We are taken back to our garden metaphors: life in the garden comes as a result of severe pruning; of breaking up the soil; of stripping out the dead wood to give the new growth room to breathe. This is the work we are called to as individuals and as the Church in this season of life from death. 'Can these bones live? O Lord God, only you know.'

Beyond the image of the garden that stands as a kind of metaphor for our Lenten disciplines and journey, there are other gardens. There is the garden of Gethsemane, a garden of desolation, of betrayal and loss but also of the deepest prayer: the most intimate of relationships between the Father and the Son and a heavy sense of vocation. It is important to stay for a while in this garden whether we fall asleep or watch. We need to find ourselves here, witnessing the prayer of the Son to the Father, remembering our own cries of anguish at burdens too hard to bear and hearing the cries of God's people through time for liberation and freedom. There is then the hillside on which the crucifixion takes place, where the grain of wheat falls to the earth and dies. We need to stand in this place also and call to mind the death Christ suffered for our sake. We need to recognize the finality of death in order to understand the meaning of the resurrection.

Resurrection

Then there is the garden of the resurrection, where angels guard the entrance to the tomb just as in the beginning they stood guard over the exit of the Garden of Eden. Here Jesus is mistaken for a gardener – not without rich resonance, since Adam was a gardener and Jesus is referred to as the second Adam. Here Mary comes to tend the dead with spices and finds instead that Christ is risen and life is restored. As Christ calls Mary by her name in this place of death, we hear again our own names being called as they were when we began our journey of faith at baptism and as they are time and time again when God calls us into his covenant of grace.[1] 'I have called you by name, you are mine.' We might recall some words from the Song of Songs:

My beloved speaks and says to me:
'Arise, my love, my fair one, and come away;
for now the winter is past,
the rain is over and gone.
The flowers appear on the earth;
the time of singing has come,
and the voice of the turtle-dove is heard in our land.'
(Song of Solomon 2.10-12)

This is the kind of lost innocence restored that was prefigured in the Exsultet, sung at the Easter Vigil. And we sing much the same thing in a well-known Easter hymn:

Now the green blade riseth from the buried grain,
wheat that in the dark earth many days has lain:
love lives again that with the dead has been:
love is come again
like wheat that springeth green.

What is lost has been restored, he who was dead is alive again and the tree of death becomes the tree of life once more. And what is generally true – that life can spring forth from the place of death – is also particularly true for all the dead parts of our own hearts and lives, as the same Easter hymn testifies:

When our hearts are wintry, grieving or in pain,
thy touch can call us back to life again.
Fields of our hearts that dead and bare have been:
love is come again
like wheat that springeth green.
(J. M. C. Crum 1872–1958)

Maybe it is also true of those dead parts of the Church: 'Can these bones live? O Lord God, only you know.'

As the Easter season moves on

Later, on the Fifth Sunday of Easter (at least in Year C!) we are led to think of the new creation and the tree at the heart of it:

Then the angel showed me the river of the water of life, bright as crystal, flowing from the throne of God and of the Lamb through the middle of the street of the city. On either side of the river is the tree of life with its twelve kinds of fruit, producing its fruit each month; and the leaves of the tree are for the healing of the nations.
(Revelation 22.1-2)

The abundance of hope and of life that bursts from the tomb[2] might lead us to forget all that had gone before, were it not for the Ascension, for Pentecost and then for Trinity, adding their own grace notes[3] to the story we have followed so far in this part of the year. The Ascension is itself an occasion with two sides. We like to think on the ascended Christ, triumphant and in glory. But it is nevertheless an occasion of loss, of departure, of nothing going on as it was before, of the disciples being left for a second time. We need to hold the passion and death in our minds together with the Ascension, for the wounds are 'yet visible above'.[4] But it is through this leave-taking and the pain of it that the gift of the Spirit becomes possible. Similarly, there are two sides to the Pentecost experience. The Spirit is poured out at Pentecost with tongues of fire and the rushing of a mighty wind but the feel-good factor does not last long. Soon the disciples are arrested or imprisoned for their faith and the burgeoning Christian community is tested to its limits and then remains in the shadow of persecution for many years.

The Easter legacy

And Trinity Sunday? It is perhaps this day that most helps us to read our journey backwards. Rublev's icon of the Holy Trinity can enable us here to look over the events we have witnessed in the preceding weeks, through the lens that this image into the heart of God and the purposes of God provides. And it is a glimpse that is both welcoming and challenging. The three figures sit around a table and their gaze moves around the circle of intimacy one to the other. Their heads are inclined, each one bending as if to give honour to the others. It is a dance of loving intimacy and of openness … Look! there is a space open at the front and into which we are invited. The figures are grouped around a table and in the centre of that table is a cup. It is a symbol both of the hospitality offered to us (and to all who stand there) and the suffering that this open love costs its giver. It serves too as a reminder of all that our journey has taught us so far: would you drink the cup I am about to drink?

God who is relationship goes out to seek and to save the lost, calling them back to the intimacy of this kind of love and relationship for which they were designed. It is this love – sparing nothing in its searching out of the beloved – that is at the heart of both the incarnation cycle and the passion cycle of readings and liturgical experiences. It is this love that meets us when we are still far off and that meets us in the breaking of the bread and the outpouring of wine – gifts that are for us the signs and symbols of love that gives its all and opens its arms on the cross to call us home.

Lent

Seasonal introduction

Giving something up?

'Are you giving something up for Lent?' This concept of Lent as a time of self-denial occupies a curious place in the consciousness of many people, whether or not they are churchgoers. Perhaps it reflects the view that church people 'go without' something such as a bar of chocolate or a bag or crisps with their morning coffee because Christians are a bit miserable – more interested in 'can't' and 'shouldn't' than in embracing life. Or is it rather that Christians are perceived as doing strange and slightly arcane things – that faith in itself is actually rather bizarre. Or perhaps Christians are perceived to be exercising a personal lifestyle choice. Giving up something can be seen as simply a personal choice, rather than a manifestation of a movement that seeks to challenge the world.

Or taking something on?

And what of the beginning of Lent for Christians themselves? Are you giving something up … or are you taking something on? Ash Wednesday reminds us of our own mortality, of the fact that life is short, that opportunities are fleeting and that we are accountable for our own life choices. We are signed with the cross in ash, a potent symbol of the dust from which we are created, of the dust into which so many of our dreams and efforts crumble and of the dust to which we shall all return when mortal life is ended. Nevertheless, we are dust that dreams – capable of ascending the heights of heaven as well as plumbing the depths. When we think too highly of ourselves, we are called to remember that we are but dust and to remember the cross. When we think too little of ourselves, we are called to remember that dust can be inspired with the breath of life and to remember the cross. We need these reminders as we embark on our journey through this part of the church year, a journey that may test to the limits our discipleship and the steadfastness of our commitment to the faith of our baptism. It is a journey we will need to travel together, sometimes shouldering one

another's crosses, and all the while remembering that we are called into community to work out the meaning of what our baptismal calling means in daily life.

If Christians are to rediscover a counter-cultural witness in Lent, then we may need to consider ways for taking something up. It might be appropriate to take up a particular practice of prayer – exploring Ignatian or Julian spirituality for example – or at least to make more room for prayer. This could involve creating physical space – some form of space set apart in the home or in the church. It might also involve temporal space – creating time in the day for regular prayer. According to your tradition, you may wish to offer confession and absolution or prayer ministry at specific times during Lent. Some churches set up a labyrinth.

Facing the cross

Lent is a time for facing the cross itself, and for peeling away some of the layers of disguise with which we are wont to cover it. It is time to remove our decorated crosses, our jewelled crosses, our crosses with softened edges. Instead, we are asked to consider the bare harsh wood on which the saviour bled and died. The cross becomes central in this part of our journey so it is important to find ways of enabling people to engage with its symbolism and to contemplate its mysteries. Because it is an image of horror that is difficult to face, careful thought needs to be given to establishing appropriate boundaries for prayer and for liturgy during this time. The cross is not only a way into understanding the suffering and death of Christ, but it also helps us to confront our own sufferings. But it is also a screen – a means of shielding some things from our gaze because they are quite simply too awful to look upon. Nevertheless, the cross is a focus for penitence that assumes a particular emphasis during this season. The near-silent Eucharist provided within these materials is one liturgical way of allowing this symbolism to speak. The silent witness involved in watching others make their confession is potent in a context where no words are spoken and the confession is made in silence, in symbolic and multisensory ways. It is a reminder too that, though our sins may be individual acts, the effects can be felt within a whole community. Services of healing and reconciliation are also a form of liturgical expression that can find rich resonance within this season.

A spring clean

Spring is naturally a time for clearing up and for clearing out – we are familiar for example with the idea of spring-cleaning. During this season we might consider ways of doing this work in the church building and we might also consider reviewing our life commitments – meeting with a spiritual director, evaluating vocation and reconsidering our giving of time and money. The Scriptures for Lent 1 remind us of the reality of evil, the pressure of temptation and the need to recognize and tackle all that would deflect us from following Jesus. There is also the opportunity to consider the wilderness places in our hearts and to consider how these places can be made to live again. These themes are picked up in different ways and run like a refrain through the lectionary Scriptures for Lent: 'If any want to become my followers, let them deny themselves and take up their cross and follow me' (Mark 8.34 Lent 2 Year B). Yet in the midst of these harsh messages and warnings there are still notes of tenderness. As the much loved Prayer after Communion,[1] and the readings for Lent 4 Year C remind us, it is while we are still far off that God sees us, has compassion, and goes in search of us. Trying to grasp the nature of the love that God has for us gives a different slant on the pain and anguish of the cross.

Study and reflection

Lent is also known as a time dedicated to study and reflection. This is an ancient tradition, originating from the use of this time as a period of catechesis, when new converts prepared for baptism and communion at Easter. Reflecting on some of the key Scriptures of the season might be appropriate: one route might be to examine the people of the Lenten Gospels: Nicodemus; the woman at the well; the blind man healed; the prodigal son. A study of Rembrandt's painting of *The Return of the Prodigal* is an imaginative way to explore the key scriptural

theme of loss and restoration and, if you are in a church that works with Godly Play, the stories of the Good Shepherd and the World Communion have resonance here (see Resources).

Journeying together

While there is an introspective aspect to Lent, the corporate dimension of the journey we travel in this season is nonetheless significant and presents evangelistic opportunities. Liturgically, the season begins as Jesus journeys into the wilderness after his baptism, and may reach its climax with the renewal of baptismal vows at Easter. We might take the opportunity to explore Lent in the context of what it means to be a community of the baptized. Providing space and people to accompany others might be a helpful way of encouraging reflection on vocation and we should not forget to think of ways in which children and young people can be supported in considering their sense of vocation. Opening up the building to make it available for people might be a contribution from the church to the wider local community. Some parishes practise an open-door retreat – a planned series of talks or meditations with regular corporate worship and prayer exercises for practice in the home. This is a helpful way to combine the inner and the corporate journeys of this time in the church year. We need the support of the community as we enter the rigours of Holy Week.

Reaching out

Mothering Sunday (also as the fourth Sunday of Lent sometime called Refreshment Sunday), as well as being a day of respite from the rigours of our Lenten fast, is an opportunity to reach out to those who attend worship for this particular celebration. Simnel cake was traditionally linked to Mothering Sunday – perhaps this is an opportunity to serve something other than biscuits with coffee after church and to share some hospitality. Mothering Sunday can be sensitive for some, especially if the emphasis is on motherhood alone. There are some examples of liturgies in this book for you to consider.

Lent:
Stand-alone seasonal material

Before Lent

We tend to think of Lent as a time of preparation for Easter. However, Lent itself needs careful preparation so that Christians are not suddenly accosted by it, but instead are made ready to use it to its maximum effect. Here is one scheme you might like to use, though there may be more appropriate processes for your particular community.

Sunday before Lent

The readings in the *Common Worship* and *Revised Common* lectionaries for the Sunday before Lent focus on the transfiguration of Jesus and therefore on our transformation, which is the purpose of Lent. A proper use of the days before Lent can build up a right sense of expectation and can help people to approach the season in a mature and realistic way.

If palm crosses are used in the church, members of the congregation could be asked to bring their palm crosses to the service on this day. These palm crosses, together with any the church might have left over from the year before, will then be used later to prepare the ash that will be used to mark the beginning of Lent.

They could be brought forward at some point towards the end of the service and dropped in front of the holy table. If the service is eucharistic, this could be on the way to communion. If it is a Service of the Word, an opportunity could be structured into the service for this to happen as part of the Conclusion.

It is customary not to decorate the church with flowers in Lent, reinforcing the notion of a season of abstinence. At the very end of the service, therefore, as part of the Dismissal, any flower arrangements might be carried out behind the ministers. The following is an example of the kind of liturgical structure based on a Dismissal Gospel that might be used.

A Concluding Rite for the Sunday before Lent

After the post-communion prayers the following acclamation is used:

To you, O Lord, I lift up my soul;
O my God, in you I trust.
You are the God of my salvation,
To you, O Lord, I lift up my soul.
In you I hope all the day long.
O my God, in you I trust.
Remember, Lord, your compassion and love,
for they are from everlasting.
To you, O Lord, I lift up my soul;
O my God, in you I trust.

[DP 241]

People each bring a different flower arrangement to the front of the church. Large arrangements may need to be carried by more than one person. A hymn or song may be sung.

Hear the Gospel of our Lord Jesus Christ according to Luke (9.43b-45)
Glory to you, O Lord.

While everyone was amazed at all that he was doing, he said to his disciples, 'Let these words sink into your ears: the Son of Man is going to be betrayed into human hands.' But they did not understand this saying; its meaning was concealed from them, so that they could not perceive it. And they were afraid to ask him about this saying.

At the end the reader says
This is the Gospel of the Lord.
Praise to you, O Christ.

The president blesses the people saying
Christ walked the way of obedience and sacrifice.
May he draw near to guide your feet into the way of peace; and the blessing ...

Go in peace ...

The ministers leave, followed by those carrying the flowers, which could then be distributed to the housebound, the sick, local hospitals, etc.

Shrove Tuesday

The name *Shrove Tuesday* derives from the ritual of *shriving*, when a person confesses his or her sins and receives absolution for them.

Shrove Tuesday, often called Pancake Day or Mardi Gras (Fat Tuesday), is the day before Ash Wednesday, when traditionally the house is emptied of fatty food so that temptation to eat rich food is minimized in preparation for the Lenten fast. It is the final day of feasting before we begin 40 days of fasting. Pancakes are associated with this day because they are a good way of using up eggs and butter.

Across the world Shrove Tuesday is a day of celebration, traditionally marked by fun and games. The first pancake race is thought to have been in 1445 when a woman had lost track of the time on Shrove Tuesday, and was busy cooking pancakes. When she heard the church bell calling people to confession, she ran all the way to the church wearing her apron and carrying her frying pan!

This is a perfect opportunity for the Church to get together to play, and, as Shrove Tuesday is deeply embedded in the traditions of our culture, it offers the possibility to invite other members of the wider community to share in the festivities.

Why not arrange a pancake party that involves cooking, eating, games, crafts, and ends with simple prayer? Possible craft activities might involve creating a Lenten calendar with 40 windows to open, each with a flower behind it so that, as Lent progresses, it becomes more and more colourful. A simple cut-out activity to which children might revert if they want some time out is the Lenten nun. The 'nun' has seven legs sticking out below her skirt so that she can 'walk' towards Easter. As each week of Lent passes, a leg is torn off so that by Easter they are all gone. A simple figure with the seven legs, each with a foot, could be drawn onto a piece of paper and then copies made so that children who want a cutting and colouring activity can use them, and take home the result to be used through Lent (See page 243 for a template). Further ideas of craft activities for Lent can be found on the Internet: type 'Lenten crafts' into a search engine.

Suggestions for activities at a party might include:
- **explaining** the origins and meaning of Lent;
- **sharing** with one another what each person's Lenten discipline might entail. People might explain to others what they are going to take on or what they are going to give up. It is worth preparing this quite carefully and providing suggestions for the inexperienced so that they can make realistic choices. You may want to talk about the possibilities that your church offers to people so you can make community choices as well as individual ones.
- **preparing** the Lenten tree, if it is going to be used through Lent (see instructions on p. 34).
- **making** the ash for the service on Ash Wednesday or the beginning of Lent. It is important to remember that, first and foremost, this is simply ash but a tradition has developed where the ash of Ash Wednesday is made by burning palm crosses that were distributed on the Palm Sunday of the previous year. The newer rites of Palm Sunday avoid the 'blessing' of palm crosses but using them in this way offers an appropriate way of disposing of items that for many hold deep significance. It also mirrors the cycle of life and death.

  This is best done at the end of the evening, and outside, because of the residual smell of the burning palms. The palm crosses, handed in on the Sunday before Lent, burn more easily if they are placed in a metal dish and a domestic kitchen blowtorch is used. White spirit is also helpful.

At this point, after the fun and the feasting, everyone and everything is ready for Lent.

A service for the beginning of Lent

Ideally this service is to be held on Ash Wednesday but, universally, people are finding that, as pressure on family life increases, these midweek festivals are less well attended. It might be worth considering whether the ceremony of the imposition of ashes should be used on Ash Wednesday or the first Sunday of Lent or even both. One solution might be to use the rite on Ash Wednesday but to make the ash available throughout the season at any point by leaving the ash as one of the symbols by the Lenten tree. This may offer a resolution to the tension between the focus on Ash Wednesday and the cultural trend away from midweek celebrations.

Preparatory notes

LENTEN TREE, HEAD, HANDS AND HEART OR STATIONS: WHICH PATHWAY?

It is suggested that the Lenten tree is carried into the church at the beginning of this service. The Sorry Stations tie in well with the Stations theme. There is nothing particularly focused on the Head, hands and heart pathway in this service.

What needs to be prepared leading up to the service?

ASH

The ash needs to be prepared. It could be made on Shrove Tuesday by burning the palm crosses handed in on the previous Sunday (see Preparing for Lent).

SORRY STATIONS

If you are to use the Sorry Stations idea described in this service, these must be prepared beforehand. Allow plenty of time so that you can get hold of all the things you need.

- A large **sand spread** can be created by placing a sheet of plastic on the ground and covering it with a 5 cm layer of sand. People may go to the sand and make a handprint in it representing the print of sin they have left on the world. You can get sand at the garden centre or a toy shop. You will also need a rake to rake the sand smooth again at the Absolution.
- A metal **waste bin** where there are pieces of paper on which people can write or draw their sins and place them in the bin. You will also need pieces of paper and pens. If you plan to burn the pieces of paper, you will need matches. Make sure you also have a volunteer who will take them outside to do this.
- A **repentance rope** is needed where people can tie small pieces of red wool onto a larger red rope. You will need a piece of rope and lengths of red wool. It might be helpful to determine whether there is a place where the rope can be hung up or laid out so it is all accessible. You can buy lengths of rope in DIY stores, though someone with a tow rope in their car might be pleased to lend it. You would need to decide whether you want it to look new and clean, or whether the fact that it is worn and dirty provides a relevant metaphor.
- For the **sin stones** station you will need a collection of large pebbles or cobbles, big enough to feel weighty when held in one hand, and a large bowl where they can be collected. If you don't have anything appropriate around your church or in a garden, you can buy bags of stones at garden centres. You will also need a jug with water to pour over the stones at the Absolution.

What needs to happen before the service?

You will need to ensure that you have everything you need for making the ash: burnt palm crosses, water and oil. You will need to ensure that the Sorry Stations are set up with everything that is required. If you are going to use incense at the Absolution, you will need a bowl with charcoal in it and a means of lighting it before the service begins. Put the charcoal blocks on some crinkled tinfoil in a bowl that can withstand heat. Light the charcoal with a cook's blowtorch or gas lighter. If you do this as the service begins, the charcoal should be adequately glowing by the time of the Absolution, when grains of incense can be sprinkled on it.

You will need to decide who is going to ask the questions about the purpose of Lent. These are asked just after the Greeting. It may be done by individuals or by the whole congregation.

What needs to be made ready immediately before the service?

The charcoal should be lit.

A note about participation

In the layout of these services we have provided a column called 'Participation'. Clearly, watching is a form of participation but it works effectively only if the watchers are able to identify with some aspect of the action. The leader may suggest points of contact but in the end it is the 'watcher' who needs to make the connections. One way of helping people to make those connections is to give them various tasks within a particular ritual, such as carrying items in procession. Once people have done that, they will always have a relationship with that action in the future. Consequently, the greater the number of people who can be used in that way, the greater the number who have a stake in the service.

Structure, movement and flow	Words/text	Multisensory	Participation
THE GATHERING	*At the entry of the ministers, a hymn may be sung.* *The president may say* In the name of the Father, and of the Son, and of the Holy Spirit. **Amen**. [CW 167]	If possible, the procession could be led by a person carrying the Lenten tree/ cross. Ash, water and olive oil could also be brought into church as part of the entry procession and placed at the base of the Lenten tree or some other suitable place.	Singing and watching.
Greeting	Grace, mercy and peace from God our Father and the Lord Jesus Christ be with you **and also with you.** [T&S 470]		

The meaning of Lent is explained in a question and answer format. The questions may be asked by the congregation as a whole, by one or more members of the congregation from their places, or by one of the ministers other than the president. The president replies.

Why is Lent so important for the Church?
Brothers and sisters in Christ, since early days Christians have observed with great devotion the time of our Lord's passion and resurrection and prepared for this by a season of penitence and fasting.

Why is Lent so important for me?
By carefully keeping these days, Christians take to heart the call to repentance and the assurance of forgiveness proclaimed in the gospel, and so grow in faith and in devotion to our Lord.

How can I best use this season?
I invite you, therefore, in the name of the Church, to the observance of a holy Lent, by self-examination and repentance; by prayer, fasting and self-denial; and by reading and meditating on God's holy word.

The Trisagion or another suitable penitential song may be used
Holy God,
holy and strong,
holy and immortal,
have mercy upon us.

[T&S 223]

One musical version of this ancient song can be found in Many and Great *published by Wild Goose Publications. It is called 'Agios, O Theos' (see Resources, p. 241).*

The song ends when the activity has finished.

Asking the question means people are more likely to listen to the answer.

As the song is sung, the burnt palm crosses are crushed using a pestle and mortar.

Once the leaves have become powder, a small amount of water is added to make a paste. Olive oil is then mixed into the paste to give it a thicker consistency.

Singing.

Depending on the manageability of numbers, members of the congregation may come forward and help at any point during the process.

The Collect	Let us pray for grace to keep Lent faithfully. *Silence is kept.* Holy God, our lives are laid open before you: rescue us from the chaos of sin and through the death of your Son bring us healing and make us whole in Jesus Christ our Lord. **Amen.** [T&S 224]		The president should encourage people to pray themselves during the silence.
THE LITURGY OF THE WORD			
Reading	*At the end the reader may say* This is the word of the Lord. **Thanks be to God.**		This reading and/or the Gospel reading could be done dramatically using, for example, *The Dramatised Bible* or the methods illustrated in chapter 3 of *Children at Worship* by Caroline Fairless (see Resources, p. 240).
Hymn/song			Singing
Gospel Reading	*This acclamation may herald the Gospel reading* Praise to you, O Christ, King of eternal glory. Jesus said, 'Repent for the kingdom of God has come near.' *Matthew 4.17*	The Gospel might be read from beside the Lenten tree or in the middle of the congregation.	The reading of the Gospel in the middle of the congregation, or in a significant place in the

	Praise to you, O Christ, King of eternal glory. *When the Gospel is announced the reader says* Hear the Gospel of our Lord Jesus Christ according to *N*. **Glory to you, O Lord.** *At the end* This is the Gospel of the Lord. **Praise to you, O Christ.** [T&S 225]		worship space, such as by the Lenten tree, opens the possibilities for hearers and watchers to give extra meaning to the reading. The reading might even be introduced by the comment 'The Gospel reading is proclaimed from beside the Lenten tree because …' Or this comment might be written in a service sheet if there is one.
Sermon			
Questions	*What are your questions about the Liturgy of the Word?*		
THE LITURGY OF PENITENCE			
Self-examination and Confession	Let us now call to mind our sin and the infinite mercy of God. *All kneel* God the Father, **have mercy on us.** God the Son, **have mercy on us.** God the Holy Spirit, **have mercy on us.** Trinity of love, **have mercy on us.** [T&S 226] *Silence for reflection.*		

		Congregational prayer.
Most merciful God, Father of our Lord Jesus Christ, we confess that we have sinned in thought, word and deed. *The congregation is encouraged to move around the 'Sorry Stations'.*	A number of **Sorry Stations** may be created before the service begins, to which people can go during this time of prayer. These may include such prayers activities as: Large **sand spread** created by placing a sheet of plastic on the ground and covering it with a 5 cm layer of sand. People may go to the sand and make a handprint in it representing the print of sin they have left on the world. A metal **waste bin** where there are pieces of paper on which people can write or draw their sin and place them in a waste bin. A **repentance rope** where we can tie small pieces of red wool onto a larger red rope. **Sin stones** where people can select a stone and in their imagination use it to represent their sin. They place it in a large bowl.	Engaging with, and moving around the Sorry stations.
As the movement around the stations comes to an end, the president encourages the congregation to finish the prayer of confession **We have not loved you with our whole heart.** **We have not loved our neighbours as ourselves.**	Members of the congregation are encouraged to use at least one of the Sorry Stations to own their sin. For a period of time they are encouraged to move around the Sorry stations and then return to their place.	Congregational prayer

	In your mercy **forgive what we have been,** **help us to amend what we are,** **and direct what we shall be;** **that we may do justly,** **love mercy,** **and walk humbly with you, our God.** **Amen.** [CW 169]		

The Imposition of Ashes	*The prepared ash is brought to the president.*
	
	The president says
	Dear friends in Christ,
	I invite you to receive these ashes
	as a sign of the spirit of penitence with
	    which we shall keep this season of Lent.
	
	God our Father,
	you create us from the dust of the earth:
	grant that these ashes may be for us
	    a sign of our penitence
	    and a symbol of our mortality;
	for it is by your grace alone
	that we receive eternal life
	in Jesus Christ our Saviour.
	Amen.
	
	[T&S 230]
	
	The ash is administered to each person with these words
	Remember that you are dust, and to dust
	    you shall return.
	Turn away from sin and be faithful to
	    Christ.
	
	[T&S 230]
	
	or, particularly if people are ashing each other, the ashes may imposed without the use of words.
			This is best done by members of the congregation.
			
			Everyone might share in the imposition of ashes.
			The president could invite people to come forward and she or he makes the sign of the cross on the forehead of the first person to come forward.

	During the imposition, silence may be kept, or a hymn, anthem or psalm may be sung.		*The ash is then handed to that person, who then imposes the ash on the next person, and so on.* *The final person makes the sign of the cross on the president.* *This should be done by everyone if possible, regardless of age.*
		At the end of the Imposition of Ashes, the ash is placed at the foot of the Lenten tree. It remains there throughout Lent for anyone to use at any point. People are particularly invited to make the sign of the cross with the ash.	*Some people with sensitive skin have raised questions about this act. A beautician might be consulted or an alternative 'ash' might be made available.*
	At the end of the Imposition of Ashes the president says The Lord enrich *you* with his grace, and nourish *you* with his blessing; the Lord defend *you* in trouble and keep *you* from all evil; the Lord accept *your* prayers, and absolve *you* from *your* offences, for the sake of Jesus Christ, our Saviour. **Amen**. *This may be accompanied before or after by singing.* [T&S 230]	*As the president begins the Absolution, incense may be placed on lighted charcoal. The person with the incense plus one other person moves around the Sorry Stations:* • *the sand at the sand spread is raked;* • *the paper on which sins were written and placed in the waste bin is set alight (beware of smoke and smoke alarms – the bin may need to be taken outside for this);* • *the red repentance rope is coiled and placed on the Lenten cross; and* • *water is poured into the bowl containing the sin stones.*	Members of the congregation perform these acts. Others watch as their involvement in each station creates connections with the action.

Questions	What are your questions about the Liturgy of Penitence?		
THE LITURGY OF THE SACRAMENT			
The Peace	Since we are justified by faith, we have peace with God through our Lord Jesus Christ, who has given us access to his grace. The peace of the Lord be always with you **and also with you.** Let us offer one another a sign of peace. *All may exchange a sign of peace.* [T&S 231]	Human contact	Everyone shares the peace
Preparation of the Table	*A hymn may be sung.* *The gifts of the people may be gathered and presented.* *The table is prepared and bread and wine are placed upon it.* *At the Preparation of the Table this prayer may be said* Risen Lord and Saviour, present among us with the wealth of your love. Cleanse us from sin and give us the faith to offer our praise and grow in your grace. **Amen.** [T&S 231]		Singing If the layout of the church and the size of the congregation permit, the congregation may be invited to gather around the holy table for the Eucharistic Prayer, remaining there until the dismissal. This prayer may be said by all or the president alone.

Taking of the bread and wine	*The president takes the bread and wine.*		
The Eucharistic Prayer	*The president uses one of the authorized Eucharistic Prayers with an appropriate proper preface.*		See the notes on how to use a Eucharistic Prayer in an all-age context (see pp. 3ff).
The Lord's Prayer	Lord Jesus, remember us in your kingdom and teach us to pray. *The Lord's Prayer is said.*		
Breaking of the Bread	*The president breaks the consecrated bread.* Every time we eat this bread and drink this cup, **we proclaim the Lord's death** **until he comes.** [CW 179] *Agnus Dei may be used as the bread is broken.*	The president breaks the consecrated bread.	Watching the action

Giving of Communion	*The president says*
	Jesus is the Lamb of God
	who takes away the sin of the world.
	Blessed are those who are called to his
	    supper.
	Lord, I am not worthy to receive you,
	but only say the word and I shall be
	    healed.
	
	[CW 180]
	
	During the distribution hymns and anthems may be sung.
			Coming for communion.
			
			Singing.

Prayer after Communion	*Silence is kept.* *All may say this prayer* **God of our pilgrimage,** **you have fed us with the bread of** **heaven.** **Refresh and sustain us** **as we go forward on our journey,** **in the name of Jesus Christ our Lord.** **Amen.** [T&S 233]		Praying together

Questions	*Do you have questions about the Liturgy of the Sacrament?*		
The Dismissal	*A hymn may be sung.*		During which everyone moves to the door.
Responsory	*This Responsory may be used* This is love, not that we loved God, **but that he loved us and sent his Son.** He is the sacrifice for our sins, **that we might live through him.** If God loves us so much **we ought to love one another.** If we love one another **God lives in us.** *cf 1 John 4.12* [NP G50]		This could be led with different members of the congregation saying the leader's parts.
Dismissal Gospel	*This Dismissal Gospel may be used* Hear the Gospel of our Lord Jesus Christ according to Luke **Glory to you, O Lord.** Which one of you, having a hundred sheep and losing one of them, does not leave the ninety-nine in the wilderness and go after the one that is lost until he finds it? When he has found it, he lays it on his shoulders and rejoices. And when he comes home, he calls together his friends and neighbours, saying to them, 'Rejoice with me, for I have found my sheep that was lost.' Just so, I tell you, there will be more joy in heaven over one sinner who repents than over ninety-nine righteous people who need no repentance. *Luke 15.4-7*		*This Gospel could be read dramatically as follows:* Which one of you, having a hundred sheep and losing one of them, does not leave the ninety-nine in the wilderness and go after the one that is lost until he finds it? When he has found it, he lays it on his shoulders and rejoices.

			And when he comes home, he calls together his friends and neighbours, saying to them, 'Rejoice with me, for I have found my sheep that was lost.' Just so, I tell you, there will be more joy in heaven over one sinner who repents than over ninety-nine righteous people who need no repentance.
	This is the Gospel of the Lord **Praise to you, O Christ.**		
Blessing	Christ give you grace to grow in holiness, to deny yourselves, take up your cross, and follow him; and the blessing … [CW 309]		
Dismissal	Go in … [CW 183] *The ministers and people depart.*		Everyone goes.
Questions	*What are your questions about the Dismissal?*		

A near-silent Eucharist

The purpose of this service is to provide an opportunity to worship together in a contemplative setting, focusing particularly on the action of Eucharist and our physical relationship with one another as we share together. The service is quite short, but includes all the required parts of the liturgy. Words are kept to a minimum, and as much of the rite as possible is enacted by gesture.

It is particularly appropriate for use during Lent and Passiontide.

Introduction

This service follows the usual order of service for a *Common Worship* Eucharist Order 1 but it uses very few words. The service is almost silent in order to be quite visual. Where there is a need for instruction, it should be provided either verbally or by a physical sign.

Because absolute silence is sometimes intimidating, you may wish to provide some sort of music, either by using appropriate recorded music played where it is needed, or by using a choir or instrumentalists. The music should be carefully chosen and appropriate to the part of the service that it accompanies.

THE GATHERING

The ministers enter and turn to face the people. They all make the sign of the cross.

Any necessary announcements are made and explanations provided.

CONFESSION AND ABSOLUTION

At the front, on the ground, is a large cross, and to the side of it is a pile of stones. Those who wish to make their confession are invited to come forward in silence and select one of the stones to represent all that they wish to confess to God. They place the stone on the cross itself and pray silently for forgiveness.

On the other side of the cross is a bowl of water with the words, 'Wash and be clean' next to it. After making their confession, worshippers wash their hands in the bowl then return to their seats.

The Absolution is said by the president

*May almighty God have mercy on you,
forgive you your sins,
and bring you to everlasting life.* **Amen**.

GLORIA

This might be sung by a choir or a recorded version is played.

THE COLLECT

Silence is kept and then the Collect for the day is said.

GOSPEL – *LECTIO DIVINA*

There is no address or sermon given in this service. Instead the wisdom of the Holy Spirit is sought through an ancient form of reading Scripture. A short passage will be read three times with directions to follow for meditation.

The Gospel is read.

LISTENING FOR THE GENTLE TOUCH OF CHRIST THE WORD – THE LITERAL SENSE

One person reads aloud (twice) the passage of Scripture. All present listen and then reflect in the silence on one segment to which they feel drawn and which, for whatever reason, seems significant to them. So in the silence (1 to 2 minutes) they hear and silently repeat a word or phrase from the reading that attracts them.

HOW CHRIST THE WORD SPEAKS TO ME – THE ALLEGORICAL SENSE

Second reading of the passage.

In the silence (for 2 to 3 minutes) people now reflect on the question, 'Where does the content of this reading touch my life today?'

WHAT CHRIST THE WORD INVITES ME TO DO – THE MORAL SENSE

Third reading of the passage.

In the silence (for 2 to 3 minutes) people reflect on the question, 'From this passage, what is God calling me to do?'

INTERCESSORY PRAYERS

The intercessions are the place where the Church brings the needs of others to God. A pile of contemporary newspapers, pairs of scissors and drawing pins are provided. People may search through the newspapers, seeking items for prayer and then cut out those they select. These can be pinned to a board. As people complete the task, they sit down. When all are seated, the service continues.

THE PEACE

In quietness and in trust shall be your strength.

Isaiah 30.15b

The ministers and the congregation all stand:

The president then shares the peace with those near him/her and they pass the peace on into the congregation.

TAKING OF THE BREAD AND WINE

The table is prepared. The president takes the bread and wine and lifts them up to God.

THE EUCHARISTIC PRAYER

Use a short Eucharistic Prayer; for example, Prayer H is used here. Although this part of the service is not silent, significant space and silence are given after the sections for each person to reflect on the meaning of the words and actions.

The Lord is here.
His Spirit is with us.
Silence

Lift up your hearts.
We lift them to the Lord.
Silence

Let us give thanks to the Lord our God.
It is right to give thanks and praise.

It is right to praise you, Father, Lord of all creation;
in your love you made us for yourself.
Silence

When we turned away
you did not reject us,
but came to meet us in your Son.
You embraced us as your children
and welcomed us to sit and eat with you.
Silence

In Christ you shared our life
that we might live in him and he in us.
He opened his arms of love upon the cross
and made for all the perfect sacrifice for sin.
Silence

On the night he was betrayed,
at supper with his friends
he took bread, and gave you thanks; (bread elevated)
he broke it and gave it to them saying: (bread offered around room)
Take, eat; this is my body which is given for you;
do this in remembrance of me.
Father, we do this in remembrance of him:
his body is the bread of life.
Silence

At the end of supper, taking the cup of wine,
he gave you thanks (cup elevated), and said:
Drink this, all of you; this is my blood of the new
    covenant, (cup offered around the room)
which is shed for you for the forgiveness of sins;
do this in remembrance of me.
Father, we do this in remembrance of him:
his blood is shed for all.
Silence

As we proclaim his death and celebrate his rising in
    glory, (hands laid on bread and wine)
send your Holy Spirit that this bread and this wine
may be to us the body and blood of your dear Son.

As we eat and drink these holy gifts
make us one in Christ, our risen Lord.
Silence

With your whole Church throughout the world
we offer you this sacrifice of praise
and lift our voice to join the eternal song of heaven.

Sanctus
Holy, holy, holy Lord,
God of power and might,
Heaven and earth are full of your glory.
Hosanna in the highest.

[CW 204–5]

THE LORD'S PRAYER

In silence we pray together the Lord's Prayer.

BREAKING OF THE BREAD

The bread is broken in silence and elevated for all to see.

The president and assistants receive communion.

The president and assistants come in front of the table and stand ready to give communion to the people.

The president beckons to the people to come and receive in silence.

When people have received, they sit down. When all have received and all are seated, the president and the assistants return to the holy table. The table is cleared and the elements are disposed of reverently.

BLESSING

The president makes the sign of the cross to the assistants, and they cross themselves.

The president makes the sign of the cross to the people and they cross themselves.

DISMISSAL

Go in peace to love and serve the Lord.
In the name of Christ. Amen.

Lent:
The Lenten tree pathway

Introduction

What is a Lenten tree?

It is an actual tree, or possibly a cross, around or on which symbols relating to Jesus' suffering and death are placed from Ash Wednesday through Lent. If the tree is in church, the symbols for each Sunday are used. If the tree is at home and so the focus on household prayers, a different symbol is used each day.

The origins of the Lenten cross and tree

In his 'Sermon 205', Augustine of Hippo considers the 'cross of Lent'[2]. He suggests that what a Christian does in Lent is really the same as during the rest of the year, but more intensely so. He says that the cross is where Christians should be for all their life, and to emphasize the point he used a number of scriptural passages. Perhaps here lie the origins of the Lenten cross, where Scripture passages are used daily to help us enter more deeply into the events of Christ's suffering and death.

The cross to which Augustine referred was probably meant to be no more than a mental construct, which, in popular devotion, became an actual cross, on which symbols are placed throughout Lent. Eventually it evolved into an elaborately decorated object with beautiful carvings. More recently, though, there has been a trend towards simplicity, and the decorative cross has been replaced by a more simple, plain one.

The origins of the Lenten tree are shrouded in even more mystery. The 'classic books' tend to deal exclusively with its meaning and use rather than to explore its origins. A quick Internet search suggests that it became popular in free church circles in the early 1990s.

The Lenten tree mirrors almost exactly the liturgical use of the Jesse tree in Advent (you can read more about this in the first volume of *Together for a Season*) in that it is concerned with the placing of symbols on or around a tree or cross. There is therefore a strong likelihood that one derives from the other and clearly the Jesse tree has a longer history.

There seems to have been a cross-fertilization of ideas between the Lenten cross and the more modern Lenten tree to the point where the two are inextricably linked.

Practical inclusive ideas

A path through Lent

The use of the Lenten tree, like the Jesse tree in Advent, offers us a possibility of an integrated pathway through Lent. By using the symbols on the key days throughout the season, we can make a coherent liturgical journey that is easy to navigate.

Making the Lenten tree

Ideally, the Lenten tree is a cross made out of the church's Christmas tree. This makes the subtle yet profound link between the incarnation of the Christ and his suffering and death.

The branches are stripped off until only the trunk is left. This is then cut into two pieces, one twice as long as the other. The longer section forms the vertical part of the cross and the shorter the horizontal piece. It is either nailed together or held together by some kind of twine.

It then needs a base substantial enough to hold it upright, large enough to carry symbols and high enough to be seen. Depending on size, it could be held upright by whatever means the church Christmas tree was supported. Alternatively, a simple Christmas tree stand, available in most shops around Christmas, could be used. Remember though, that these are unlikely to be available in the weeks before Lent!

If the Lenten tree model based on the Christmas tree is not an option, another alternative is to use a free-standing cross with a piece of purple material draped

1. The branches are stripped off until only the trunk is left.

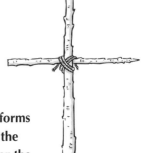

2. This is then cut into two pieces, one twice as long as the other.

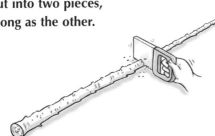

3. The longer section forms the vertical part of the cross and the shorter the horizontal piece. It is nailed together or held by some kind of twine.

over the arms. The symbols are placed around the base. This is called the Lenten cross.

Another possibility is to make a large banner with a tree drawn or painted on it. This could be hung in a prominent position at the front of the church. The symbols could then be stuck on to the 'tree' using hooked Velcro™. The symbols should be pictures made as part of activities in the service.

Whichever model is adopted, it is important that the Lenten tree (or cross) should be large, prominent and visible.

The Lenten wreath

A Lenten wreath is a variant of the Lenten cross that is clearly derived from the Advent wreath tradition. Here a cross is laid out on a flat surface with places to light a candle on each of the six Sundays through Lent, and space for a larger, white, candle to be lit on Easter Day (see diagram).

The candles can be lit each day in the home at a suitable point. This might be a more appropriate construction for the Lenten tree/cross in the home.

Making a Lenten wreath

The Lenten wreath is often made of rose, vines and thistles, representing the crown of thorns placed upon our Lord's head by Pontius Pilate. There are six candles (these can be white or purple), which are lit consecutively on the six Sundays in Lent. There can be room in the centre for a large candle to be lit on Easter Day. Other variations have a black candle that is lit on Good Friday and/or a pink candle to be lit on Mothering Sunday (replacing one of the white or purple ones. Some wreaths also have three nails depicting those used to nail Christ on the cross.

A WARNING

Lent is a time when candle use is restrained because it could be seen to pre-empt, and even detract from, the dramatic use of light and candles at the Easter Liturgy. If a Lenten wreath is used in church, any conflict of this nature should be avoided.

The wreath can be made from twining and thorny branches, vine, rose or brambles.   **pieces of wood**

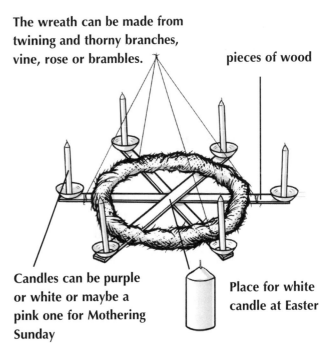

Candles can be purple or white or maybe a pink one for Mothering Sunday

Place for white candle at Easter

The symbols

There are many different sequences of readings and symbols for the Lenten tree. Nothing should be seen as being prescriptive, and the suggestions given here probably need to be adapted to local circumstances.

Symbols to be placed around the base of the tree or cross are suggested for each of the Sundays in Lent, plus Maundy Thursday, Good Friday, Holy Saturday and Easter Day. There are also notes and brief liturgical suggestions for each occasion.

A decision needs to be made about whether the symbols will be left around the cross throughout the whole of Lent, so building up a picture of the passion of Jesus, or whether only the symbols for that particular Sunday will be used when we highlight their presence and meaning. Each has its own strengths and weaknesses.

One way of keeping these themes in the mind of the congregation is to give people a representative token each week to remind them of what has been placed around the Lenten tree.

The readings and prayers below could be used in any year, as they are independent of the lectionary readings.

The symbols could be brought in at various points during the service, though the material below assumes that it will form part of the gathering rite and would lead into the prayers of penitence. Other possible places might be:

- After the Liturgy of the Word, providing a liturgical context for the Intercessions;
- At the Offertory as part of the Preparation of the Table;
- At the end of the service, as part of the Dismissal.

If these other places are used, the liturgical material offered here will need to be adapted.

Although the presentation of the symbols can take place at a number of different points within the liturgy, for consistency and continuity we recommend that the same place be used throughout Lent unless there is a good reason to deviate from the usual pattern, such as on Ash Wednesday.

For each of the occasions below it is suggested that the symbols are carried in so that they are clearly visible. If they form part of an entrance procession, this would be helped if they were held aloft and placed at or near the front of the worship area.

The Sunday scheme of readings and symbols

Ash Wednesday

ASH FROM BURNT PALM CROSSES

The containers of ash are brought forward during the opening hymn. They are taken to the Lenten tree.

The president greets the congregation and the service continues in the customary way.

As part of the opening part of the service, the ash from the burnt palm crosses is mixed with water and oil in preparation for the ashing, which comes later in the service as part of the Liturgy of Penitence.

At the end of the imposition of ashes, the ash is returned to the base of the Lenten tree. It is left there through Lent and may be used by worshippers during the season as an act of private devotion.

Week 1 – The First Sunday of Lent

BREAD AND WINE

The bread and wine are brought forward during the opening hymn. They are taken to the Lenten tree, where the bearers hold them.

The president greets the congregation and an opening prayer may be used.

The bread is laid at the foot of the cross with these words
Bread to feed the hungry in a starving world.

The wine is laid at the foot of the cross with these words
Wine to gladden the heart in a painful world.

The prayers of penitence are introduced with these or other suitable words
God has given bread for the world, enough for all to be filled.
Let us call to mind the ways we keep God's gifts for ourselves.

The service continues with the Confession.

If the bread and wine are to be used for the Eucharist, they are placed on the holy table during the Preparation of the Table.
We say together
These gifts of pain and celebration
shall be for us the body and blood of Christ.

The service continues with the Eucharistic Prayer.

Week 2 – Second Sunday of Lent

PERFUME FOR ANOINTING

The perfume is brought forward during the opening hymn. It is taken to the Lenten tree, where the bearer holds it.

The president greets the congregation and an opening prayer may be used.

These words are used as the perfume is poured into a bowl at the foot of the Lenten tree, allowing the fragrance to permeate the church

Perfume, poured out to prepare our Lord for his death.

We say together
May the fragrance of Jesus fill this place.
May the fragrance of Jesus fill my life.

The prayers of penitence are introduced with these or other suitable words
God calls us to be a fragrant offering to his glory.
Let us call to mind the way our living exudes the odour of death.
The service continues with the Confession.

After the president has pronounced the Absolution, members of the congregation may be invited to come to the Lenten tree and have the perfume spread on their hands. This may be accompanied by singing.

Once the congregation has finished using the perfume, the singing ends and the service continues with the Collect.

Week 3 – Third Sunday of Lent

THIRTY PIECES OF SILVER

A bag of money is brought forward during the opening hymn. It is taken to the Lenten tree, where the bearer holds it.

The president greets the congregation and an opening prayer may be used.

The bag of money is laid at the foot of the cross with these words
Money: for the relief of poverty, and a root of evil.

We say together
May our riches be in our love of the Lord.

The prayers of penitence are introduced with these or other suitable words
God chose the poor in the world to be rich in faith

and to be heirs of the kingdom that he has promised to those who love him.
Let us call to mind the way we dishonour the poor.
The service continues with the Confession.

If a monetary collection is offered, it could be laid at the foot of the Lenten tree with these words
Yours, Lord, is the greatness, the power,
the glory, the splendour, and the majesty;
for everything in heaven and on earth is yours.

All things come from you,
and of your own do we give you.

[CW 291]

Week 4 – Fourth Sunday of Lent

CROWN OF THORNS

The crown of thorns is brought forward during the opening hymn. It is taken to the Lenten tree, where the bearer holds it.

The president greets the congregation and an opening prayer may be used.

The crown of thorns is placed over the cross with these words
The crown of thorns – a sign of mockery and the truth of his reign.

We say together
May we wear with Christ
the crown of eternal life.

The prayers of penitence are introduced with these or other suitable words
Jesus says, 'Be faithful until death, and I will give you the crown of life.'

Let us call to mind the ways we are unfaithful to our Lord.
The service continues with the Confession.

If a suitable crown of thorns can be made, an opportunity might be provided for individuals who wish gently to place it on their head to experience a little of what our Lord suffered. Extreme care needs to be taken if this is done.

If Mothering Sunday is celebrated, the same scheme should be continued so that our journey towards the cross is uninterrupted, though some explanation may be necessary especially if there are visitors in the church.

Week 5 – Fifth Sunday of Lent

WHIP

The whip is brought forward during the opening hymn. It is taken to the Lenten tree, where the bearer holds it.

The president greets the congregation and an opening prayer may be used.

The whip is placed on the cross with these words
The whip of oppression that tortured our Lord and tore his flesh.

We say together
He bore our pain.
May we relieve the pain of others.

The prayers of penitence are introduced with these or other suitable words
He was wounded for our transgressions, crushed for our iniquities;
upon him was the punishment that made us whole, and by his bruises we are healed.
Let us call to mind the way we cause pain to others.
The service continues with the Confession.

Week 6 – Palm Sunday

PALMS

After the procession commemorating our Lord's entry into Jerusalem has entered the worship area, the congregation processes past the Lenten tree, where they drop the palms or branches that have been used. This is done without words during the singing of a hymn or song, such as 'All glory, laud and honour'.

It is recommended that palm crosses are NOT used for the procession but palms or branches are used. If palm crosses are to be distributed, they could form part of the Dismissal as people ready themselves for their walk with Jesus through Holy Week.

Maundy Thursday

BOWL AND TOWEL

The bowl and towel are brought forward during the opening hymn and are taken to the Lenten tree.

If the holy oils are to be received into the church, the bearers simply place them at the foot of the Lenten tree without words or ceremony and go to their places. The service continues with the reception of the oils.

If there is no reception of the holy oils, the bearers hold them and remain by the Lenten tree.

The president greets the congregation and an opening prayer may be used.

The bowl and towel are placed at the foot of the Lenten tree with these words
The bowl and towel for the washing of the feet of his disciples – a sign of Jesus' love.

We say together
May we love one another as Christ has loved us.

The prayers of penitence are introduced with these or other suitable words
The Son of Man came not to be served but to serve, and to give his life a ransom for many.
Let us call to mind the ways we fail to serve others but expect others to serve us.
The service continues with the Confession.

The bowl and towel are used later in the service for the washing of feet.

Good Friday

As every service on Good Friday inevitably and rightly focuses on the cross of Christ, it might be considered unnecessary to add any extra ceremony regarding the Lenten tree.

If the Lenten tree is to be used, it should be the cross that is used throughout the service. Ensure it is in a place central to the worship and any extraneous cloths removed. The Good Friday Liturgy offers a number of different ways in which the cross might be used.

Holy Saturday

FLOWERS

This day should be marked by as minimal a liturgy as possible. If the church is open, flowers (daffodils) might be left near the cross for any visitors to place at the foot of the cross, as often happens near the site of a tragedy.

Alternatively, a time could be advertised when people might come into church to place flowers around the cross and spend some time in prayer.

Easter Day

TRANSFORMING THE CROSS

Before the service begins, the symbols of Jesus' suffering and death are removed and the cross is covered with florist's foam.

At an appropriate point in the service, each member of the congregation is invited to place a flower on the cross. The appropriate point will depend upon the nature of the service. If it is the Easter Liturgy, returning from communion might be the most suitable occasion.

The Lenten tree in groups

Children

There is a session for each of the weeks of Lent. The opening part of the session is drawn from Prayer During the Day in Lent from *Common Worship: Daily Prayer*. This provides an opportunity for the children to become familiar with some significant liturgical texts used in the familiar setting of their group. This material is suitable for use either on Sunday or during the week. The material provided will last for between 45 minutes and an hour.

Opening part of the meeting (common to every session)

Before the meeting begins, place three small candles on a table in the middle of the space where the children gather

PREPARATION

Make sure there is someone at the door to greet each child on arrival. Ask if they have had a good week and if there is anything special they want to share this week. When each child is ready to sit down, direct them to join a circle where the leader greets them too and encourages them to join in the discussion of the circle.

When everyone has arrived, light the first candle.

Leader: *Let us share anything we especially want to say thank you to God for this week.*

Light the second candle.

Leader: *Let us remember anyone we know who is sad or ill or frightened at the moment.*

Light the third candle.

Leader: *If any other thoughts come into your mind while we are saying these prayers, just tell God about them quietly in your mind.*

Now let's say our opening prayers:

O God, make speed to save us.
O Lord, make haste to help us.
Hear my prayer, O Lord, and give ear to my cry;
hold not your peace at my tears.

Psalm 39.13

PRAISE

Each week a different person could say this and by the end of Lent most people may be able to say it all together

Jesus, like a mother you gather your people to you; you are gentle with us as a mother with her children. Lord Jesus, in your mercy heal us; in your love and tenderness remake us.

Shortened from Anselm (1109)

[DP 66]

You could sing a short song that you all know here.

PRAYER

Say this prayer together
Lord Jesus, be with us as we travel through these weeks of Lent, so that we will be ready to enter the mystery of Easter. Amen.

Different material for each week

ON OR AFTER ASH WEDNESDAY – SYMBOL: ASH

(If no meetings are planned until after the first Sunday of Lent, this session could be omitted.)

THE WORD OF GOD IN THE STORY OF JONAH

If the group of children is familiar with the story of Jonah, retell it together. If it is not a story they know, then you should tell it to them. There are several lovely picture books that tell the story and details are provided in the Resources section. Or you could use the Godly Play version of the story.

Spend time particularly on the part of the story in chapter 3, when Jonah obeys God's second call for him to go to Nineveh.

Symbols and reflection

A member of the group places a container with ash used at the Ash Wednesday service in the middle of the three candles. You might like to add a piece of sacking cloth to this.

Think about the story together. You may like to use the four questions used in the Godly Play method of thinking about sacred stories:

- I wonder which part of the story you liked best?
- I wonder what was the most important part of the story?
- I wonder if there is any part of the story that is about you, or I wonder where you are in the story?
- I wonder if there is any part of the story we could leave out and still have all the story we need?

When you have finished wondering together, you could take the container of ash out of the middle of the circle and invite the children to pass it round and make a cross on one another's hands, saying 'dust you are and to dust you shall return' as they do so. You should demonstrate with the first child and invite that person to mark your hand also before they pass it on to the next person. No one should be obliged to take part in this.

Art, craft and other activities

Invite children to choose what they do to respond to the story. Allow a free choice and make sure you have plenty of paper, paint, clay and so on for them so that they can each choose their own activity. Invite them to use the ash and sackcloth also if they would like to.

NB This ending is used for each session.

Final prayer

We all say this famous prayer together. Use this prayer every week so that, by the end of Lent, the children will know it

**Teach us, good Lord, to serve you as you deserve;
to give and not to count the cost;
to fight and not to heed the wounds;
to toil and not to seek for rest;
to labour and not to seek for any reward,
save that of knowing that we do your will.**

After Ignatius of Loyola (1556)

The Lord's Prayer is said.

The Conclusion

*May God bless us and show us compassion and
    mercy.*
Amen.

[DP 70]

On or after Lent 1 – Symbol: Bread and stones

A member of the group places some bread and some large (and not beautiful) pebbles in the middle of the three candles.

The Word of God in the story of Jesus' temptation in the wilderness

Tell the story of Jesus' temptation in the wilderness. This story is the Gospel reading for the first Sunday in Lent each year. In Year A it is heard from Matthew's Gospel, in Year B from Mark and in Year C from Luke. Each of these accounts has its own emphasis. You may like to use the account directly from the Bible. Each is quite short, so they are not too difficult for children to listen to. Use a version that is easily accessible. You could use the *Good News* version, or Eugene Peterson's *The Message*. If you use a children's Bible, try not to use one that adds unfounded details to the story.

Think about the story together. You may like to use the four questions used in the Godly Play method of thinking about sacred stories (as before).

When you have finished wondering together, you could pass a stone round the circle. Invite each person to weigh it in his or her hand and feel how hard it is. As children pass it on to the next person, they say, 'Remember not to be hard hearted.' Then invite them to pass round the bread and to break off a piece each. Before they eat it, they can each say, 'Give us this day our daily bread.'

Art, craft and other activities

As before, but also invite the children to use stones if they would like to.

Conclude with the session ending (see above).

On or after Lent 2 – Symbol: Perfume

A member of the group places a bottle of perfume or a bowl of perfumed oil in the middle of the three candles.

THE WORD OF GOD IN THE STORY OF THE WOMAN WHO POURED PERFUME ON JESUS' HEAD

The story is found in Mark 14.3-9. You could read it from *The Message*, tell it in your own words or from a children's Bible (though many do not carry an account of this incident). If you are going to use your own words, do not add unwarranted details.

Think about the story together. You may like to use the four questions used in Godly Play (as before).

When you have finished wondering together, you could pass the bottle of perfume around the group and invite each person to smell it. Those who would like to put some one should be invited to do so.

ART, CRAFT AND OTHER ACTIVITIES

As before (see p. 40).

Conclude with the session ending (see p. 40).

ON OR AFTER LENT 3 – SYMBOL: THIRTY PIECES OF SILVER

A member of the group places money in the middle of the three candles. You will need to judge whether to use 30 coins, or whether to use a pile of large denomination notes, indicating that this was a significant amount of money.

THE WORD OF GOD IN THE STORY OF JUDAS ISCARIOT'S BETRAYAL OF JESUS

Tell the story of Judas betraying Jesus from Matthew's Gospel. Read chapter 26 verses 14-16 (Judas agrees to betray Jesus), 47-50 (in the garden of Gethsemane) and chapter 27 verses 1-10 (Judas hangs himself). You could find it in a version such as *The Message*, or you could tell the story in your own words. You might want to tell the story only as far as the arrest of Jesus, looking just at the betrayal of Jesus for money, though the question of Judas' response to what he had done and how the authorities dealt with the money they reacquired would be a suitable issue for a group of older children or teenagers.

Think about the story together. You may like to use the four questions used in the Godly Play method of thinking about sacred stories (see p. 40), but today do not pass anything round the group.

ART, CRAFT AND OTHER ACTIVITIES

As before (see p. 40).

Conclude with the session ending (see p. 40).

ON OR AFTER LENT 4 – SYMBOL: MARY THE MOTHER OF JESUS

This session falls either on or after Mothering Sunday and so we use the image of Mary at the foot of the cross.

A member of the group places a picture of Mary in the middle of the three candles.

THE WORD OF GOD IN THE STORY OF MARY THE MOTHER OF JESUS AT THE FOOT OF THE CROSS

Tell the story of Mary and John at the foot of the cross from John 19.25-27.

Think about the story together. You may like to use the four questions used in the Godly Play method of thinking about sacred stories (see p. 40).

After the story and your reflections, give each person in the circle a little figure to hold in the palm of his or her hand. These could be figures cut out of paper, or they could be Lego™ or Playmobil™ figures or Godly Play people of God. It doesn't matter what they look like, just that everyone should have one. Ask people to hold the figure in the palm of their hand and then ask the question 'I wonder who you need to care for and to look after?'

ART, CRAFT AND OTHER ACTIVITIES

As before (see p. 40) but also make the figures you have used available.

Conclude with the session ending (see p. 40).

ON OR AFTER LENT 5 – SYMBOL: CROWN OF THORNS

A member of the group places a circle of barbed wire or a crown made of thorny twigs in the middle of the three candles.

THE WORD OF GOD IN THE STORY OF JESUS BEING CROWNED WITH THORNS

Tell the story of Pilate having a crown of thorns put on Jesus' head, from John 19.1-6,12-16. You might choose to read it from a translation such as *The Message*, from a children's Bible or you could tell it in your own words. However, try not to add unwarranted detail to the story.

Think about the story together. You may like to use the four questions used in the Godly Play method of thinking about sacred stories (see p. 40).

After the story and your reflections, pass a thorn taken from (perhaps a rose) bush around the circle.

You may want to put it in a tiny box or on a little dish. As people pass the thorn to the next person, they say: 'Remember how easy it is to hurt other people.'

ART, CRAFT AND OTHER ACTIVITIES

As before (see p. 40).

Conclude with the session ending (see p. 40).

Adults

The following group materials are designed to follow on from the Sunday symbols that are placed around the Lenten tree during Lent

Each session is designed to be self-contained. Any one session could be missed with no effect on the weeks that follow. In some churches it might be impossible to hold a meeting on the days between Ash Wednesday and the first Sunday of Lent, or on the Monday, Tuesday or Wednesday of Holy Week. In those situations you simply omit those sessions.

Each session is planned to last an hour and fifteen minutes, though this could be expanded or contracted to fit the time available.

The whole group meeting is an 'Office of prayer'. The material below uses the office of Prayer during the Day for Lent from *Common Worship: Daily Prayer*. The session begins with the Preparation and Praise from the first part of the office. The group work then forms part of the central section where we engage with the Word of God in Scripture. It then ends with the Response, Prayers and the Conclusion. In this way the whole meeting becomes an extended Office.

The opening part of the Office is to be found at the beginning of the next section. From that point onwards simply follow the pattern for each week.

Opening part of the meeting (common to every session)

Here is a format for prayer with which each evening might begin.

Before the meeting begins, place three small candles on a table in the middle of the space where people will meet.

PREPARATION

A short piece of quiet, reflective music may be played on a CD player.

During the music
Leader: *Take a moment to be still before God.*

A candle may be lit.
Leader: *Be aware of the many people who are sharing in prayer throughout the world.*

A candle may be lit.
Leader: *Remember before God the significant events of the day/week and offer them and the people involved into the hands of God.*

A candle may be lit.
Leader: *If any thoughts or concerns enter your mind during this quiet time, do not try to block them but allow them to emerge. As they form, imagine you take hold of them, look at them, and then place them into the greater hands of God.*

When the music stops, a short silence is kept then the leader begins
O God, make speed to save us.
O Lord, make haste to help us.
Hear my prayer, O Lord, and give ear to my cry;
hold not your peace at my tears.

Psalm 39.13

PRAISE

All are invited to say
Jesus, like a mother you gather your people to you;
you are gentle with us as a mother with her children.

Despair turns to hope through your sweet goodness;
through your gentleness we find comfort in fear.

Your warmth gives life to the dead,
your touch makes sinners righteous.

Lord Jesus, in your mercy heal us;
in your love and tenderness remake us.

In your compassion bring grace and forgiveness,
for the beauty of heaven may your love prepare us.

After Anselm (1109)

[DP 66}

A song or a hymn may be sung
From Psalm 103
Bless the Lord, O my soul,
and all that is within me bless his holy name.
The Lord is full of compassion and mercy,

slow to anger and of great kindness.
For as the heavens are high above the earth,
so great is his mercy upon those who fear him.

Glory to the Father and to the Son
and to the Holy Spirit;
as it was in the beginning is now
and shall be for ever. Amen.

[CW 714]

The Collect may be said by the leader or by everyone
Almighty God,
by the prayer and discipline of Lent
may we enter into the mystery of Christ's sufferings,
and by following in his Way
come to share in his glory;
through Jesus Christ our Lord.
Amen.

[DP 424]

Different material for each week

AFTER ASH WEDNESDAY – SYMBOL: ASH

(If no meetings are planned until after the first Sunday of Lent, this session could be omitted.)

SCRIPTURE PASSAGE JONAH 3.1-10

Read the Scripture passage out loud, but try to make sure people can see it either in their own Bibles or on a specially printed sheet.

Allow a short silence for reflection on the reading.

COMMENT

Allow anyone who wishes to offer a question that emerges from the reading to which they would like an answer. If possible, write them down and then use them in turn as discussion starters.

SYMBOL AND REFLECTION

A member of the group places a container with ash used at the Ash Wednesday service in the middle of the three candles.

Each member of the group is invited to reflect on what that ash means to them. Each person could ask questions such as:

- What is there in my life that feels like that ash at this moment?
- What is there in my life that I would like to commit to the purifying flames of the Holy Spirit?

- Which elements of my life or behaviour patterns do I wish weren't there?

Those who feel able are invited to share their thoughts with the rest of the group. Be aware that this may stir up some very personal thoughts that people may not want to share, so this part of the exercise should not be forced.

Silence is kept for further reflection.

COMMENT ON ASH

REPENTANCE AND SORROW

In the Old Testament, the covering of the head with ash, or even suiting in ashes, is a sign of repentance or sorrow:

- The prophet Jeremiah, for example, calls for repentance this way: 'O my poor people, put on sackcloth, and roll in ashes' (Jeremiah 6.26).
- 'I turned to the Lord God, to seek an answer by prayer and supplication with fasting and sackcloth and ashes' (Daniel 9.3).

Perhaps the best known example of repentance in the Old Testament that involves sackcloth and ashes is that which we heard earlier. When the prophet Jonah finally obeyed God's command and preached in the great city of Nineveh, his preaching was amazingly effective. Word of his message was carried to the king of Nineveh. 'When the news reached the king of Nineveh, he rose from his throne, removed his robe, covered himself with sackcloth, and sat in ashes' (Jonah 3.6).

In the New Testament, Jesus refers to the use of sackcloth and ashes as signs of repentance:

Woe to you, Chorazin! Woe to you, Bethsaida! For if the deeds of power done in you had been done in Tyre and Sidon, they would have repented long ago in sackcloth and ashes.

Matthew 11.21, Luke 10.13

This Old Testament tradition became a significant feature of medieval piety when it became the practice to use ash to mark the beginning of Lent. Traditionally, the ash of Ash Wednesday is made from the burning of the palm leaves that were used to mark Palm Sunday the previous year.

MOURNING

Ash was also associated with mourning:

- 'Then Jacob tore his garments, and put sackcloth on his loins, and mourned for his son for many days' (Genesis 37.34).
- 'Then David said to Joab and to all the people who were with him, "Tear your clothes, and put on sackcloth, and mourn over Abner." And King David followed the bier' (2 Samuel 3.31).
- 'When Mordecai learned all that had been done, Mordecai tore his clothes and put on sackcloth and ashes, and went through the city, wailing with a loud and bitter cry' (Esther 4.1).

WORTHLESSNESS

The term 'ashes' is often used to signify worthlessness, insignificance or evanescence (Genesis 18.27; Job 30.19).

PURIFICATION/CONSECRATION

There is also another tradition in which ashes are used as a source of purification. In Numbers chapter 19 the ashes from a red heifer that is completely burned, when sprinkled on the unclean, makes them ceremonially clean.

In the medieval period ashes were mixed with a special blessed water called 'Gregorian water' and then used in the consecration of churches.

BUILDING UP

Ash was also used in the construction industry in Roman times to make cement that was used to make buildings stronger. Today, fly ash, which is a by-product of burning powdered coal, forms a constituent part of concrete, without which many of the buildings of today could not be constructed.

DISCUSSION

Ask: Which of the different meanings of ash strikes you most forcefully? Why?

We return to the Office of Prayer …

RESPONSE

A song may be sung or a quiet piece of music played.

Blessed are the merciful,
for they will receive mercy.

Matthew 5.7

[DP 69]

PERSONAL PRAYER

Of the many different uses for ash, all present are invited to decide which for them personally is the most significant. The leader explains that in a moment all are going to be invited to use the ash and it can mean for them whatever they want it to mean from the possibilities suggested above or from other possibilities that may have emerged through the discussion.

Silence is kept as people decide what significance the ash has for them.

Some music is played as each person uses the ash individually.

When the music stops, a short silence is kept.

NB The section below should be used to end each session.

We all say this prayer
Teach us, good Lord, to serve you as you deserve;
to give and not to count the cost;
to fight and not to heed the wounds;
to toil and not to seek for rest;
to labour and not to seek for any reward,
save that of knowing that we do your will.

After Ignatius of Loyola (1556)

The Lord's Prayer is said.

THE CONCLUSION

May God bless us and show us compassion and mercy.
Amen.

[DP 70]

AFTER LENT 1 – SYMBOL: BREAD AND WINE

SCRIPTURE PASSAGE 1 CORINTHIANS 11.23-26 (29)

Read out the Scripture passage, but try to make sure people can see it either in their own Bibles or on a specially printed sheet.

Allow a short silence for reflection on the reading

COMMENT

Allow anyone who wishes to offer a question that emerges from the reading to which they would like an answer. If possible, write them down and then use them in turn as discussion starters.

SYMBOL AND REFLECTION

A member of the group places bread and wine in the middle of the three candles.

Each member of the group is invited to reflect on what the bread and wine means to them. Each person could ask questions such as:

- Is there anything special about bread and wine?
- Could other food and drink have the same meaning?
- Do bread and wine mean something different when used in the Eucharist?

Those who feel able are invited to share their thoughts with the rest of the group. Be aware that this may stir up some very personal thoughts that people may not want to share, so this part of the exercise should not be forced.

Silence is kept for further reflection.

COMMENT ON BREAD AND WINE

ORDINARY 'STUFF'

In one sense bread and wine are not special. They were the ordinary food and drink of ordinary people, and had been since earliest times.

There are many references to bread and wine in the Bible: Noah was the first biblical character to be described as drunk (Genesis 9.21); bread and wine are often mentioned as signs of well-being (e.g. Judges 19.19); and Psalm 104.15 represents a fairly typical view – 'wine to gladden the human heart, oil to make the face shine, and bread to strengthen the human heart.'

Bakers had a significant role in households where they had 'staff' – the best known early example in the Bible is the baker in Pharaoh's household, who met Joseph in prison and had a dream interpreted by him. His fellow-prisoner was the 'cup-bearer to the king' – so bread and wine featured in that story (if you have seen *Joseph and his Amazing Technicolour Dream Coat* you will be familiar with these characters).

Just a thought: if bread and wine were the ordinary food and drink in Jesus' day at the time of the Last Supper, would he have used different elements if he were doing it today. If so, what? Pizza and beer? Something else?

SPECIAL 'STUFF'

The significant event in the history of God's people, which first made the ordinary 'special', was the Exodus and, in particular, the Passover, which celebrated that event. In memory of the Israelites making unleavened bread as they travelled, escaping from Egypt, at the Passover unleavened bread is eaten and wine is prominent too. Thus bread and wine in this particular context have become 'special'.

EXTRA-SPECIAL 'STUFF'

It was the Passover meal that Jesus and his disciples were eating the night of his betrayal – they were eating bread and wine. But Jesus now gave it a new significance: taking the bread (which the host at Passover normally did) he said: 'This is my body which is for you.' Similarly, taking the wine he said: 'This cup is the new covenant in my blood.' From now on, for Christians, bread and wine had an extra-special significance: rather than remembering the Passover, they were to remember him – and they were to go on doing so.

DOING THE 'STUFF'

Ever since then, Christians have taken bread and wine in remembrance of Jesus. In different traditions the service is called by different names: Mass, Eucharist, Communion, the Lord's Supper. And there is a variety of practice, too: because it is a special activity, some do it often (weekly or daily) while others do it less often (monthly, quarterly, or even annually). Some believe in 'transubstantiation' – the bread and wine become the body and blood of Jesus; some believe in 'consubstantiation' – the body and blood of Jesus are united to the bread and wine; others focus on remembering in the dynamic way the Jews do – that is, as if I were there and it happened for me; others simply use bread and wine to remember what happened in the past. Some use real bread, some use wafers; some use real wine, some use Ribena™ (or something similar).

However it is done, whatever it is called, whenever it happens, that it is done is the important thing: in the context of Christian worship, the ordinary (bread and wine) has become special (the body and blood of Jesus) – and we are called to 'do this in remembrance of me'.

DISCUSSION

Ask: Both Passover and Eucharist celebrate God's saving actions: Passover the escape of the Israelites from slavery in Egypt, Eucharist the death of Jesus 'to save us from our sins'. In view of that, how do the symbols of bread and wine help you think about Jesus' death?

We return to the Office of Prayer …

RESPONSE

A song may be sung or a quiet piece of music played.

Blessed are the merciful
for they will receive mercy.

Matthew 5.7

[DP 69]

PRAYER

Of the different possible meaning of the symbols of bread and wine, all present are invited to decide which for them personally is the most significant at this moment in their life.

The leader explains that in a moment all will be invited to taste the bread and wine for themselves.

Silence is kept as people decide what significance the bread and wine have for them.

Some music is played as the leader informally breaks the bread into the right number of pieces and pours the wine into a glass or glasses.

Each person tastes the bread and wine.

When the music stops a short silence is kept.

Conclude with the session ending on (see p. 44).

AFTER LENT 2 – SYMBOL: PERFUME

SCRIPTURE PASSAGE MARK 14.1-9

Read out the Scripture passage, but try to make sure people can see it either in their own Bibles or on a specially printed sheet.

Allow a short silence for reflection on the reading.

COMMENT

Allow anyone who wishes to offer a question that emerges from the reading to which they would like an answer. If possible, write them down and then use them in turn as discussion starters.

SYMBOL AND REFLECTION

A member of the group places perfume in the middle of the three candles.

Each member of the group is invited to reflect on what that perfume means to them. Each person could ask questions such as:

- What kind of perfume do I give off through my life?
- Could I ever be as extravagant in expressing my feelings for Jesus as the woman in the story was?
- Who are the poor who are 'always with me' and what should I do about them?

Those who feel able are invited to share their thoughts with the rest of the group. Be aware that this may stir up some very personal thoughts that people may not want to share, so this part of the exercise should not be forced.

Silence is kept for further reflection.

COMMENT ON PERFUME

SMELLING NICE

Products that enhance the feel of the skin and the smell of the body have been highly valued in every culture.

The earliest form of perfume was incense. It was first discovered by the Mesopotamians and quickly made its way to Egypt, where it became very popular. Incense and other perfumes were used extensively on both the living and the dead, and in both mystic and religious ceremonies!

The Romans also used perfumes, their public baths containing shelves of various perfumes that were used frequently and extravagantly.

Today, perfumes are evident in our society as people look for the physical and spiritual help they find in aromatherapy and similar practices where perfumes are used.

FRAGRANT WORSHIP

Perfume, particularly incense, has featured throughout the Judaeo-Christian tradition.

Moses, for example, in his instructions for the creating of the tabernacle and all the paraphernalia of worship, was told: 'Take sweet spices, stacte, and onycha and galbanum, sweet spices with pure frankincense, (an equal part of each), and make an incense blended as by the perfumer, seasoned with salt, pure and holy' (Exodus 30.34-35).

When Solomon was about to build the Temple, he explained what it was for: 'I am now about to build a house for the name of the Lord my God and dedicate it to him for offering fragrant incense before him …' (2 Chronicles 2.4).

Indeed, so significant was perfume in the worship of God that one way in which people demonstrated their sinfulness and spiritual waywardness was to burn perfume to other gods: '… provoking me to anger, in that they went to make offerings and serve other gods that they had not known, neither they, nor you, nor your ancestors' (Jeremiah 44.3).

The best known biblical example of perfume being used in worship is the bringing by the wise men of gold, frankincense and myrrh to the infant Jesus (Matthew 2).

Traditionally, incense has been symbolic of the prayers and worship of God's people, e.g. 'Let my prayer be counted as incense before you' (Psalm 141.2) and 'Each [living creature] holding a harp and golden bowls full of incense, which are the prayers of the saints' (Revelation 5.8).

Incense is used today widely in Christian worship in Orthodox and Roman Catholic churches and in some Anglican churches. It is used at Christian festivals to heighten the liturgical ambience, particularly in Eucharistic celebrations where it is symbolic of the cleansing of priest, people and altar in readiness to celebrate the sacrifice of Christ in the Eucharist.

Some would explain the benefit of burning incense in worship as simply offering the possibility of involving another sense (other than just sight and sound) in worship.

Discussion

Ask: If perfume (particularly incense) is symbolic of prayer and used liturgically in the Eucharist, how might you find it an aid to your own consideration of the sacrifice of Jesus for you?

We return to the Office of Prayer …

Response

A song may be sung or a quiet piece of music played.

Blessed are the merciful
for they will receive mercy.

Matthew 5.7

[DP 69]

Prayer

The leader pours some perfume out of a bottle and into a bowl or open container.

Silence as the fragrance of the perfume is allowed to spread around the room.

Some music is played as each person takes some of the perfume and rubs it on his or her hands. We are invited to reflect on what 'fragrance' we would like to give off to other people.

When the music stops, a short silence is kept.

Conclude with the session ending (see p. 44).

After Lent 3 – Symbol: Thirty pieces of silver

Scripture passage Matthew 26.14-16; 27.1-10

Read out the Scripture passages, but try to make sure people can see them either in their own Bibles or on a specially printed sheet.

Allow a short silence for reflection on the reading.

Comment

Allow anyone who wishes to offer a question that emerges from the reading, to which they would like an answer. If possible, write them down and then use them in turn as discussion starters.

Symbol and reflection

A member of the group places a small bag of money in the middle of the three candles.

All present are invited to reflect on what that money means to them. Each person could ask questions such as:
- If I had been in Judas' shoes, would I have done what he did?
- If I am honest, do I betray Jesus in other ways?
- Has Judas been unfairly 'picked on' as the 'rotten apple'?

Those who feel able, are invited to share their thoughts with the rest of the group. Be aware that this may stir up some very personal thoughts that people may not want to share, so this part of the exercise should not be forced.

Silence is kept for further reflection.

Comment on the 30 pieces of silver

How much?

The story of Judas' betrayal of Jesus' for 30 pieces of silver is well known even by many who know little of the rest of the Christian story. In fact, 30 pieces of silver was 'cheap' – it was the price paid to the owner of a slave if he/she was gored by a bull (Exodus 21.32). If the silver pieces were denarii, each of them a day's wage for a Roman soldier, 30 would be the equivalent of a month's wages, in modern terms perhaps £1,000–£1,500.

WHY?

But why did Judas do it? There have been various theories:

a) if, as it is thought, he was a Zealot (they were a fundamentalist Jewish group who bitterly resented and resisted the occupation of the Romans), perhaps he became disenchanted because he came to see that Jesus was not going to fulfil his specific hopes;

b) it is possible he simply wanted to force Jesus' hand, to make him 'come out' as the Messiah;

c) since John tells us that he was the disciples' treasurer (John 13.29) and that he was greedy and a thief (John 12.6), the betrayal of Jesus may simply have been one way to 'make a quick buck'.

EXPECTED?

What makes the incident all the more significant and poignant is that Judas was chosen by Jesus as one of his twelve special followers, 'to be with him, and to be sent out to proclaim the message' (Mark 3.14). Yet in every Gospel, when Judas is mentioned he has that unfortunate gloss added to him, that he would betray Jesus (Mark 3.19; Matthew 10.4; Luke 6.16; John 18.2,5). John's Gospel implies that Jesus knew all along what Judas would do (John 13.18-30).

What is more, Matthew suggests that the whole thing was a fulfilment of prophecy (Zechariah 11.13).

(It has been suggested that, if you were to put the twelve disciples through an aptitude test – the kind would-be executives might have to do – Judas would have been the only one to show real leadership potential!)

REMORSE? REPENTANCE? OR WHAT?

Matthew records the outcome. Once Judas sees what results from his treachery, he takes the money back and goes and hangs himself. What is going on? A sense of failure? Remorse? A kind of repentance?

The 30 pieces of silver are used to buy a field that becomes a burial place – a fitting outcome.

TODAY?

Key words and phrases from this story are with us still today. 'Judas', '30 pieces of silver', the 'Judas kiss' are heard from time to time to imply some act of treachery.

The challenge for us is that, while we may not be guilty of selling Jesus for 30 pieces of silver, all too often in a variety of ways we betray him: we fail him in word and action.

DISCUSSION

Ask: If the bag of money is symbolic of the betrayal of Jesus by Judas, what alternative items might we place among the candles as symbols of our betrayal of Jesus?

We return to the Office of Prayer …

RESPONSE

A song may be sung or a quiet piece of music played.

Blessed are the merciful,
for they will receive mercy.

Matthew 5.7

[DP 69]

PERSONAL PRAYER

The leader spreads the coins around on the table among the candles.

Each person is invited to pick up a coin.

Music is played and personally people say sorry to God for the times when they have 'sold out' on their faith. When each person is ready, they place the coin back on the table and say to themselves or aloud 'The price for our sin is more than money – it is the life of Christ.'

When the music stops, a short silence is kept.

Conclude with the session ending (see p. 44).

AFTER LENT 4 – SYMBOL: CROWN OF THORNS

SCRIPTURE PASSAGE JOHN 19.1-6,12-16

Read out the Scripture passages, but try to make sure people can see them either in their own Bibles or on a specially printed sheet.

Allow a short silence for reflection on the reading.

COMMENT

Allow anyone who wishes to offer a question that emerges from the reading, to which they would like an answer. If possible, write them down and then use them in turn as discussion starters.

SYMBOL AND REFLECTION

A member of the group places a circle of barbed wire in the middle of the three candles.

All present are invited to reflect on what that barbed wire means to them. Each person could ask questions such as:

- If this was happening today, what mocking symbol would I give him?
- How would it feel to be mercilessly mocked about something that was true?
- Jesus did not react to this cruelty. How would I have handled it?

Those who feel able, are invited to share their thoughts with the rest of the group. Be aware that this may stir up some very personal thoughts that people may not want to share, so this part of the exercise should not be forced.

Silence is kept for further reflection.

COMMENT ON THE CROWN OF THORNS

The catalogue of painful physical actions, not to mention the mental and spiritual anguish, inflicted on Jesus even before being crucified is appalling to consider. He had already experienced arrest followed, in all probability, by ill-treatment and a sleepless night; and then there was the travesty of the trial with its false accusations and the jeering of the crowd baying for his death. Seeking to appease the crowd, Pilate ordered Jesus to be scourged (flogged) (John 19.1).

If that were not sufficient indignity, the Roman soldiers took up the claim that he was a king, and they stripped the bleeding Jesus, dressed him in a robe (Mathew says it was scarlet, Mark and John say it was purple), gave him a stick (staff) as a sceptre, and as the *pièce de résistance* they took flexible branches with long thorns (commonly used as firewood) and plaited them into the shape of a crown. They pressed it into his scalp, which would have caused copious bleeding, the scalp being one of the most vascular areas of the body. They knelt before him paying mock homage, called out, 'Hail, king of the Jews!', spat on him, and struck him repeatedly – Mark says 'on the head' (Mark 15.19), John says they 'slapped him in the face' (John 19.3).

Such indignity! Such excruciating pain! Is that any way to treat any human being? Yet there was added irony: he really was a king, the most gentle, compassionate, self-sacrificing, grace-ful king you could possibly ask for. And here he was wearing a crown of thorns, blood pouring down his bruised, disfigured face.

What is more, he apparently took it all without complaint. Peter, reminiscing later, wrote: 'When he was abused, he did not return abuse; when he suffered, he did not threaten' (1 Peter 2.23). And the writers of the New Testament, the theologians of Christian history, and writers of Christian hymns and poetry have all agreed: 'He did it for us.' 'We may not know, we cannot tell what pains he had to bear; but we believe it was for us he hung and suffered there.'

The crown of thorns is one painful symbol of all that Jesus suffered for us.

DISCUSSION

Ask: 'He did it for us' What does that mean for you?

We return to the Office of Prayer …

RESPONSE

A song may be sung or a quiet piece of music played.

Blessed are the merciful,
for they will receive mercy.

Matthew 5.7

[DP 69]

PERSONAL PRAYER

Silence as we each reflect on what may have emerged through the discussion that is of relevance for each of us.

Silence is kept as each person is invited to ask the question, 'How have others suffered for me?'

Some music is played as the reflection continues.

When the music stops, a short silence is kept.

Conclude with the session ending (see p. 40).

AFTER LENT 5 – SYMBOL: WHIP

SCRIPTURE PASSAGE MARK 10.32-34; 15.1-5,12-15

Read out the Scripture passage, but try to make sure people can see it either in their own Bibles or on a specially printed sheet.

(In the first passage, Jesus foretells his death and resurrection; in the second, Jesus is before Pilate)

Allow a short silence for reflection on the reading.

COMMENT

Allow anyone who wishes to offer a question that emerges from the reading to which they would like an answer. If possible, write them down and then use them in turn as discussion starters.

SYMBOL AND REFLECTION

A member of the group places something representing a whip in the middle of the three candles.

All present are invited to reflect on what that whip means to them. Each person could ask questions such as:

- Just how painful would it have been?
- We use the word 'whip' in colloquial language today. Does that linguistic use have any link to the actual meaning and use?
- The whip was a cruel form of torture. What weapons of torture do we use today – not just physical ones?

Those who feel able, are invited to share their thoughts with the rest of the group. Be aware that this may stir up some very personal thoughts that people may not want to share, so this part of the exercise should not be forced.

Silence is kept for further reflection.

COMMENT ON THE WHIP

A whip is our symbol this time, something that in contemporary use can be relatively harmless – horse riders use whips, for example. The Gospels tell us that Jesus was flogged, which sounds rather more serious – and painful! In fact, in line with the practice of his day, Jesus experienced scourging, arguably the most painful form of torture ever devised by human beings to inflict on other human beings – with the possible exception of crucifixion.

The scourge was a vicious instrument. It comprised a stick/rod with several braided leather thongs attached, in the ends of which were lead, bone, glass and nails. The prisoner was tied to a post to expose and stretch the back and the torture was normally inflicted by two soldiers who were medically trained for the purpose. Repeated whipping with the scourge resulted in intense bleeding. The skin was reduced to ribbons, sometimes muscles were torn and, in the very worst cases, even the gut was exposed.

In view of this, is it any wonder that criminals often died during or shortly after scourging? Jesus, amazingly, survived the painful experience.

It was a punishment the Romans used to try to extract the truth from the prisoner. It is significant, therefore, that according to John's account, it was after Pilate's enigmatic question 'What is truth?' that he had Jesus scourged and that, when he saw Jesus survive, he tried all the harder to have him released. Jesus had not given in to torture or changed his story – Pilate could find no fault in him, no basis for charging him. In the end it was the combination of the crowd's persistence and Pilate's weakness that resulted in Jesus' crucifixion.

The Mel Gibson film *The Passion of the Christ* was difficult for some because of the graphic way it portrayed the suffering and pain of Jesus. The likelihood is that the reality was even worse, not least the scourging.

DISCUSSION

Ask: In Isaiah 53 (usually seen as a prophetic glimpse of the suffering of Jesus) we read: 'Surely he has borne our infirmities and carried our diseases … he was … crushed for our iniquities … and by his bruises we are healed.' (vv. 4,5). Was it really necessary for Jesus to suffer to save us?

We return to the Office of Prayer …

RESPONSE

A song may be sung or a quiet piece of music played.

Blessed are the merciful,
for they will receive mercy.

Matthew 5.7

[DP 69]

PRAYER

People look at the whip and first of all the leader encourages each person to ask how they have borne the lashes of others.

As people continue to look at the whip, the leader encourages each person to ask how they have lashed out at others.

Some music is played as each person is invited to hold the whip for few seconds. First people are invited to ask God for healing from the pain others have caused to them. Then they are invited to ask forgiveness for the ways they have lashed out at others.

When the music stops, a short silence is kept.

We conclude with the session ending (see p. 40).

The Lenten tree at home

Just as the Jesse tree can be used both in church and at home, so too can the Lenten tree and it offers a simple way of encouraging families to start praying together, albeit briefly.

Again, you can use either a cross or a tree format. You could use a banner with Velcro™ for holding the symbols onto the tree or a wooden cross with small hooks or nails. A piece of laminated card could also be used and the symbols stuck onto it using sticky tack or a similar substance. However, you need to be aware that, because there are daily symbols, there will need to be a lot more 'spaces' than on the tree in church – 40 in all! This number is arrived at by counting each day from Ash Wednesday to Holy Saturday inclusive, but omitting the Sundays in Lent. On Sundays the theme for the Lenten tree in church is used.

If you are working with a tree format, the symbols can be placed anywhere on the tree each day.

With a cross format, it works best if the cross piece is 8 units long by 3 units wide, and the central piece is 14 units tall by 2 units wide. You can then divide the cross into 40 sections (one for each day of Lent – not including Sundays), as in the diagram.

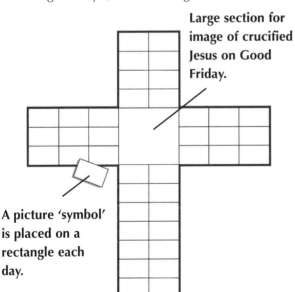

Large section for image of crucified Jesus on Good Friday.

A picture 'symbol' is placed on a rectangle each day.

A 'picture symbol' is placed in each square, which relates to the reading for that day. The unmarked, larger central section is for an image of the crucified Christ on Good Friday.

It might be helpful to create a special space that the Lenten cross occupies to become a prayer focus for the whole household. A candle could be placed there to be lit each day when the family gathers for the Lenten cross prayers. It might also be the centrepiece of the dining table if the household eats together.

The readings and symbols

There are different schemes of readings and symbols that can be used for each day during Lent. One useful resource book with its own pattern of memory verses, suggested songs, prayers, and activites can be found in *The Lenten tree: Devotions for children and adults to prepare for Christ's death and his resurrection* (see Resources, p. 240). There are also daily readings and devotions for adults and children. It is set out in a daily pattern that is easy to follow and use.

The following scheme of readings and pictures is adapted from one used by Catherine Fournier and is printed here with permission. (See Resources, p. 241, for web site details.)

Ash Wednesday

Reading: Even now (Joel 2.12-13)
Picture: The sign of the cross made on our foreheads on Ash Wednesday

2nd day of Lent (Thursday)

Reading: Original sin (Genesis 3.1-20)
Picture: A fruit

3rd day (Friday)

Reading: Cain and Abel (Genesis 4.1-12)
Picture: Two men fighting

4th day (Saturday)

Reading: Noah's ark (Genesis 9.8-11)
Picture: Noah's ark

5th day (Monday)

Reading: Abraham and Isaac (Genesis 22.1-18)
Picture: A lamb

6th day (Tuesday)

Reading: Jesus and Abraham (John 8.31-40)
Picture: A chain – symbol of the slavery from which Christ frees us

7th day (Wednesday)

Reading: Moses and the Ten Commandments (Exodus 20.1-21)
Picture: The two stone tablets

8th day (Thursday)

Reading: The covenant with Abraham and Moses (Jeremiah 31.31-33)
Picture: An outstretched arm with open hand

9th day (Friday)

Reading: A new covenant (Luke 22.15-20)
Picture: Two hands clasped together

10th day (Saturday)

Reading: The two great commandments (Matthew 22.34-40)
Picture: The words 'The two great commandments'

~~~~~~~~~~~~~~~~~~~~~~~~~~~~~~~~~~

11th day (Monday)

Reading: Manna in the desert (Exodus 16.4-12)
Picture: A small piece of bread to represent manna

12th day (Tuesday)

Reading: Jesus in the desert (Luke 4.1-13)
Picture: A stone

13th day (Wednesday)

Reading: The day of the Lord (Joel 2.10-16)
Picture: A trumpet

14th day (Thursday)

Reading: Jonah and the whale (Jonah 1.1 – 4.11)
Picture: A large whale

15th day (Friday)

Reading: Whom shall I send? (Isaiah 6.8-10)
Picture: A burning piece of coal

16th day (Saturday)

Reading: Trust and rescue (Psalm 22.1-5)
Picture: The earth

~~~~~~~~~~~~~~~~~~~~~~~~~~~~~~~~~~

17th day (Monday)

Reading: The call of Jeremiah (Jeremiah 1.4-8)
Picture: A shepherd's staff

18th day (Tuesday)

Reading: Story of Elijah (2 Kings 2.9-12)
Picture: A chariot and horses

19th day (Wednesday)

Reading: Story of Elisha (2 Kings 4.38-44)
Picture: A pot of soup

20th day (Thursday)

Reading: Loaves and fishes (Mark 6.34-44)
Picture: A basket of bread and fish

21st day (Friday)

Reading: Gabriel and the anointed one (Daniel 9.15-24)
Picture: The angel Gabriel

22nd day (Saturday)

Reading: Anointing of David (1 Samuel 16.1-13)
Picture: A jug (or horn) of oil

~~~~~~~~~~~~~~~~~~~~~~~~~~~~~~~~~~

23rd day (Monday)

Reading: Anointing at Bethany (Matthew 26.6-13)
Picture: A vial of perfume

24th day (Tuesday)

Reading: John the Baptist (Luke 1.13-17,80)
Picture: A pitcher of water

25th day (Wednesday)

Reading: Prophecy of peace (Micah 4.1-4)
Picture: A sword and a pruning hook

26th day (Thursday)

Reading: Jesus fulfils all prophecies (Luke 24.44-48)
Picture: The Bible

27th day (Friday)

Reading: Transfiguration (Luke 9.28-36)
Picture: A blinding, radiant light

28th day (Saturday)

Reading: Entry into Jerusalem (Matthew 21.1-9)
Picture: A donkey with palms in the background

~~~~~~~~~~~~~~~~~~~~~~~~~~

29th day (Monday)

Reading: Zeal for your house consumes me (Psalm 69.6-25)
Picture: A musical instrument

30th day (Tuesday)

Reading: Cleansing the Temple (John 2.13-25)
Picture: A knotted piece of rope

31st day (Wednesday)

Reading: Judas (Matthew 26.14-25)
Picture: A bag of money

32nd day (Thursday)

Reading: The innocent victim (Isaiah 53.1-12)
Picture: A white lamb

33rd day (Friday)

Reading: The Last Supper (Luke 22.14-20)
Picture: A cup and plate

34th day (Saturday)

Reading: Agony in garden (Matthew 26.36-46)
Picture: Olives – from the garden of Gethsemane

~~~~~~~~~~~~~~~~~~~~~~~~~~

35th day (Monday)

Reading: Peter denies Jesus (Mark 14.66-72)
Picture: A cockerel

36th day (Tuesday)

Reading: Crown of thorns (Matthew 27.27-31)
Picture: The crown of thorns

37th day (Wednesday)

Reading: Jesus is scourged (Matthew 27.20-26)
Picture: A whip

38th day (Maundy Thursday)

Reading: The footwashing (John 13.1-15)
Picture: A jug with water pouring over feet

39th day (Good Friday)

Reading: The two thieves (Luke 23.32-43)
Picture: A row of three crosses

40th day (Holy Saturday)

Reading: Death of Jesus (Matthew 27.45-54)
Picture: Shaking buildings – reminder of the earthquake

Here is a very short order for prayer around the Lenten tree/cross.

Short prayer around the Lenten tree/cross

When everyone is ready, a candle may be lit.

Blessed are the merciful,
for they will receive mercy.

Matthew 5.7

Reading

The reading for the day is read.

The picture

The picture is placed on the Lenten cross/tree. Anything else may be said or shared here.

PRAYER

Someone asks
Who is in our thoughts today?
Names or situations are mentioned.

Silence is kept as we share our thoughts about them with God.

Say The Lord's Prayer together.

Someone says
May God show us compassion and mercy.
Amen.

The Lenten tree in outreach

A Lenten garden

Some churches create a Lenten garden (which might later be reconfigured as an Easter garden). This can then be a part of the prayer space on offer to visitors, with some guidance as to how they might use it as an aid to reflection. A Lenten tree standing in such a garden would work well. You could make your garden either inside or outside. The location will determine the material you use. Inside you might like to use sand, whilst outside you could use stones and gravel. The garden will begin its life very barren and bare but, as Lent progresses towards Easter, it will begin to flower. The tree will mirror this. You could use a bare branch, proportionate to the size of the garden, or you could use a small, potted deciduous tree that will come to life naturally as Lent progresses. The latter route is a little precarious when Easter is early as the tree may not come into leaf in time. You may like to add a few 'home-made' leaves each day if the natural route is not going to be practicable. You could do this simply by tying appropriately sized bits of green cloth to the tree.

Useful desert images to work with are:
- the temptations of Christ in the wilderness;
- John the Baptist as a wandering preacher of the desert;
- the desert as a wilderness and as a place where God speaks to his people;
- the valley of the dry bones;
- the ash that reminds us of mortality;
- things that are dried up and barren (thorns; dry land; empty hearts; the place of the skull);
- the theme of journey (the journey of God's people through the wilderness; our journey through Lent; our Christian journey; footsteps in the sand or earth to remind us that we are travelling and that we have not arrived);
- the cross.

The tree might be made a central feature of a successive set of changing scenes.

You might like to create an explanatory leaflet to accompany your garden, which could be left beside it, either for people to read in situ, or to take away. Even if it is outside, this is possible: simply laminate those to be left outside.

Lent:
The Head, hands and heart pathway

Introduction

I will put my law within them, and I will write it on their hearts; and I will be their God, and they shall be my people. No longer shall they teach one another, or say to each other, 'Know the Lord', for they shall all know me, from the least of them to the greatest, says the Lord; for I will forgive their iniquity, and remember their sin no more.

Jeremiah 31.33-34 Lent 5 Year B

A work of integration

This pathway is concerned with the outworking of the Lenten call to live lives that are worthy of the gospel. It is about seeking to bring into harmony what we say with our lips, what we believe in our hearts and what we show forth in our lives. The Lenten journey and its disciplines are concerned with this work of integration. Through the practice of self-denial and prayer, through reviewing our lives and commitments and considering again God's call, including perhaps personal confession and absolution, we are making space for God to transform us and to write the law on our hearts. Throughout the events that lead up to the arrest of Jesus, the crucifixion and then the post-resurrection appearances, the disciples were challenged to believe what they saw with their own eyes though it contradicted what they thought to be true. They were called to reconcile the cross and the empty tomb with the words spoken by Christ as they accompanied him throughout his ministry, and then to flesh out this gospel in shared lives and costly witness in the world. To the question 'Who do you say that I am?' is required a response that costs no less than everything, just as the cross of Christ had demonstrated.

A work of transformation

This difficult emotional work of bringing together the words that the disciples had heard and the reality of experience is demonstrated powerfully in the account of the journey to Emmaus described in Luke's Gospel (Luke 24.13-35). As they walk along the road, the disciples are 'talking with each other about all these things that had happened'. Surely, they seem to be saying, it wasn't supposed to end like this. Jesus draws alongside them as they travel. And he said them 'What are you discussing as you walk along?' The disciples are struggling to make sense of their experience of Jesus in the light of his death: 'We had hoped that he was the one to redeem Israel.' And now? The disciples explain that there are reports that Jesus has been seen alive. Clearly this is almost too good to be true for the grieving disciples who seem afraid to accept these accounts. Jesus calls them 'slow of heart to believe all that the prophets have declared', and then 'he interpreted to them the things about himself in all the scriptures'. However the realization does not come through the words alone. Noticeably, it is in the action of the breaking of bread that memory, past experience, the Scriptures and an encounter with the risen Lord collide and represent to their senses the truth that Christ is risen. The moment when Christ took bread, blessed and broke it transformed their experience and enabled them to make the link between what they knew in their heads with what was now written into their senses and their very being: 'Were not our hearts burning within us while he was talking to us on the road?'

The same physicality that characterized the supper at Emmaus is also evident in many of the post-resurrection appearances. This resurrection is bodily and tangible. 'Look at my hands and my feet. See that it is I myself. Touch me and see; for a ghost does not have flesh and bones as you see that I have' (Luke 24.39.) 'He showed them his hands and feet,' (Luke 24.40). Or again in the encounter between the risen Christ and Thomas in John's Gospel 'Put your finger here and see my hands. Reach out your hand and put it in my side. Do not doubt but believe' (John 20.27). Look … see … touch … believe … isn't this the pattern not only for our experience of faith – a faith that goes beyond words – but also for our liturgical action?

Another head-to-heart transformation is revealed in the post-resurrection encounter between Jesus and Peter described in John's Gospel. Peter's threefold avowal of love matches his earlier threefold denial and works in him both forgiveness and a recommissioning for ministry: 'Feed my sheep'. Our own journey through Lent and through following in the footsteps of Christ during Holy Week brings us all to a place where we recognize our 'manifold sins and wickedness' and we are led to seek the forgiveness of Christ so that we might live in newness of life – the 'new birth into a living hope' that Peter writes about in his letter (1 Peter 1.3). It is perhaps this sense of being forgiven much that underpins the theme of Head, hands and heart – the desire to serve God that springs from being much beloved. This depth of forgiveness that is a kind of kenosis finds its fullest expression in the cross of Christ and it is also powerfully demonstrated in the washing of the feet of the disciples and suggested in the extravagant love of the woman who pours costly ointment of nard over the head of Jesus in an act of intimacy and devotion that scandalized the assembled company. God's love above all is a love that goes out in search of the least and the lost to bring them home – as the parable of the Prodigal Son (The Fourth Sunday of Lent Year C) tells us. It is there, too, in Rublev's icon of the Holy Trinity where the cup of suffering indicates to us the cost of the mutual self-offering and self-giving that is at the heart of the Trinitarian life that we are called to represent to the world.

Images of head, hand and heart

The images of head, hands and heart are plentiful: the head of Jesus anointed with ointment of nard, bowed in prayer in Gethsemane, crowned with thorns … the hands of Jesus healing the blind man, touching those to whom he ministered, overturning the tables in the Temple, breaking bread at table, healing the soldier's ear, carrying the cross, holding the reed, fastened to the cross … the hands of others reaching out to Jesus in the crowds, pouring out the nard for anointing, waving in praise, wielding a whip for flogging, casting lots for the garments of Christ, helping to carry the cross, lifting the body down, wrapping the body for burial … the wounds of Christ that are a focus for contemplation in Holy Week and on Good Friday and the wounds that remain on Christ's post-resurrection, post-ascension body – 'rich wounds yet visible above' that cause the angels to worship.[3] And hearts? This part of our journey through the church year faces us perhaps more than any other with the fickleness of the human heart. Those who shout the praises of Christ turn the next minute to yell 'Crucify!'; Christ's own disciple betrays him with a kiss; they fail him at Gethsemane and

Peter denies him three times. However, it is of such people that the Church is made, people transformed by finding forgiveness for faithlessness at the foot of the cross; grace and healing by the blood of the Lamb, and transformation by the power of the Spirit to fulfil the new commandment to love as he loved us and to open out this love to the world.

Symbolic expression for Head, hands and heart

These themes focus our attention on the cross and the outworking of the forgiveness and love shown there in lives worthy of the gospel to which we have been called. It is appropriate, then, to spend time in meditation centred on the cross and to find ways of encouraging congregations to respond to the symbolism of the cross and to a personal engagement with the events surrounding it. A variety of interactive approaches is suggested for this in the group work session 'Proclaiming the Lord's death' and in materials provided for Good Friday. Celebrating a near-silent Eucharist (you will find the order for this in the Lent stand-alone section on page 31) is a way of helping people to focus their attention on the sensory dimensions of communion. When we did this at Greenbelt[4] with 200 people, the silence as people made their confession was almost tangible and the silent witnessing of other people engaging in confession was a moving part of the whole experience.

It is important as far as is possible in your context to engage the whole church community in projects, groups and reflective practices that will enable them to do the work of integration in their lives. Practising the Examen is one such way. It is a simple practice involving reflection on a regular basis on what Ignatius would have termed the movement of consolation and desolation in our lives, thus helping us to discern the presence and the leading of God in our lives. This practice is suitable for use by individuals as well as in families and it has been used in children's groups and youth groups in recognition of the need for more reflective practice in these contexts.[5] In keeping with this theme it is worth considering ways of helping people – including children – to engage with the Stations of the Cross and to reflect upon the particular aspects of the passion, crucifixion and death of Christ represented there.

Included in this section is the description of the programme undertaken by one parish in the Diocese of Southwark. What is clear from their story is that theology is often done as we work together on creative projects and that we learn an enormous amount from engaging with children over these difficult parts of our journey through the church year. Following in the way is not an easy option and this path of discipleship in the shadow of the cross – and the resurrection – needs to belong to the whole people of God, children as well as adults.

Head, hands and heart in groups

Children

The Instruments of the Passion: a way of exploring Lent and Holy Week

This activity focuses on the last week in Jesus' life. The aim is to construct a physical place to represent Jerusalem and to explore the events of Holy Week through references to the instruments of Jesus' Passion. (This project might be good to take up if you followed the ideas for modelling Bethlehem described in the Crib pathway in the first volume of *Together for a Season*.)

As you explore each of the references in which the instruments are alluded to, and create a place in which to put them, the story will begin to assemble itself.

In Christian art 'The Instruments of the Passion' are the objects associated with Jesus' Passion, which become symbols in themselves. (See Resources, p. 241, for web sites that give more information on these instruments.) Traditionally they are:
- The pillar or column where Jesus was whipped;
- The whips that were used;
- The crown of thorns;
- The cross on which he was crucified;
- The title, attached to the cross, inscribed in Hebrew, Latin and Greek: 'Jesus Christ, the King of the Jews';
- The nails, inflicting four wounds;
- The spear by which a Roman soldier inflicted the final of the five wounds, in his side;
- A symbolic cup, for his suffering, also the cup in which his redeeming blood is caught.

It is possible to add other items to these. For example:
- the dice used by the soldiers to cast lots for Jesus' clothing;
- the robe, woven in one piece, and so on;
- the purple robe.

When you look at paintings, windows or sculptures of Jesus' crucifixion, you can often find these items there, and they sometimes feature on altar frontals for Lent and Passiontide. *The Agony in the Garden*, painted by Andrea Mantegna, is a good example of this (see Resources).

Addressing violence – with children?

You (and parents and carers) may need some convincing that an activity like this is suitable for children. At one level, a project based on these items could be deemed terribly gruesome.

Moreover, it has sometimes been the case that, in working with children, preachers and teachers have emphasized the violence of Christ's Passion in a way that is inappropriate and insensitive. There is no intention of doing that here.

However, there are reasons for including this activity:

First, Jesus' last week is a very physical and passionate event. What happened to him was cruel and uncompromising. The emotions of all involved were pushed to the limits. Yet it is important to remember that, during the course of our lifetime, we shall each experience physically and emotionally taxing situations. The keeping of Holy Week is, in a manner of speaking, a way of rehearsing for this and discovering how people cope, in the hope that we can learn from this. This is one of the key 'tasks' of any religion and Christianity is no exception.

In the traditions that have been handed down to us, the benefit of the experience of generations who have gone before us is something on which we draw. These traditions are handed down to us in a number of ways and Christian art has a significant contribution to make.

Second, during their childhood, boys (in particular) pass through phases of interest in violence, which need to be acknowledged, addressed and considered. This may be one way in which this can be undertaken. We may be familiar with the palm crosses that are instantly turned upside down to become swords, even before their dedication is over! Rather than being perplexed or scandalized by this, at times, inevitable behaviour, this project might be one means of engaging with it.

Timescale

This material is designed to be used at any time. It could be used on a Sunday morning or it might be used in a midweek group. It could even be used all together in one long session. There are six Sundays between Ash Wednesday and Easter Day. The fourth Sunday is Mothering Sunday and may, perhaps, be used in a different way from the other Sundays of Lent. The Sunday before Easter is Palm Sunday and may again be used differently. It may be that, if you use this material on a Sunday, you will not meet as a group on every Sunday of Lent; if you meet midweek, you may not meet in the school holidays. The material is therefore divided into four weekly blocks. If you need another session, simply divide it up further. The activity of making the city is completely flexible in any case and will depend on the number of participants you have and how long you meet for. It will also depend in part on the age and competence of the children involved.

Planning the activity

THE CITY OF JERUSALEM

You will need to find a map or plan of the city of Jerusalem at the time of Jesus. Many Bibles have such a plan in them. You can also find one at www.bible-history.com/maps/jerusalem.html. It is not necessary to reproduce this exactly, but to have some kind of capacity for identifying the significant places in some sort of relationship in whatever modelling space you decide to use.

HELPFUL PICTURES

It might be helpful to have a copy of a picture like Mantegna's *Agony in the Garden* as a reference document. Search the Internet for one that you would like to use, or you could use several and compare them. One of the values of this is that you see there is no 'final document' but that the paintings are all the result of a 'dialogue' between the painter, the received symbolism, what the painter knows of the story and what the painter wishes to convey. This is the kind of process in which you and the community of children will engage as you create your model.

THE GARMENTS OF JESUS

At the time of Jesus, most garments worn in the Middle East region were made of woven strips of material that were about 20 cm wide and included decorative braids from 5 to 10 cm wide. Hence the tradition of the stripy tea towel for nativity play shepherds! The garments could be disassembled

and turned into new one. The strips of cloth were frequently recycled. Archaeology has revealed that a single garment might hold sections of many different dates. However, cloth from Damascus and Bethlehem was woven on wider looms. Damascene cloth was particularly prized for its width, pieces being around 100 cm wide. Bethlehem cloth was woven in stripes and was wide also. So it seems likely that Jesus' seamless robe so prized by the soldiers was made of cloth from either Bethlehem or Damascus.

WHERE?

You will need to decide where to create your 'place' that is to represent Jerusalem. It might be at the entrance of the place where you meet, so that as it grows it becomes a talking point. It could be in a space in a church if that is where you meet or if that is where you can place the things you make and collect. You could choose a public space in which to create your place if you can find a welcoming host.

WHAT TO DO

Having determined the site of your 'place' representing Jerusalem, you will need to symbolize the city.

CREATING THE CITY WALLS

Build a wall indicating a boundary: there are any number of ways to do this, depending on the scale you are using. One simple way might be to use the bricks that form the game Jenga™ (as long as you can manage Lent without playing it!). As stated above, the shape of your 'place' does not need to correspond exactly with the shape of first-century Jerusalem, as this may not be possible in your chosen space. You simply need to make a site for all the symbols and the places with which they are associated.

CREATING SPECIFIC SITES

There will be an assortment of tasks to be done each week as you set out to make your place resemble a city. You could build roads and gates. There could be buildings. A simple way to do this is to use rectangular blocks (of concrete, wood or polystyrene) and simply draw on windows and doors with black felt pen. Two particular sites outside the city will be important – the Garden of Gethemane, where Jesus was arrested, and Golgotha, where he was crucified.

Discuss during the first week what you might use to represent all this and see what people feel they can contribute. Once you begin to talk about it, children will think of all sorts of things that they can bring to help in this task, and their contributions add to their ownership of the site. It might also be a good idea to provide a bag of play sand and a bag of pebbles as basic building materials. It would be a good idea to draw up a rota of construction site workers for each week, so that everyone gets a turn if they would like it. You might also allocate different areas of the city to these teams, starting with those that are needed first.

ITEMS FOR THE INSTRUMENTS OF THE PASSION

You will also need to decide on a way to procure each of the items needed to show the Instruments of the Passion and tell the story, which will bring your place to life. If you think that people will be committed enough to remember, you could ask the children to bring in contributions each week. You would need to provide a list. If you judge that family life is so busy that this is too much of an imposition, then you will need to gather them yourself. Lay them attractively in a basket or box so that they can be brought out after the act of worship during the session. If you decide to ask children to bring contributions, put this container in a place where they can add their contributions on arrival.

During each session

Begin by sharing news of the week and then move to the act of worship.

After this, place the basket with your Instruments of the Passion on the table and begin to tell the story by sharing the references and looking at the items. After this, the week's team of builders will need to begin their construction work, while other people work with the things that have been brought. The items brought will also need to be prepared for inclusion in your place.

You could include each in a little scene modelled onto a small piece of board to provide a visual context. You might use everyday items to help with this or you could use a modelling medium – air hardening clay, Model Magic (made by Crayola™), or Fimo™. Or if people prefer to do so, they could write about the items, or draw a picture or print out the relevant quote from the Bible. Different people might choose to do different things and that is fine.

ACT OF WORSHIP

(Used each week)

O God, make speed to save us.
O Lord, make haste to help us.

The Lord is merciful and gracious; slow to anger and abounding in steadfast love.

Psalm 103.8

In this time of Lent, we especially spend time remembering the things we have done wrong, and asking God to forgive us:

Lord,
We confess to you our selfishness and lack of love.
Fill us with your Spirit.
Lord, have mercy.
Lord, have mercy.

We confess to you our fear and failure in sharing our faith.
Fill us with your Spirit.
Christ, have mercy.
Christ, have mercy.

We confess to you our stubbornness and lack of trust.
Fill us with your Spirit.
Lord, have mercy.
Lord, have mercy.

May the Father forgive us
by the death of his Son
and strengthen us
to live in the power of the Spirit
all our days.
Amen.

We pray for ourselves and for other people:
We pray to the Lord for courage to give up other things
and to give ourselves to him this Lent, saying
Lord, meet us in the silence,
give us strength and hear our prayer.

Give us the courage to give up quarrels, strife and jealousy
in our families, neighbourhoods and communities.
May the presence of the risen Jesus,
his body once broken and now made whole,
bring peace and direction as we live with one another.
Lord, meet us in the silence,
give us strength and hear our prayer.

*Give us the courage
to give up our selfishness as we live for others,
and to give time, care and comfort to the sick.*

*May the wounded hands of Jesus bring his healing
   touch,
and the light of his presence fill their rooms.
Lord, meet us in the silence,*
give us strength and hear our prayer.

[T&S 216–17]

*May God bless us and show us compassion and
   mercy.*
Amen.

[DP 70]

Here are the items that will need to be contributed.

Week 1

The anointing at Bethany, the triumphant entry into Jerusalem and the Last Supper:

- Small perfume sample bottles (you could use the sort that come in packs of six for Christmas). Reading: John 12.2-8 or tell this in your own words.
- Small palm trees or small branches (you could use house plants or they could be gathered from gardens and hedgerows). If pussy willow is available to gather this would be particularly appropriate. Reading: Matthew 21.1-11 or tell this in your own words
- The bread and wine of the Last Supper. You might also provide a bowl and a towel as a reminder of the foot washing. 'Bread' might be made from salt dough or you could use matzos, which are used today by the Jews for Passover and would be an apt reminder of the connection with Passover, and, as in the original story where the bread was unleavened, so it would keep on the journey – it does keep well. A small cup or chalice. It is probably not a good idea to use a real silver one if it is to be left out! It will be possible to find something of an appropriate shape made from clay, wood or another metal. Readings: John 13.1-20 and Matthew 26.26-29.

Week 2

The betrayal and arrest and trial of Jesus:

- 30 silver coins. Here you could ask for contributions and see if you can manage an assortment of interesting small coins. You will also need something to keep them together. A drawstring purse left partly open would be appropriate. Reading: Matthew 26.14-16 and 27.3.
- A symbolic cup. Reading: Mark 14.32-36.
- Something to represent the pillar or column to which Jesus was tied when he was whipped and the whips that were used. Reading: Mark 15.1-15.
- The crown of thorns and the purple robe. A length of shiny purple lining material might make the purple robe, or you could ask people to bring in purple cloths and then arrange the pieces together. The coordinating colours would be an important feature. For the crown of thorns, gather thorny twigs and branches. If you have older children, they might be able to weave these into a crown. You must provide gardening gloves! Reading: Mark 15.16-20.

Week 3

The crucifixion and death of Jesus (this account is in all the Gospels – try John 19.17-37):

- The cross on which he was crucified;
- The title, attached to the cross, inscribed in Hebrew, Latin and Greek: 'Jesus Christ, the King of the Jews';
- The nails, inflicting four wounds;
- The spear by which a Roman soldier inflicted the final one of the five wounds, in his side;
- The robe, woven in one piece, with the dice used by the soldiers to cast lots for Jesus' clothing;
- Small pieces of natural sponge (Reading: Matthew 27.34);
- You might also add a small container of vinegar.

Week 4

The burial of Jesus:

- Small balls of cinnamon dough (Reading: John 19.40).
- Burial spices. You could use myrrh, perfume and oils from aromatherapy stores and also at Christmas from present shops. Or you could use things that are more easily obtainable: cinnamon sticks, cloves, star anise and similar items.

- Strips of white linen (Reading: John 20.6-7). Several lengths of white sheeting.
- A 'round' stone of an appropriate size (Reading: John 20.1).

AFTERWARDS

When your place is finished it might be used in a number of ways:

- If it is in a public space, you might like to provide a written explanation for anyone who is going to come across it.
- If it is in a church, it might be the focal point for a service during Holy Week.
- It could be turned into an Easter Garden at the end of Holy Week.

Adults

Introduction

The Beatitudes are a helpful way into an exploration of the themes of Head, hands and heart. The life we are asked to live, the qualities we are asked to demonstrate, require that we do with our hands what we say with our lips; that we act in accordance with the gospel we preach; that we live out the acts of justice and mercy in real relationships and costly loving.

Each session here is based on a theme from the Beatitudes and uses other 'link' Scriptures to explore that theme. The Scriptures used are uncompromising. We have costly choices to make – not only in Lent but in the whole of the direction that our lives take.

Preparing your meeting place

Give time to arranging the place in which the meetings are to take place. Remove clutter to establish a clear focus and use colours and symbols appropriate to this time of the church year. Create a focal table. A piece of sackcloth will recall penitence and simplicity. Clearly the cross is important during this season and should be a key symbol in the focal arrangement. You could use some of the imagery and symbols described in the material provided for the Lenten tree or you might draw inspiration from the images of the lectionary readings.

The lectionary readings of Lent often reflect choices, and the contrast between seeing and not seeing, between darkness and light. For example, in the Gospel for Lent 2 Year B we read that 'If any want

to become my followers, let them deny themselves and take up their cross and follow me' (Mark 8.34). Again, in the Gospel for Lent 4 Year A, the account of the healing of the blind man in St John's Gospel concludes with the healed man opting for belief in Jesus and the Pharisees choosing not to see Jesus. In Year B we read 'the light has come into the world, and people loved darkness rather than light because their deeds were evil' (John 3.19). These Scriptures suggest a candle, together with an icon or picture of Christ as a particularly suitable focal point.

Week 1: Blessed living

PREPARATION

Create the focal table for the session. A piece of sackcloth covering the table would provide a suitable link with the liturgical colours and focus of the season. Add a cross and a bowl of ash.

Provide a variety of media for reflection and response after the meditative reading. These might include paper; card; colouring pencils; pens; paints; fabrics; glue; scissors; clay; versions of Scripture.

SCRIPTURE REFERENCES

Matthew 5.1-12

Link Scripture: Joel 2.1-2,12-17 (one of the readings for Ash Wednesday)

FOR GROUP REFLECTION

You may wish to use the following ways of reflecting upon the Scriptures.

Ask the group to think of their faith journey. Where have they come from and where will they go? Where has the road been easy and where has it been difficult? The following questions used slowly and meditatively might help:

- Where is God calling me to go in this season of Lent?
- Am I being led into new pathways?
- What am I being asked to do today?
- What do I hold in my hand today – what can I offer to others; what do I need to take hold of for myself?
- What blessing am I being asked to give to others?
- What word of God needs to take root in my life today?

REFLECTION USING LECTIO DIVINA

One helpful way into the Scriptures is *lectio divina*. Here is a simple version of this process of reading and reflecting on the Scriptures.

Spend a few minutes introducing the practice and settling people. Encourage them to put down any papers or books and to sit comfortably in their seats.

Listening for the gentle touch of Christ the Word
First hearing of the passage.
One person reads aloud the passage of Scripture twice. Those present listen and then, in the silence, reflect on one segment to which they are drawn and which seems significant to them. In the silence (one to two minutes) invite members of the group to hear and silently repeat a word or phrase from the segment that has attracted them.

Reflecting on how Christ the Word speaks to me
Second hearing of the passage.
The passage is read again.
In the silence (for two to three minutes) invite the group to reflect on the question: Where does the content of this reading touch my life today?

Reflecting on what Christ the Word invites me to do
Third hearing of the passage.
In the silence (for two to three minutes) people reflect on the question: What is God calling me to do?

Allow time for people to choose their own response to what they have thought about or been challenged by, using one or more of the media offered.

WORSHIP

As much of this session has been concerned with individual responses, which have been private, it is important to provide some sense of gathering as a group at the end of the session. Space needs to be provided for people to share anything they wish to offer to the whole group and then closure offered in formal prayers and liturgy, which can perform the function of holding the group.

You might like to end by using Prayer During the Day in Lent on page 66 of *Common Worship: Daily Prayer*.

Close with a suitable prayer. You might like to use the following:

God of all our growing,
take our roots down deep
in the long, dark winter season of our grief.
Nurture the resurrection life in us
in the secret places of the soil,
in the barren frozen earth, underground
where no eye can see.
Send your Spirit where the cold season rages
and speak to us the promise of spring.

© Nicola Slee

Week 2: Justice and righteousness

PREPARATION

For your focal table, you may wish to use sand, twisted thorn, stones; a platter with broken bread and water.

For the worship activity, you will need a tray of damp compost ready for planting seeds and enough seeds for each member of the group.

SCRIPTURE REFERENCES

Matthew 5.6: 'Blessed are those who hunger and thirst for righteousness, for they will be filled.'

Link Scripture: Isaiah 58.1-12

FOR GROUP REFLECTION

Discuss the following questions:
- What does it mean to 'do justly'?
- How do our ideas of what is fair and unfair, just and unjust, compare with what we see of God's ideas?
- What situations can we think of where these two ways of seeing and doing collide?
- What does this passage of Scripture have to say to us about linking our religious practices with our life choices, our attitude to ourselves and to those we are responsible for, including those who work for us?
- What challenges are there here to our integration of public and private?
- In what ways can we as individuals and as the Church 'share our bread with the hungry'?
- What might characterize churches that are like a 'watered garden'?
- How can churches like this be created and grown?

WORSHIP

Have your tray of damp compost ready. Give each person a seed.

You might like to use Prayer During the Day in Lent in *Common Worship: Daily Prayer*, page 66. (Isaiah 58.6-9a is one of the short readings set.) Use the seeds in the way suggested below in the context of the prayers.

or

Light a candle by the focal table.

Jesus said: 'Very truly, I tell you, unless a grain of wheat falls into the earth and dies, it remains just a single grain; but if it dies, it bears much fruit.'

John 12.24

Keep silence together.

Hold the seed in your hand. Say something like:

Look carefully at this seed. It is so small and yet so full – full of potential and possibility; full of life. Who knows what this seed will become? Perhaps a flower – a sunflower maybe or a wallflower? Perhaps an aubergine or maybe a carrot ... the seed may grow easily, may have plenty of water and careful attention ... or it may struggle for life and nourishment.

Planting is an act of trust. We plant seeds of faith not knowing whether they will come to fruition. The seed must be left in the earth and being buried brings forth a life of its own; in its own time and at its own pace. Seeds cannot be hurried or made to be other than what they are.

Think for a moment of those who have planted seeds of faith in your life; those who have nurtured you physically and emotionally, and give thanks for the faith they had in you.

All of us carry the seeds of faith. They were planted in us a long time ago in some cases and for some of us very recently. What is it that God might want to bring to fruition in your life now and what is getting in the way of the new life that he wants to bring forth?

Waiting for the seeds to grow is an act of patience and waiting. God waits for life to come out of death; for new things to spring up in the place of disappointments. The Lenten and Easter journeys are all about this. Where is God calling you to action and where is he asking you to wait?

Look again at the seed in your hand. It is small but it contains many things. As you place your seed in the earth, let it be for you a symbol of change and growth; of possibility and new life; of the challenge to grow and the challenge of waiting.

Invite the members of the group to come and plant their seeds in the soil.

Close with a suitable prayer. You might like to use the following:

God of all our growing,
call our shoots up from the soil
in the sharp spring season
of our awakening.
Nurture the resurrection life in us,
in the fragile, burgeoning thrust of green,
in the delicate bud, the trembling leaf,
the first tentative signs of our growth.
Send your Spirit where the new season dances
and bring us into the promise of spring.

© Nicola Slee

Week 3: Mercy

PREPARATION

For your focal table: a copy of the painting by Rembrandt of *The Return of the Prodigal Son* (see Resources, p. 241) – set this as the focal image with a candle either side of it.

SCRIPTURE REFERENCES

Matthew 5.7: 'Blessed are the merciful, for they will receive mercy.'

Link Scripture: Luke 15.11-32, The parable of the lost son.

FOR GROUP REFLECTION

If you are familiar with Godly Play, the Good Shepherd would be suitable here. This session would then follow the usual Godly Play pattern with free response time and a feast.

Otherwise you might like to focus the work of the group on the figures in Rembrandt's painting, drawing attention to each of the figures in turn: the father; the older son; the bystanders; the returned younger son, and inviting group members to ask themselves:

- What can we learn from each of them about ourselves and about God?
- Where are we in this painting?

• What might these figures and their perspectives have to teach us about how we are in our relationships with one another and with those outside our community?

WORSHIP

You might like to use the Prayer after Communion on page 182 of *Common Worship* as a focus in the closing prayers:

Father of all,
we give you thanks and praise,
that when we were still far off
you met us in your Son and brought us home.
Dying and living, he declared your love,
gave us grace, and opened the gate of glory.
May we who share Christ's body live his risen life;
we who drink his cup bring life to others;
we whom the Spirit lights give light to the world.
Keep us firm in the hope you have set before us,
so we and all your children shall be free,
and the whole earth live to praise your name;
through Christ our Lord
Amen.

Week 4: Devotion

PREPARATION

For your focal table: white cloth, silver cloth, netting or similar.

For the worship activity: an earthenware jar or pot; burner for aromatherapy oils; sandalwood, rose and neroli oils; myrrh. carrier oil.

SCRIPTURE REFERENCES

Matthew 5.8: 'Blessed are the pure in heart, for they will see God.'

Link Scripture: Mark 14.3-9, The woman anointing the feet of Jesus.

FOR GROUP REFLECTION

Finding ourselves in the story.

Look at each of the characters in the story in turn:
• The host – what can we learn here about hospitality and the lack of it? What does Jesus have to say about this?

• The woman – how do we respond to the woman's actions? Do we consider her embarrassing? Foolish? Extreme? Over-emotional? When were we last motivated to this kind of extravagant love?
• The disciples – do we sympathize with their responses?
• Jesus – how might this encounter have been for Jesus? In the Gospel of John, Jesus talks about anointing for burial. Talk about the intimacy of the woman's devotion and the meaning that Jesus gives to it in the context of his approaching death.

Which person in the story do you identify with the most?

WORSHIP

Have rose, sandalwood and neroli oils mixed together in a bowl with a carrier oil and in a separate bowl have drops of myrrh in a carrier oil. Invite members of the group to come forward and to use the oils to anoint themselves with whichever oil resonates for them.

Play a recording of 'The King of love my Shepherd is' as a closing act of meditation and worship.

Week 5: Peace through the cross

This session differs from the others in that it explores the cross in the context of the Eucharist.

PREPARATION

For your focal table: a crown of thorns (can be made from thorn branches, barbed wire, thin branches or shrubbery); red cloth.

You will also need:
• a large variety of pictorial representations of the crucifixion, including the famous Salvador Dali's *Christ on a Hypercube Cross*. You could find these in books, in postcards bought from churches and museums and also on the Internet;
• a variety of crosses, ideally from different cultures and traditions;
• a number of cinematic representations of the events of the Passion;
• bread and wine.

SCRIPTURE REFERENCES

Matthew 5.9: 'Blessed are the peacemakers, for they will be called children of God.'

Link Scripture: The Passion reading (John 18.12 – 19.42).

GROUP ACTIVITY

INTRODUCTORY EXERCISE

Ask everyone to draw an X on a piece of paper and to think of a reason why they might do this in everyday life: what does X symbolize?

Answers might include:

an unknown (in algebra);

a sign for multiplication;

a spot on a map where there is a crossroads or buried treasure;

a mark to indicate something is wrong or cancelled;

a mark to indicate a vote in an election – a kind of signature;

a kiss on a letter or a text message.

Ask which of these might be applied to the crucifixion and in which ways.

DISCUSSION

Pass around the images of the crucifixion and allow the group some time to examine and reflect on them. Ask all present to select the one they like the most and explain why, then the one they like the least and why.

There is an amazing array of variations on the theme of the simple cross and, as is apparent from even a cursory study of the images and examples handed out, the smallest change to the symbol can create significantly different associations. For example: What is conveyed by choosing to depict the crosses of Golgotha as tall or hilltop silhouettes and what changes when they are shown to be at head height to the crowd of onlookers?

Ask the group to place together crosses and images that seem to convey the same theme, or highlight the same aspect of the cross and its significance.

Some of the themes that may emerge, as they have emerged through the history of Christian representations of Christ's death, include:

- The cross as part of a bigger story – Many South American crucifixes, Celtic crosses, icons and triptych paintings portray other key incidents and figures from the history of God's interaction with humankind on or around the cross.
- Suffering – In the representation of the agony on the face of Christ or in his twisted body, or in the grief of the onlookers, or in the identification of Christ with the oppressed of a local culture, many, though certainly not all, examples focus on the theme of suffering.
- Cruelty – Equally, sometimes simultaneously, there is a related focus on the cruelty of those crucifying or taunting Jesus, whether in paintings like Bacon's *Three Studies for Figures at the Base of a Crucifixion*, modelled on Nazi leaders, or in crosses made of nails or featuring barbed wire, thorns, and so on.
- Absence – a common theme is the absence from the cross of Christ's body and the connected question of the absence of life, God, etc. represented by cut-away shapes, empty vessels and the like.
- Invasion (Breaking in/Tearing through) – The surprising presence of something that is revealed or emerges or intrudes through a tear in the fabric of things recurs in easily identified imagery.
- Paradox – Not surprisingly, given the juxtaposition of life/death, human/divine, love/ hatred, day/night, etc. at the crucifixion, tension and paradox feature repeatedly in the image systems of crosses (for example, the circle and cross of the Celtic tradition) and paintings.
- The cross as meeting and gathering point – Both in terms of the meeting of things in opposition (above) and in terms of gathering different cultures, peoples and generations (many images include individuals and things from different periods of history congregated around the cross) there is often a theme of gathering woven into the depictions of the Passion.

PROCLAIMING THE LORD'S DEATH

Then, in each of these categories, use one image, and find Bible passages and points in the communion service that highlight some of the ways in which the Eucharist 'proclaims Christ's death'. Below are two examples:

1. Absence

Images:	Claes Oldenburg, *Soft drainpipe – Blue (Cool) version*; Richard Long, *England*.
Scriptures:	Psalm 22; Isaiah 53.12; Philippians 2.1-11.
Eucharistic action:	The pouring of wine into an empty cup.
Questions:	The most startling thing about encountering death is the sudden and absolute sense of absence. In what ways are the birth, death and resurrection of Jesus about absence, or emptying? In what ways are they about presence and fullness?

2. Invasion/Tearing

Images:	Salvador Dali, *Crucifixion (Hypercubic Body)*.

A note about this painting – Dali's stated desire was to react to the gruesome 'ugliness' of the crucifixion scenes of painters like Grünewald. What is there to recommend or criticize about this desire to depict the cross as 'beautiful'?

The hypercube is a theoretical mathematic construct – just as we can draw a two-dimensional representation of a three-dimensional object, so, in theory, it should be possible to make a three-dimensional model of a four-dimensional reality. A hypercube is a two-dimensional representation of a three-dimensional model of a four-dimensional reality. What does Dali's imagery suggest about what was happening at the moment Jesus cried out in death, when the Temple curtain tore and the dead walked abroad?

Scriptures:	Matthew 9.16-17; Matthew 27.50-54; Revelation 5.
Eucharistic action:	The breaking of bread.
Questions:	When something is torn open, something else is revealed; when something bursts its seams, something else emerges.

What do the images of tearing and breaking symbolize for us in our communion liturgies?

CONCLUSION

Read the following extract from *Orthodoxy* by G. K. Chesterton on 'Circles and crosses' and discuss how the symbolic associations of the cross, particularly in the paradoxes they create, might lead us away from purely 'rational' thinking into an ability to glimpse something more like the full picture.

As we have taken the circle as the symbol of reason and madness, we may very well take the cross as the symbol at once of mystery and of health. Buddhism is centripetal, but Christianity is centrifugal: it breaks out. For the circle is perfect and infinite in its nature; but it is fixed for ever in its size; it can never be larger or smaller. But the cross, though it has at its heart a collision and a contradiction, can extend its four arms forever without altering its shape. Because it has a paradox in its centre it can grow without changing. The circle returns upon itself and is bound. The cross opens its arms to the four winds; it is a signpost for free travellers.[6]

CLOSING WORSHIP

Use Prayers at the Foot of the Cross on page 317 of *Common Worship: Daily Prayer*.

Place a large cross centrally and surround it with night lights in holders.

Where the rubrics suggest that silence is kept or there might be singing or appropriate actions, you might

either

sing or read 'When I survey the wondrous cross' as a meditation

or

You could give each member of the group a 'holding cross' (see Resources, p. 241). Ask them to hold the crosses in their hands and to reflect on the shape and the feel of the wood. Invite them to share their feelings and observations.

Head, hands and heart at home

Films

A film night could be organized with showings of films that relate to the themes of the season. Good examples are *The Shawshank Redemption*; *Chocolat*; *Babette's Feast*. Clearly, you can buy these as DVDs or videos but they are also mostly available from large video hire shops. There are many films that deal with the life of Christ. *The Miracle Maker* is a good mixed audience film. It is particularly suitable for children and has supporting educational materials. *The Passion of the Christ* is a powerful film but you will need to be aware of the level of brutality and violence in the film – not to mention the amount of blood – and be prepared for the reactions of the audience to this. (The original version has an 18 certificate but an edited version with a 15 certificate is also available.) Nevertheless, if watched by a group of people, there is much to discuss afterwards. More standard though still interesting interpretations are around – try *Jesus of Nazareth* (Zeffirelli) or *The Gospel According to St Matthew* (Pasolini), which is still a very powerful film and is beautifully shot. For children, *The Selfish Giant*, an animation of Oscar Wilde's story, is very appropriate, as is *The Easter Story Keepers*. (See Resources, p. 241, for details of the films mentioned above.)

There is now a widely recognized practice of doing 'theology through film'. It is a relaxing, yet instructive, way to spend a cold spring evening or a wet weekend and provides a good reason for inviting people into your home.

Head, hands and heart in outreach

The essence of this Head, hands and heart pathway is a concern with bodily and symbolic expression of prayer and finding ways to integrate head, hands and heart in our journey through Lent, Holy Week and beyond.

The labyrinth

The labyrinth is an ancient form of spiritual practice dating from pre-Christian times. Labyrinths are found in many different cultures across the world. When the great cathedrals of northern Europe were built, many incorporated labyrinths as part of the architecture of the nave, embedding them in the floor. People would walk the labyrinths as a form of prayer and would stop to say prayers at particular points of the labyrinth. The labyrinth can be seen as a metaphor of the spiritual journey – in the Christian tradition, the geometric design of the labyrinth was seen as representing the order of the creator and the journey to the centre as being symbolic of the Christian journey towards God. In recent years, the labyrinth has been reinterpreted for postmodern

culture, employing audio-visual technology and using interactive prayer and symbolic actions at points of the journey. Many churches have set up a labyrinth in their churches or in an appropriate room nearby during Lent and have offered invitations to the local community. Some have combined this with hospitality – a coffee shop or juice bar, for example, where people can sit and chat afterwards or talk with a member of the church about their experiences.

There are several versions of online labyrinths. One example of this is at www.embody.co.uk.

You will also find information at www.labyrinth-enterprises.com, which provides links to photographs of labyrinths in churches in the USA.

A way of addressing the needs of the community for space and quiet might be to keep the church building open as much as possible during Lent. But you need to think about ways of presenting the building as a place of living worship rather than as a museum! You might want to consider the kind of publicity on offer and what is available for children to do when they come into the building. You might want to devise a prayer walk around the church building or consider an interactive prayer or worship installation of some kind.

Tending a neglected open space

As a church you might wish to explore the garden metaphor literally and consider what areas there might be in your neighbourhood that could be cleared and used to benefit the local community more fully. You might need to work with your local council on this or with neighbourhood schemes.

Exploring Christianity

As Lent is a time for study and reflection on matters of faith, it is a particularly suitable time to run not only study courses for those who are already members of the church but also courses for enquirers. *Alpha* is well documented and there are also many alternatives such as Emmaus or you may wish to base a course around images of Jesus, which could include materials such as *The Christ We Share* (see Resources, p. 241) a pack of images of Christ from a variety of cultures and traditions. These occasions are not only about sharing the faith but also about opening wide the church doors and sharing food and hospitality before raising issues of life and faith. You might like to consider running a course with a particular emphasis – for example, one for parents on raising children or one for parents of teenagers. These evenings could be centred around food – a meal could be provided – and have an agenda based on support and encouragement.

Mothering Sunday

This is a key opportunity for most churches to welcome many visitors. It is also a very difficult Sunday for some people for many reasons and pastoral sensitivity will need to be exercised. As a church, though, you might like to reflect on this day in the context of Lent and consider how it might be used as an opportunity for outreach. In some years, this coincides with the Feast of the Annunciation, which provides opportunities to reflect on the role of Mary in the Christ story. Many churches distribute flowers on this day and invite members of the congregation to take them to give to their mothers or to those who have mothered them in the faith. Gifts of flowers could be made by the church to local agencies or hospitals as there is need – and as a symbol of the love we receive from mother Church.

Lent:
The Stations pathway

Introduction

Journey

The call of our founding father, Abraham, was to make a journey. Passover recalls the culmination of that journey, with the exodus from Egypt, crossing the Red Sea, the 40 years in the wilderness, and the final taking possession of the Promised Land. The ancient escape from exile has become symbolic of every believer's journey towards God. The Israelites preserved the memory that 'A wandering Aramean was my ancestor' (Deuteronomy 26.5). The pilgrimages to Jerusalem made by Jesus, his family and his disciples, were occasions on which this history of wandering was recalled and celebrated, whilst incorporating the idea of going to the holy place.

Christianity began with a breaking out from the upper room under the guidance of the Holy Spirit, and a call to preach to all nations. This new missionary faith was known as 'the Way' (Acts 9.2) before the conversion of Saul, and its evangelists quickly spread the gospel to the ends of the known world.

However, it wasn't until the time of the Emperor Constantine that Christians began to journey freely to the Holy Land on pilgrimage, and join with those making the Way of the Cross in Jerusalem. At about the same time, the movement of large numbers of people away from cities to live as hermits in the desert took its inspiration from Jesus' forty-day journey in the wilderness.

The foundation of much of our Christian celebration of Lent, Holy Week and Pentecost lies in real journeys. So our celebration of the seasons of the Christian Church will properly involve movement, both in enriching our own faith, and also in making public demonstration of our faith outside the confines of our worship spaces.

Processions

To pew-bound Anglicans, any idea of moving during worship may feel like straying into a foreign country. However, processions have always had great significance. Taking to the streets for a march is a powerful symbol.

Remove the pews from our ancient churches and it becomes obvious that the side aisles of the nave, from which there is often no view of the altar, were designed for something else – processions. Palm Sunday was celebrated with a procession leading out of one door of the church, and returning via another. Baptism included its own procession, first from the entrance of the church to the font, and only afterwards to the body of the church to join in worship with the faithful. The signal for the start of a wedding is the entrance of the bride via the west door, following the priest to the place where the bridegroom waits for her. And our life's end is marked by the final procession, as our coffin is carried into church, and then out for burial.

Simply walking together can often say much more than words can express. It gives meaning and a sense of solidarity both to those who take part and those who witness any procession or march.

Sister Benedicta Ward[7] says: 'Humans tell stories, narratives, and go along together in order to focus the reality of their lives, to remember. People … are bodies, so to apprehend truths they need to participate in events and make reality real for themselves.'

The first accounts of Easter processions are to be found in documents from the fourth century. In Jerusalem it had become possible to stand in the place of the crucifixion, and to touch a part of the cross. Helena, the mother of the Emperor Constantine, who made Christianity the official religion of the Empire, made a pilgrimage to the Holy Land. Aided by Cyril, Bishop of Jerusalem, she popularized the idea of going to holy places associated with the life of Christ, and in particular, the following of the way of the cross from Jerusalem to the place of the crucifixion. A European nun, Egeria, travelled to the Holy Land and, in letters written home to her sisters in AD 397, provides us with the first account of Christian liturgy in Jerusalem.

So it is that the whole cycle of services from Ash Wednesday through to Pentecost lends itself to worship which involves movement:

- It begins with Jesus going into the wilderness for 40 days;
- Palm Sunday has the triumphal entry of Jesus into Jerusalem;
- The disciples go with Jesus to the place where they will celebrate the Passover;
- Jesus washes the feet of those who had walked with him from the first days of his ministry to this final meal;
- After the Last Supper, Jesus walks with them to Gethsemane;
- On Good Friday we follow the Stations of the Cross, following a pattern established in Jerusalem;
- Also following ancient custom, we come to venerate the cross;
- On Easter Eve, or before dawn on Easter Day, the new fire is brought into the church to proclaim the resurrection;
- We recall the walk to Emmaus, and the recognition of the risen Christ there when bread is broken;
- With Pentecost, the birth of the Church is celebrated by taking out the gospel on to the streets in the Whit Walks, which had such a long tradition in the north of England.

The Stations of the Cross: a brief history

A special pilgrim route through Jerusalem seems to have been marked out from the earliest times. Travellers who visited the Holy Land during the early Middle Ages write of a *via sacra*, but this is not described as the way of the cross. Indeed, it seems to have been common to begin at Mount Calvary, and walk back to the house of Pilate. However, by the sixteenth century a route probably more like that taken by Christ carrying the cross had emerged, beginning at Pilate's house and proceeding outside the city to Calvary. So the way was set for this journey to become a devotion in itself.

Meanwhile, a desire grew to create reproductions of the holy places of Jerusalem in other places. In the fifth century a Bishop of Bologna built a series of interconnected chapels in the monastery of San Stefano, which became known as 'Hierusalem'. This tradition slowly developed, and by the fifteenth century these reproductions of Jerusalem's holy

places were beginning to appear all over Europe. Alvarez of Cordoba commissioned a series of chapels in which were painted the principal scenes of the Passion and, in Nuremburg, scenes popularly known as 'the Seven Falls', because each shows Jesus falling under the weight of the cross. By the end of the seventeenth century the custom of placing the stations in churches was becoming relatively common and devotions to accompany the pictures had begun to appear.

Some stations, such as those in Antwerp cathedral, became valuable works of art and the creation of pictures or carvings of the stations has become an art form in itself. A set is to be found in most Roman Catholic churches in some form or other. At their most minimalist, there may be simply a series of numbers, the worshipper being expected to be so familiar with this act of piety that the pictures are deemed no longer necessary! In monasteries they are usually to be found in the cloister, though their absence in the Romanesque cloisters across Europe with their exquisite biblical carvings is another testimony to the fact that their popularity was established later than the early Middle Ages. Sometimes they are to be found in the open air on roads leading to a church or shrine or in a garden.

Today

A recognition of the importance of art and movement in worship has led in recent years to a new flourishing of the practice of the stations. Many new picture sets have appeared that may be reproduced in a variety of ways, and new books with pictures and devotions created together appear annually. Indeed, the value of this devotion has been so proven that Stations of the Resurrection have also been created, with art and devotional texts to support them. The feeling of journey and pilgrimage in the Lent and Easter seasons has really begun to emerge very strongly. *Times and Seasons* offers a set of Stations of the Cross drawn solely from biblical texts. It also offers a series of Stations of the Resurrection. It is suggested that these be used with pictures or carvings that are already available, or that you create your own.

The Stations of the Cross

See page 84 for a list of the Stations.

Practical inclusive ideas

Stations through Lent

Together for a Season takes this idea a step further, with an entire pathway devoted to creating stations through the seasons. These are derived from the weekly lectionary texts with suggestions for creating your own stations each week to create a visible sense of journey from Ash Wednesday to the cross and then from the resurrection to Pentecost. But it is possible to be more creative than this and the group material for adults and for children provides ideas for devising further themed stations. This approach, too, lends itself to outreach, with suggestions for pieces of 'public art' in places in the neighbourhood that are deemed to be suitable.

Stations of the Gospel for each Sunday of Lent

The table below provides suggestions for making a 'station' each week that reflects the Gospel reading. These stations can be used in a number of ways, depending on the size and shape of the place where they are to be used. Here are some possibilities:

- Build up your stations week by week through Lent, placing them around the building so that they create a physical journey around the building as time goes by. You could use the new station as a focus for part of your service each week so, for example, the Gospel might be read from the station. If there is enough room in your building, a Gospel procession to the station might be made by everyone so that people are standing around the station with the items that illustrate the Gospel account. You might want to use the font as the place for the first station and then follow around the building from there. For some of the stations there are specific suggestions about where the station might be located, but if it is not possible in your situation to follow these, then this is not necessary.

- Use the new station each week as a focus at the front of the church. The Gospel could be read from there or the station could be used as a focus for the sermon. At the end of the service, perhaps during the Dismissal, move it to another part of the building to remain until Maundy Thursday.

- You could put your station near the door of the church or even in the porch, or in a place that is normally maintained as a space for prayer. Provide some ideas for prayer to go with the items in the station, and perhaps copies of the Gospel reading might be placed there also. Thus the station becomes a focus for people as they enter the church for worship, or as a visitor.

The Stations of the Cross service in *Times and Seasons* focuses on events of Jesus' passion and these would follow on naturally from the stations you have built up during Lent.

While each reading will stand on its own, themes that relate them in each year can emerge and these have been used to create a coherence for the set of stations created each year, thereby enhancing the feeling of a journey moving relentlessly onwards towards the cross.

In Year A the theme used is colour, particularly the contrast between darkness and light. This is represented by the underlay on which the other items of the station stand, chosen to reflect the words of the Gospel.

Year A	Lectionary Gospel	Theme
Ash Wednesday	Matthew 6.1-6,16-21	**Be discreet when you fast or give alms** Use the area around the font and use dark cloth as a focus. Use a box and drape cloth over it; put dark cloth inside also and a few coins, together with some indications of giving alms: e.g. collections envelopes, collecting boxes, gift aid forms. Outside the box, a bowl of water, scented soap and a towel; and the dish of ash, once it has been used in the service.
Lent 1	Matthew 4.1-11	**Jesus was led out into the desert to be put to the test** Use dark and light fabrics. On the dark fabrics, spread out some sand and sharp, jagged stones and add pictures of inhospitable places. On the light fabric put bread and water and pictures or other representations of angels.

Lent 2	John 3.1-17	**Nicodemus came by night and Jesus said, 'God so loved the world that he gave his only Son'** Use dark and light fabrics. On the dark fabric place a small glass bowl of water and a pillar candle. On the place where the dark and light fabrics meet, place a small cross or crucifix and on the light fabric a picture of Christian people at worship – possibly from a culture other than your own.
Lent 3	John 4.5-42	**The woman at the well** Use dark and light fabric. On the dark fabric place a dark coloured jar, filled to the brim with water. On the light fabric place two very small glasses, a candle and a handful of seeds (wheat or, if you cannot get that, use a packet of linseed or pumpkin seeds or something similar, from a wholefood counter).
Lent 4 Mothering Sunday	John 9.1-41	**The healing of the man born blind and the debate that followed it** Use dark and light fabric. On the light fabric put some mud, a shallow bowl of water and a picture of some eyes. Add cards with the words 'I was blind, now I see', 'prophet' and 'Lord, I believe'. On the dark fabric put a sheaf of paper with RULES written in large letters on the top sheet. (Old paper will do for this, rolled slightly and a bit dog-eared.)
Lent 5 Passion Sunday	John 11.1-45	**The raising of Lazarus** If you have a tomb in your church, place this station on or close to it. Use dark and light fabric. On the dark fabric, place a group of small stones built up to look like a tomb. Add some 'tears': you could use tear-shaped stones or glass beads. On the light fabric place a pile of strips of cloth, a reminder of the raising, and the prayer that Jesus said, 'Father I thank you for having heard me ...'
Palm Sunday	Matthew 21.1-11	**The triumphal entry into Jerusalem** Use red fabric and make the station near the church door. Lay coloured material across the station, together with branches. Put the palm crosses there prior to distribution and put the remainder back there afterwards.
Maundy Thursday	John 13.1-17, 31b-35	**I give you a new commandment** Use a towel to cover the place where the station is to be. Put a pile of towels there and a plain, wide, large bowl and scented soap. Add the words 'Love one another' written on a card.
Good Friday	John 18 – 19	**Crucify him!** Make the station close to where the cross to be used at Good Friday services will be erected. Use red fabric to which you add the instruments of the Passion: a crown of thorns (you can make a simple one by taking a flexible thorny twig, e.g. blackberry or climbing rose, bending it round into a circle and fixing it with a piece of wire), a hammer and nails, a spear, a ladder (you could make a miniature one using stiff brown paper) and dice. You might also add a piece of torn fabric to represent the veil of the Temple.

In Year B a fabric, the traditional unbleached linen, recalling sackcloth as a symbol of repentance, is used to connect the stations.

Year B	Lectionary Gospel	Theme
		Use fabric that will resemble sackcloth or unbleached linen.
Ash Wednesday	John 8.1-11	**Let any among you who is without sin cast the first stone.** Make this first station at or somewhere near the font if possible, marking the start of a journey. Put some dampish sand onto the sackcloth and make marks in it to resemble Hebrew letters, a reminder of Jesus writing on the ground. Add a pile of rough, ugly-looking stones, each the size of the palm of a hand. Put one stone at some distance from the pile.
Lent 1	Mark 1.9-15	**You are my Son, the Beloved.** Add more dampish sand on top of the sackcloth. Add some shimmering blue or silver fabric around one side and put a dove onto this as a reminder of the baptism of Jesus. On the other side stand up some black card or black-painted hardboard cut into menacing shapes. You can add 'animal footprints' into the damp sand to create the impression of the wild beasts. This can be done by tying together a number of cotton buds, which then create a paw shape when pressed into the sand.
Lent 2	Mark 8.31-38	**If any want to become my followers** Use a standing cross and a piece of fabric to represent a road: it could narrow towards the back of the station, as though going into the distance. At the end of this road put a pool of gold cloth and some angels. Put the cross about halfway down the road and the words 'Get behind me, Satan' at the beginning of the road. You may wish to use uneven and hesitant lettering.
Lent 3	John 2.13-22	**The cleansing of the Temple** Place the cross in one corner at the back of the station. Make a whip of plaited cords and lay this in the centre of a scene of chaos: money thrown down, pots and vessels overturned, some broken pieces of plantpot. If you could manage an empty bird cage, that would be excellent, otherwise a few feathers strewn around would be fine.
Lent 4	John 3.14-21	**For God so loved the world that he gave his only Son** Use a crucifix (a cross with a statue of Christ on it). Use two strips of fabric, one light and shining, one dark, and intertwine them, laying them unevenly across the station. Use a lit pillar candle at the end and add the words 'For God so loved the world that he gave his only Son'.
Lent 5 Passion Sunday	John 12.20-33	**The hour has come for the Son of Man to be glorified** Use a cross with a statue of Christ in Majesty on it. Put a pile of earth and a pile of grain seeds side by side below the cross. Add the words 'Unless a grain of wheat falls into the earth and dies, it remains just a single grain, but if it dies, it bears much fruit' and 'Father save me from this hour'.
Palm Sunday	John 12.12-16	**The triumphal entry into Jerusalem** Use red fabric and make the station near the church door. Lay coloured material across the station, together with branches. Put the palm crosses there prior to distribution and put the remainder back there afterwards.
Maundy Thursday	John 13.1-17, 31b-35	**I give you a new commandment** Use a towel to cover the place where the station is to be. Put a pile of towels there and a plain, wide, large bowl and scented soap. Add the words 'Love one another' written on a card.

Good Friday	John 18–19	**Crucify him!** Make the station close to where the cross to be used at Good Friday services will be erected. Use red fabric to which you add the instruments of the Passion: a crown of thorns (you can make a simple one by taking a flexible thorny twig, e.g. blackberry or climbing rose, bending it round into a circle and fixing it with a piece of wire), a hammer and nails, a spear, a ladder (you could make a miniature one using stiff brown paper) and dice. You might also add a piece of torn fabric to represent the veil of the Temple.

In Year C, the stations are united by the theme of place, so the underlays all relate to geography with maps and plans.

Year C	Lectionary Gospel	Theme
Ash Wednesday	John 8.2-11	**The woman taken in adultery** Use a plan of the Temple in Jerusalem as the underlay for the station. Put on it a pile of ugly-looking stones, with one set apart from the rest. Add some sand and create some scribbles in it. Add the words 'Neither do I condemn you. Go on your way, from now on do not sin again' written on red paper with a black pen.
Lent 1	Luke 4.1-13	**The temptations** Use a map of the world or a picture of the earth from space as the underlay for the station. Add a pile of smooth stones and then one stone set apart from the pile. Next to it put a bread roll of a similar size. Add also a picture of someone very high up in a precarious place, for example, one of the pictures of the men building skyscrapers in the 1930s. Use the words 'Do not put the Lord your God to the test'.
Lent 2	Luke 13.31-35	**As a hen gathers her chicks** Use a plan of the city of Jerusalem for the underlay. (Find one on the Internet and blow it up on a photocopier, unless you can find someone who has one from a visit.) Add something to indicate a prophet: a 'scroll' can be made from two small cheap rolling pins with part of a roll of lining paper attached to them. Add also a model of a hen and some chicks (or a picture) and the words 'Jerusalem, Jerusalem, how often have I desired to gather your children …'
Lent 3	Luke 13.1-9	**Repent!** Use a plan of the city of Jerusalem again. Build a tower with small wooden bricks and then knock it down, leaving the bricks where they fell. Use some red colouring and smear it at random over the plan. Add a small saw (if security is an issue, use a hacksaw with the blade removed) and a branch in a vase (if you can find a fig tree branch so much the better). Add the word 'Repent'.
Lent 4	Luke 15.1-3, 11b-32	**The Prodigal** Use an Internet search engine earth-type picture of the Holy Land/Israel-Palestine. In a lush-looking area put two equal piles of coins – pennies will do. Then in a mountainous and barren looking area, put some old bean pods (buy a few runner or broad beans from a supermarket and dry them out a bit in an airing cupboard). Then add a splendid robe (a piece of fine material will be appropriate), a ring, sandals and a picture of a fine plate of beef. Add the words 'Father I have sinned against heaven and before you' next to the beans.

Lent 5 Passion Sunday	John 12.1-8	**The woman with ointment** Use a picture or plan of a first-century Jewish house as the underlay. Put on it symbols of a banquet: a pile of napkins, a pile of tempting fruit, etc. Add a towel and then a tile, with a large blob of perfumed handcream on it. Next to this put a pretty jar, empty and on its side.
Palm Sunday	Luke 19.28-40	**The triumphal entry into Jerusalem** Use a plan of the city of Jerusalem and its surroundings and make the station near the church door. Lay coloured material across the station, together with branches. Put the palm crosses there prior to distribution and put the remainder back there afterwards.
Maundy Thursday	John 13.1-17, 31b-35	**I give you a new commandment** Use a picture of the last supper where the station is to be. Put a pile of towels there and a plain, wide, large bowl and scented soap. Add the words 'Love one another' written on a card.
Good Friday	John 18–19	**Crucify him!** Make the station near to the pace where the cross to be used on Good Friday is to be. Use a plan of the city of Jerusalem and its surroundings. You could make an outline of the wall with pebbles. Add the instruments of the Passion: place the hammer and nails, ladder, spear and dice outside the city and the crown of thorns inside the city. You may also like to add a small cross.

The Stations in groups

Children

Although the Stations of the Cross are familiar to very many adults, they will be less familiar to most children. They may see the representations of the stations around church buildings either during Lent and Passiontide or perhaps constantly, but very often the services or observations of these stations will be adult-only affairs. The ideas in this pathway therefore provide the opportunity for children to make a set of pictures to accompany the Stations of the Cross service that is included in *Times and Seasons*. The service in *Times and Seasons* provides a Gospel reading and a prayer for each of the stations. The incidents portrayed are all to be found in the Gospels and so vary slightly from those that are commonly shown around churches or in some books. The observation at each station begins with the response

We adore you, O Christ, and we bless you,
because by your holy cross you have redeemed the world.

and concludes with the response

Holy God,
holy and strong,
holy and immortal,
have mercy on us.

[T&S 239ff]

It is suggested that these responses are used each week with the children so that they are learnt and become part of their 'spiritual vocabulary', to be drawn upon when the need arises.

This material is designed to be used at any time. It could be used on a Sunday morning or it might be used in a midweek group. It could even be used all together in one long session. There are six Sundays between Ash Wednesday and Easter Day. The fourth Sunday is Mothering Sunday and may, perhaps, be used in a different way from the other Sundays of Lent. The Sunday before Easter is Palm Sunday and may again be used differently. It may be that, if you use this material on a Sunday, you will not meet as a group on every Sunday of Lent; if you meet midweek, you may not meet in the school holidays. The material is therefore divided into four-week blocks. If you need another session, simply divide it up further. The activity of making the stations is completely flexible in any case and will depend on the number of participants you have and how long you meet for. It will also depend in part on the age and competence of the children involved, and how far you want the material to look 'finished' or are happy to display as work in progress. You may need to have a team of adults and older children who are prepared to meet towards the end of Lent to finish things off and tidy up each panel ready for it to be hung.

Hanging the panels will depend on their location. You could use a cane through a channel in the top of each and then attach a cord to each end of the cane to hang them by. If they are to be hung against a soft surface, they could be mounted onto it with pins. Or they could be mounted onto board or really stiff card and propped up, say, in a window alcove.

Preparation

YOU WILL NEED

- Hessian rectangles or squares as the background for the scenes. You will need to decide on a size and then cut 15 pieces the same size. It frays quite easily so it might be a good idea to secure the sides first. You could sew them, but if time is an issue then simply use iron-heat activated bonding ribbon (sometimes called hemming tape), which can be bought very easily now from sewing shops and even from supermarkets.
- Scraps of coarse, roughly-cut fabric; some smoother gentler fabrics also – felt is good as it sticks easily, doesn't fray and can be drawn on. You could use silk or something similar for faces, hands and feet. You might like to cut out lots of these so people can help themselves to what they need. Another possibility is to use the flesh-coloured paper people shapes that are now available in stationers and in educational catalogues. They come in different skin tones, which adds diversity.
- All sorts of little sticks and twigs: these can be used to symbolize the garden of Gethsemane, for example, to make the cross, or crown of thorns and to portray various aspects of other scenes.
- Shapes of figures to copy: the pictures in *The Good News Bible* are really helpful from this point of view as they are simple and easy to emulate, yet very communicative. You might enlarge some on a photocopier to use as an inspiration.
- Adhesives: bonding fabric may be good to use with older children (in which case you will also need an iron); PVA glue sticks just about anything and can be bought in a washable variety; sewing cotton and needles might be helpful and staplers can also be used; scissors and pencils.

Have all these materials laid out on flat surfaces around the meeting room in preparation for each session.

The worship time (a standard pattern for each week)

THE FOCAL TABLE

Cover the table with either Lenten purple cloth or sackcloth each week. Use a cross as the main focus. If you have access to different crosses, each of which is distinctive, you might like to use a different one on each occasion that you meet. If you can make a collection of small crosses, so much the better. Invite the children each week on arrival to choose one, which they will hold during the worship time. Add something to represent each of the incidents you will be considering and responding to on that particular occasion.

Open with a greeting
The Lord be with you
and also with you.

Use the cross response
We adore you, O Christ, and we bless you,
because by your holy cross you have redeemed the world.

[T&S 239]

Sing a short song. Here are some suggestions:

'For God so loved the world' (*34 Songs for All Occasions*);

'O Christe Domine Jesu' ('Christ Jesus Lord and Saviour') (Taizé);

'Jesus' love is very wonderful' (*Jump Up if You're Wearing Red* and *Junior Praise*);

'He came down that we may have love' (*Jump Up if You're Wearing Red*);

'Thank you Jesus' (*Kidsource 1*);

'When I think about the cross' (*Kidsource 1*);

'My Lord loves me' (*Kidsource 2*).

Read the short version of each of the stories that are to be considered for this week, each with their pondering questions. Provide time for pondering together if people wish to respond to the questions. If you have children who enjoy reading aloud, you could ask a child each week to come having prepared one of the Bible texts to read to everyone, so that they hear part of the story read from the Bible. (Do this only if it is going to be really well read, however. Listening to other people stumbling through Bible readings just for the sake of hearing the words read is a not a good experience for anyone, and particularly not for children, and does not commend the Bible to people at all. However, if different people each week can contribute this really well, it does give a thrill to Bible reading, and a growing ownership of the text.)

Have a time of prayer. If you are accustomed to praying aloud, then do so. If you are used to using particular prayers, you may wish to use the simplified short versions of the prayers that accompany each station and you could say the Lord's Prayer together.

Conclude with this response
Holy God,
holy and strong,
holy and immortal,
have mercy on us.

[T&S 239]

Spend time making the stations.

The different stations in sequence allocated by week

Remember that you can change the groupings if you wish.

Week 1:

First Station: Jesus in agony in the Garden of Gethsemane

Jesus took his disciples to a garden to pray. They fell asleep.
He was very frightened.
What makes you feel afraid? Who helps you?

A reading from the Gospel according to Mark (14.32-36)
They went to a place called Gethsemane; and he said to his disciples, 'Sit here while I pray.' He took with him Peter and James and John, and began to be distressed and agitated. And he said to them, 'I am deeply grieved, even to death; remain here, and keep awake.' And going a little farther, he threw himself on the ground and prayed that, if it were possible, the hour might pass from him. He said, 'Abba, Father, for you all things are possible; remove this cup from me; yet, not what I want, but what you want.'

Prayers
Lord Jesus, you entered the garden of fear
and faced the agony of your impending death:
be with those who share that agony
and face death unwillingly this day.
You shared our fear and knew the weakness of our
*   humanity:*

give strength and hope to the dispirited and
*   despairing.*
To you, Jesus, who sweated blood,
be honour and glory with the Father and the Holy
*   Spirit,*
now and for ever.
Amen.

[T&S 239]

An adapted version of the prayer
Lord Jesus, in the garden of fear
you faced the agony of death:
be with those who are afraid or who are dying today.
You know fear and weakness:
give strength and hope to those in despair.
Amen.

Second Station: Jesus betrayed by Judas and arrested

Judas arrived with soldiers who had come to arrest Jesus. Judas kissed Jesus, so that the soldiers would know which person to arrest.
Judas betrayed Jesus. He let him down.
Have you ever let anyone down? Has anyone ever let you down?

A reading from the Gospel according to Mark (14.43-46)
Immediately, while he was still speaking, Judas, one of the twelve, arrived; and with him there was a crowd with swords and clubs, from the chief priests, the scribes, and the elders. Now the betrayer had given them a sign, saying, 'The one I will kiss is the man; arrest him and lead him away under guard.' So when he came, he went up to him at once and said, 'Rabbi!' and kissed him. Then they laid hands on him and arrested him.

Prayers
Lord Jesus, you were betrayed by the kiss of a friend:
be with those who are betrayed and slandered and
*   falsely accused.*
You knew the experience of having your love
thrown back in your face for mere silver:
be with families which are torn apart by mistrust or
*   temptation.*
To you, Jesus, who offered your face to your betrayer,
be honour and glory with the Father and the Holy
*   Spirit,*
now and for ever.
Amen.

[T&S 240]

An adapted version of the prayer
Lord Jesus, you were betrayed by Judas' kiss:
be with those who are betrayed and accused though
they have done nothing wrong.
Be with families that are torn apart by mistrust or
temptation.
Amen.

THIRD STATION: JESUS CONDEMNED BY THE SANHEDRIN

Jesus was taken to the court. People told lies about him.
Then they condemned him to death.
Do you sometimes feel like telling lies?

A reading from the Gospel according to Mark (14.55-64)
Now the chief priests and the whole council were
looking for testimony against Jesus to put him to death;
but they found none. For many gave false testimony
against him, and their testimony did not agree. Some
stood up and gave false testimony against him, saying,
'We heard him say, "I will destroy this temple that is
made with hands, and in three days I will build another,
not made with hands".' But even on this point their
testimony did not agree. Then the high priest stood up
before them and asked Jesus, 'Have you no answer?
What is it that they testify against you?' But he was
silent and did not answer. Again the high priest asked
him, 'Are you the Messiah, the Son of the Blessed One?'
Jesus said, 'I am; and "you will see the Son of Man
seated at the right hand of the Power", and "coming
with the clouds of heaven".' Then the high priest tore
his clothes and said, 'Why do we still need witnesses?
You have heard his blasphemy! What is your decision?'
All of them condemned him as deserving death.

Prayers
Lord Jesus, you were the victim of religious bigotry:
be with those who are persecuted by small-minded
authority.
You faced the condemnation of fearful hearts:
deepen the understanding of those who shut
themselves off from the experience and wisdom
of others.
To you, Jesus, unjustly judged victim,
be honour and glory with the Father and the Holy
Spirit,
now and for ever.
Amen.

[T&S 241]

An adapted version of the prayer
Lord Jesus, you were the victim of religious bigotry:
be with those who are persecuted.

You faced the condemnation of fearful hearts:
help those who do try to learn from people who are
different from them.
Amen.

FOURTH STATION: PETER DENIES JESUS

Peter followed and sat in the courtyard. He stayed
there all night, until the morning began to break.
When the cock had crowed twice, he remembered
what Jesus had said: 'You will say three times that
you do not know me.' Peter began to cry.
Have you ever let anyone down?
Have you ever done anything you were really sorry
about?

A reading from the Gospel according to Mark (14.72)
At that moment the cock crowed for the second time.
Then Peter remembered that Jesus had said to him,
'Before the cock crows twice, you will deny me three
times.' And he broke down and wept.

Prayers
Lord Jesus, as Peter betrayed you,
you experienced the double agony of love rejected
and friendship denied:
be with those who know no friends and are rejected
by society.
You understood the fear within Peter:
help us to understand the anxieties of those who fear
for their future.
To you, Jesus, who gazed with sadness at your lost
friend,
be honour and glory with the Father and the Holy
Spirit,
now and for ever.
Amen.

[T&S 242]

An adapted version of the prayer
Lord Jesus, as Peter betrayed you,
you experienced the agony of friendship denied:
be with those who have no friends and whom no
one wants to know.
Amen.

WEEK 2:

FIFTH STATION: JESUS JUDGED BY PILATE

Pontius Pilate told Jesus he was going to be crucified
even though he hadn't done anything wrong.
Jesus didn't say anything at all.
How do you feel when you get the blame for
something you haven't done?

A reading from the Gospel according to Mark (15.14,15)
Pilate asked them, 'Why, what evil has he done?' But they shouted all the more, 'Crucify him!' So Pilate, wishing to satisfy the crowd, released Barabbas for them; and after flogging Jesus, he handed him over to be crucified.

Prayers

Lord Jesus, you were condemned to death for political expediency:
be with those who are imprisoned for the convenience of the powerful.
You were the victim of unbridled injustice:
change the minds and motivations of oppressors and exploiters to your way of peace.
To you, Jesus, innocent though condemned,
be honour and glory with the Father and the Holy Spirit,
now and for ever.
Amen.

[T&S 243]

An adapted version of the prayer
Lord Jesus, you were condemned to death because it was the easy way out for the ruler:
you were the victim of injustice:
change the minds of oppressors and exploiters to your way of peace.
Amen.

SIXTH STATION: JESUS SCOURGED AND CROWNED WITH THORNS

The soldiers bullied Jesus: they dressed him up like a king but with a crown made of thorns. Then they made fun of him and laughed at him. They hit him and spat at him.

How do you feel when you are bullied or when people laugh at you?

Have you ever been involved in bullying someone else?

A reading from the Gospel according to Mark (15.17-19)
And they clothed him in a purple cloak; and after twisting some thorns into a crown, they put it on him. And they began saluting him, 'Hail, King of the Jews!' They struck his head with a reed, spat upon him, and knelt down in homage to him.

Prayer
Lord Jesus, you faced the torment of barbaric punishment and mocking tongue:

be with those who cry out in physical agony and emotional distress.
You endured unbearable abuse:
be with those who face torture and mockery in our world today.
To you, Jesus, the King crowned with thorns,
be honour and glory with the Father and the Holy Spirit,
now and for ever.
Amen.

[T&S 244]

An adapted version of the prayer
Lord Jesus, you endured unbearable abuse and barbaric punishment:
be with those who are abused and cruelly punished today.
Amen.

SEVENTH STATION: JESUS CARRIES THE CROSS

Next, the soldiers gave Jesus a heavy wooden cross to carry through the streets.
Sometimes when we have big problems people say we have a cross to carry.
Do you know anyone who has a cross to carry now?

A reading from the Gospel according to Mark (15.20)
After mocking him, they stripped him of the purple cloak and put his own clothes on him. Then they led him out to crucify him.

Prayers
Lord Jesus, you carried the cross through the rough streets of Jerusalem:
be with those who are loaded with burdens beyond their strength.
You bore the weight of our sins when you carried the cross:
help us to realize the extent and the cost of your love for us.
To you, Jesus, bearing a cross not your own,
be honour and glory with the Father and the Holy Spirit,
now and for ever.
Amen.

[T&S 245]

An adapted version of the prayer
Lord Jesus, you carried the cross through the rough streets of Jerusalem:
be with those who are loaded with burdens beyond their strength.
Amen.

EIGHTH STATION: SIMON OF CYRENE HELPS JESUS TO CARRY THE CROSS

Simon, a man in the crowd, was told by the soldiers to carry Jesus' cross for a while.
Have you ever helped someone who had a heavy load to carry and was tired out?

A reading from the Gospel according to Mark (15.21)
They compelled a passer-by, who was coming in from the country, to carry his cross; it was Simon of Cyrene, the father of Alexander and Rufus.

Prayer
Lord Jesus, you were worn down by fatigue:
be with those from whom life drains all energy.
You needed the help of a passing stranger:
give us the humility to receive aid from others.
To you, Jesus, weighed down with exhaustion and in need of help,
be honour and glory with the Father and the Holy Spirit,
now and for ever.
Amen.

[T&S 246]

An adapted version of the prayer
Lord Jesus, you needed the help of a passing stranger:
give us the humility to receive help from others.
Amen.

WEEK 3:

NINTH STATION: JESUS MEETS THE WOMEN OF JERUSALEM

There were some women standing along the roadside. They were friends of Jesus.
How do you think their faces looked when they saw Jesus in so much pain?
How do you feel when your friend is hurt?

A reading from the Gospel according to Luke (23.27-31)
A great number of the people followed him, and among them were women who were beating their breasts and wailing for him. But Jesus turned to them and said, 'Daughters of Jerusalem, do not weep for me, but weep for yourselves and for your children. For the days are surely coming when they will say, "Blessed are the barren, and the wombs that never bore, and the breasts that never nursed." Then they will begin to say to the mountains, "Fall on us"; and to the hills, "Cover us." For if they do this when the wood is green, what will happen when it is dry?'

Prayer
Lord Jesus, the women of Jerusalem wept for you:
move us to tears at the plight of the broken in our world.
You embraced the pain of Jerusalem, the 'city of peace':
bless Jerusalem this day and lead it to the path of profound peace.
To you, Jesus, the King of peace who wept for the city of peace,
be honour and glory with the Father and the Holy Spirit,
now and for ever.
Amen.

[T&S 247]

An adapted version of the prayer
Lord Jesus, the women of Jerusalem wept for you:
move us to tears at the plight of the broken in our world.
Amen.

TENTH STATION: JESUS IS CRUCIFIED

Then the soldiers nailed Jesus to the cross.
Jesus didn't blame them. He prayed that his Father in heaven would forgive them.
Is there someone you need to forgive?
Do you need to say sorry for something you have done or said?

A reading from the Gospel according to Mark (15.24)
And they crucified him, and divided his clothes among them, casting lots to decide what each should take.

Prayer
Lord Jesus, you bled in pain as the nails were driven into your flesh:
transform through the mystery of your love the pain of those who suffer.
To you, Jesus, our crucified Lord,
be honour and glory with the Father and the Holy Spirit,
now and for ever.
Amen.

[T&S 248]

An adapted version of the prayer
Lord Jesus, you suffered pain as you were nailed to the cross:
be with those who suffer today.
To you, Jesus, our crucified Lord,
be honour and glory with the Father and the Holy Spirit,
now and for ever.
Amen.

Eleventh Station: Jesus promises the kingdom to the penitent thief

Two other people were crucified at the same time as Jesus. One of them laughed at him: 'If you are really God's son, save yourself and us.' But the other said 'Jesus, remember me when you come into your kingdom.' Jesus said to him: 'Today you will be with me in Paradise.'

Have you ever laughed at someone unkindly? Who has been really, really kind to you when you were in a mess?

A reading from the Gospel according to Luke (23.39-43)
One of the criminals who were hanged there kept deriding him and saying, 'Are you not the Messiah? Save yourself and us!' But the other rebuked him, saying, 'Do you not fear God, since you are under the same sentence of condemnation? And we indeed have been condemned justly, for we are getting what we deserve for our deeds, but this man has done nothing wrong.' Then he said, 'Jesus, remember me when you come into your kingdom.' He replied, 'Truly I tell you, today you will be with me in Paradise.'

Prayers
Lord Jesus, even in your deepest agony you listened to the crucified thief:
hear us as we unburden to you our deepest fears.
You spoke words of love in your hour of death:
help us to speak words of life to a dying world.
To you, Jesus, who offer hope to the hopeless,
be honour and glory with the Father and the Holy Spirit,
now and for ever.
Amen.

[T&S 249]

An adapted version of the prayer
Lord Jesus, even in your deepest agony you listened to the crucified thief:
hear us as we share our deepest fears with you.
And help us to speak words of life to a dying world.
Amen.

Twelfth Station: Jesus on the cross; his mother and his friend

Jesus' mother, Mary, stood with his friend near the cross. Jesus knew they were sad. He said to Mary, 'Here is your son,' and to his friend, 'Here is your mother.'

When have you thought of someone else's need rather than your own?

A reading from the Gospel according to John (19.26,27)
When Jesus saw his mother and the disciple whom he loved standing beside her, he said to his mother, 'Woman, here is your son.' Then he said to the disciple, 'Here is your mother.' And from that hour the disciple took her into his own home.

Prayers
Lord Jesus, your mother and your dearest friend stayed with you to the bitter end,
yet even while racked with pain you ministered to them:
be with all broken families today
and care for those who long for companionship.
You cared for your loved ones even in your death-throes:
give us a love for one another
that is stronger even than the fear of death.
To you, Jesus, loving in the face of death,
be honour and glory with the Father and the Holy Spirit,
now and for ever.
Amen.

[T&S 250]

An adapted version of the prayer
Lord Jesus, your mother and your dearest friend stayed with you to the bitter end,
and you ministered to them even from the cross:
be with all broken families today
and care for those who long for someone to be with them.
Amen.

Week 4:

Thirteenth Station: Jesus dies on the cross

Jesus died on the cross.
He had told his friends that this would happen but that he would be alive again in three days.

A reading from the Gospel according to Mark (15.34-37)
At three o'clock Jesus cried out with a loud voice, 'Eloi, Eloi, lema sabachthani?' which means, 'My God, my God, why have you forsaken me?' When some of the bystanders heard it, they said, 'Listen, he is calling for Elijah.' And someone ran, filled a sponge with sour wine, put it on a stick, and gave it to him to drink, saying, 'Wait, let us see whether Elijah will come to take him down.' Then Jesus gave a loud cry and breathed his last.

Prayers

Lord Jesus, you died on the cross
and entered the bleakest of all circumstances:
give courage to those who die at the hands of others.
In death you entered into the darkest place of all:
illumine our darkness with your glorious presence.
To you, Jesus, your lifeless body hanging on the tree
*   of shame,*
be honour and glory with the Father and the Holy Spirit,
now and for ever.
Amen.

[T&S 251]

An adapted version of the prayer
Lord Jesus,
In death you entered into the darkest place of all:
illumine our darkness with your glorious presence.
Amen.

FOURTEENTH STATION: JESUS LAID IN THE TOMB

The body of Jesus was wrapped in a clean sheet and
then put into a tomb.
A large stone blocked the entrance to the tomb and a
soldier stood guard.
How do you imagine everyone felt?

A reading from the Gospel according to Mark (15.46)
Then Joseph bought a linen cloth, and taking down
the body, wrapped it in the linen cloth, and laid it in
a tomb that had been hewn out of the rock. He then
rolled a stone against the door of the tomb.

Prayers

Lord Jesus, Lord of life, you became as nothing for us:
be with those who feel worthless and as nothing in
*   the world's eyes.*
You were laid in a cold, dark tomb and hidden from
*   sight:*
be with all who suffer and die in secret,
hidden from the eyes of the world.
To you, Jesus, your rigid body imprisoned in a tomb,
be honour and glory with the Father and the Holy
*   Spirit,*
now and for ever.
Amen.

[T&S 252]

An adapted version of the prayer
Lord Jesus, Lord of life, you became as nothing for us:
be with those who feel worthless and as nothing in
*   the world's eyes.*
You were laid in a cold, dark tomb and hidden from
*   sight:*

be with all who suffer and die in secret,
hidden from the eyes of the world.
Amen.

FIFTEENTH STATION: JESUS RISEN FROM THE DEAD

On Sunday morning some of Jesus' friends came to
the tomb.
They found the tomb was open and, when they
looked inside, Jesus' body wasn't there.
Then they saw him and they remembered that Jesus
had told them that he would live again.
Jesus will be with us for ever and ever.

A reading from the Gospel according to Mark (16.4-8)
When they looked up, they saw that the stone, which
was very large, had already been rolled back. As they
entered the tomb, they saw a young man, dressed in
a white robe, sitting on the right side; and they were
alarmed. But he said to them, 'Do not be alarmed; you
are looking for Jesus of Nazareth, who was crucified. He
has been raised; he is not here. Look, there is the place
they laid him. But go, tell his disciples and Peter that he
is going ahead of you to Galilee; there you will see him,
just as he told you.' So they went out and fled from the
tomb, for terror and amazement had seized them; and
they said nothing to anyone, for they were afraid.

Prayers

Lord Jesus, you were dead but now you are alive:
transform the torments of this world's sin
that we may see your radiant glory.
You were raised from death to life:
may the power of your resurrection live in us,
that we may be channels of your true life beyond
*   measure.*
To you, Jesus, who have broken free from the bonds
*   of death,*
be honour and glory with the Father and the Holy Spirit,
now and for ever.
Amen.

[T&S 253]

An adapted version of the prayer
Lord Jesus,
may the power of your resurrection live in us,
that we may be channels of your true life beyond
*   measure.*
To you, Jesus, who has broken free from the bonds
*   of death,*
be honour and glory with the Father and the Holy
*   Spirit,*
now and for ever.
Amen.

Adults

This group material provides the opportunity to study the Lenten Gospels together during the weeks of Lent, and to try to relate these to our own lives. The material may be used either during the week before the Gospel reading is due to be read in worship, or during the week after it has been read.

You will need
- to set up the station items in the meeting place;
- materials for the response time: paper and pens for writing, art materials if your group enjoys using art as a response, items that may be added to the stations;
- Bibles;
- copies of the relevant psalm.

Set your considerations within the context of worship by using Prayer During the Day for Lent, beginning on page 66 of *Common Worship: Daily Prayer*.

Preparation

O God, make speed to save us.
O Lord, make haste to help us.

Hear my prayer, O Lord, and give ear to my cry;
hold not your peace at my tears.

Psalm 39.13

Praise

Jesus, like a mother you gather your people to you;
you are gentle with us as a mother with her children.

Despair turns to hope through your sweet goodness;
through your gentleness we find comfort in fear.

Your warmth gives life to the dead,
your touch makes sinners righteous.

Lord Jesus, in your mercy heal us;
in your love and tenderness remake us.

In your compassion bring grace and forgiveness,
for the beauty of heaven may your love prepare us.

Anselm (1109)

[DP 66]

The word of God

PSALMODY

Say together the psalm for the appropriate day

Sunday Psalm 51.11-end

Monday Psalm 3

Tuesday Psalm 6

Wednesday Psalm 11

Thursday Psalm 12

Friday Psalm 32

Saturday Psalm 61

Each psalm or group of psalms may end with
Glory to the Father and to the Son
and to the Holy Spirit;
as it was in the beginning is now
and shall be for ever. Amen.

[DP 67]

The reading and reflection

Read together the Gospel you have chosen to study today, with the items from the station in front of you.

Keep a short time of silence for personal reflection.

Ponder the story together:
What do you like about the scene it sets before you?
What makes you uncomfortable?
How does the story relate to you? Where are you in the story?

Respond to the story individually or as a group:
You could write something as a response or you could paint, draw or use some kind of modelling medium. You might like to add something to the contents of the station.

When people have completed their responses, gather together again.

Prayers

The Collect of the day or the prayer of St Ignatius is said
Teach us, good Lord, to serve you as you deserve;
to give and not to count the cost;
to fight and not to heed the wounds;
to toil and not to seek for rest;
to labour and not to seek for any reward,
save that of knowing that we do your will.
Amen.

After Ignatius of Loyola (1556)

The Lord's Prayer is said.

The Conclusion

May God bless us and show us compassion and mercy.
Amen.

[DP 70]

The Stations at home

You might like to use the scenes of the stations of the cross described in *Times and Seasons*. Get a notebook and put the heading of each station across a double page spread. You can print the Bible text to go with it if you like. Throughout Lent, watch the newspapers and when you find a story that you think relates to one of the stations, cut it out and stick it in on the relevant page under the right heading. You might like to write prayers to go in your book also.

First Station:	Jesus in agony in the Garden of Gethsemene:	Mark (14.32-36)
Second Station:	Jesus betrayed by Judas and arrested:	Mark (14.43-46)
Third Station:	Jesus condemned by the Sanhedrin:	Mark (14.55-64)
Fourth Station:	Peter denies Jesus:	Mark (14.72)
Fifth Station:	Jesus judged by Pilate:	Mark (15.14,15)
Sixth Station:	Jesus scourged and crowned with thorns:	Mark (15.17-19)
Seventh Station:	Jesus carries the cross:	Mark (15.20)
Eighth Station:	Simon of Cyrene helps Jesus to carry the cross:	Mark (15.21)
Ninth Station:	Jesus meets the women of Jerusalem:	Luke (23.27-31)
Tenth Station:	Jesus is crucified:	Mark (15.24)
Eleventh Station:	Jesus promises the kingdom to the penitent thief:	Luke (23.39-43)

Twelfth Station:	Jesus on the cross; his mother and his friend:	John (19.26,27)
Thirteenth Station:	Jesus dies on the cross:	Mark (15.34-37)
Fourteenth Station:	Jesus laid in the tomb:	Mark (15.46)
Fifteenth Station:	Jesus risen from the dead:	Mark (16.4-8)

The Stations in outreach

The increasing recognition of the importance of public art provides encouragement for us to take the Stations of the Cross out into the areas around our churches and indeed, further afield. The proliferation of street drama provides similar encouragement: a walk around Covent Garden in London, or down the main shopping streets in other cities both in Britain and further afield in Europe, provides us with the opportunity to see many living statues, circus artists and musical buskers. The further step of taking the Stations of the Cross out into a churchyard or nearby shopping centre is not, then, so alien.

You could gather together items in order to leave simple sculptured stations outside in a churchyard. You don't necessarily need to use figures: the use of other artefacts to tell a story can be very effective. Or you could make a series of 15 simple crosses out of plain wood and add pictures to them.

If you were prepared to try street drama, simply take a series of tableaux to the same place each Saturday throughout Lent. Cold might be a factor for those taking part, particularly at the beginning of Lent, so people may need to wear warm clothing under their costumes. You could provide groups of three stations each week, or group the stations together and tell the whole story on several occasions throughout the season. Be prepared for mixed reactions. You may take a certain amount of abuse, but it is worth remembering that there will be many people for whom this may be the first encounter with this story and, if what you do is of a high quality and done with integrity, there will be those who are engaged by the power of a very powerful story.

HOLY WEEK

Seasonal introduction

Dark places

Our journey through Holy Week takes us straight into the dark places of human experience and the dangerous depths of the human heart. We find ourselves reflected in the faces and experience of numerous people whose stories are woven through the Scriptures and liturgies of the season. Palm Sunday with its festal shouts and acclamation is shot through with ambiguity. This is not exactly the picture of a dashing hero on a white steed coming to the rescue by force or at least by force of personality. The crowd itself is full of fickle emotion. Why have they come? With the benefit of history, we know how the mood will change, but it is not hard to imagine even some of those cheering slinking away into the shadows when events turn unpredictable. Even more difficult is the realization that all of us have done something similar – we have run away when standing up for Jesus is just too costly, too embarrassing or too dangerous. We are there in this crowd of pleasure seekers, of followers and observers, of lovers of a good parade and there when the denial comes in the shouts of 'Crucify!' and in the darkness of a courtyard before dawn.

We are there in the garden where Jesus is alone with a weight of responsibility as one by one his disciples drift off to sleep. We are there in the pain of decision-making and in the loneliness of vocation. And we are there sleeping on the ground as the agony of choice is played out, because our spirits are willing but …

Dark moments

And there are other dark moments too. There are the weak-willed crowd-pleasers like Pilate, more concerned with his own reputation as a hard man than with doing the right thing. There is Judas and his zealous desire for a quick fix, for an 'end justifies the means' smashing of Roman power by force if necessary and his burning disappointment at the slow pace of change. Peter – full of swaggering confidence one minute and consumed by guilt at his own collapse the next.

There is brutality and violence – people who move under cover of dark; people who put the boot in under orders; people who obey orders above all else. This is a place of undercover operations, lanterns and whispers in the night and armies arresting a victim in a place and at a time when no one can see another person's face clearly. Christ's arrest and trial; the sense of powerlessness as we watch events unfold; the brutality of the cross, are all profoundly disturbing – all the more so because these events are both particular and universal. We are watching the Christ story but these events touch on deep terrors of mistaken arrest; of innocent victims; of the detention centre; of the rooms with blood on the floor; of the torture chamber, the chill of the silent scream sliding into the pit of your stomach, the stench of fear and the trickling of sweat down the back. Is it possible to find ourselves in this dark place?

Tender moments

However, nor should we miss the tender moments in this journey: Jesus weeping for Jerusalem and for his beloved friend Lazarus; the woman anointing Jesus, the intimacy of touch and the room full of the scent of perfume; the poignancy of a last meal between friends; Jesus washing the feet of his disciples; the strangers who carry the cross, wipe the face of Jesus and provide a tomb – all powerful images of love that reaches into the forgotten places; the words of Jesus to the thief dying next to him; the promise of paradise and of wrongdoing put right. Then there is Mary – following her beloved Jesus, standing at the foot of the cross and later cradling the dead son she once carried in her womb, to whom she gave birth and whom she nurtured. The mirror images of Mary cradling her infant son and the Pietà – Mary with the dead Christ lying across her lap – remind us that the love demonstrated in the Incarnation is the same love that is demonstrated on the cross, 'For God so loved the world … ' (John 3.16 Lent 2 Year A). In this context it is interesting to remember that the Feast of the Annunciation occurs on 25 March.

The still place

And after all that this week throws at us, after following closely or from afar the slow steps to the cross and the tomb, after all the tears we have shed have exhausted themselves, we are left at the end in the still quiet place of death. It is a moment captured exquisitely by J. S. Bach near the end of the *St John Passion*:

Lie still, lie still,
O sacred limbs lie sleeping
and I will lay aside my weeping.
Lie still, lie still.
I too may rest, I may rest in peace.
The grave that was appointed you
to close the sum of suffering due
shall be my path to heaven,
from hell my full release.

from J. S. Bach, St John Passion[1]

And we are asked to stand here for a while, painful and uncomfortable though it might be. We are asked to remain here in the place of forgotten dreams; of hopelessness; and of letting go of the loved one who is now dead and gone. We should not look to Easter morning too early – this place has much to teach us. For Good Friday and Holy Saturday are about the laying aside of the power to 'do' anything. It is about facing the root of the word passion – *passio* – to suffer, recognizing that 'the meaning is in the waiting' to borrow a well-known phrase of R. S. Thomas (from his poem 'Kneeling'). Alongside those who dwell in the shadow of death, alongside those who watch at the bedsides of the dying, alongside all who descend into their private hell where we are powerless to reach them, we are called simply to wait.

Holy Week:
Stand-alone seasonal material

The Liturgy of Palm Sunday: Commemoration of the Lord's entry into Jerusalem

Preparatory notes

This service is based on the Commemoration of the Lord's Entry into Jerusalem, which is described at the beginning of the Eucharist for Palm Sunday in *Times and Seasons*. However, it takes the liturgy out into the streets and gathering places of the neighbourhood, reflecting the journey that Christ made into Jerusalem.

A short history of the celebrations of Palm Sunday

Jesus' triumphant entry into Jerusalem before his passion has been celebrated on the Sunday before Easter since the first centuries of Christianity and has often been marked by the carrying of branches. The branches of date palms were symbols of victory from ancient times: The Romans used them to reward athletics champions and the leaders of military triumphs and, from evidence in the Hebrew Bible (Leviticus 23.40; 1 Maccabees 13.37), it seems that the Jews also carried palm branches during their festivals. In the book of Revelation, palm branches are a symbol of martyrdom and in Christian art, martyrs are often represented holding palms. There is tenth-century evidence that, in Constantinople, other kinds of branch were used also (olive or myrtle, lilac, laurel and other flowering branches) and of course, in the colder climate of northern Europe where dates did not grow and few other branches were in flower by Palm Sunday in most years, pussy willows often came to be used instead.

The fourth-century nun, Egeria, in a diary that provides a detailed description of her Easter pilgrimage to Jerusalem, gives an account of a Palm Sunday celebration. It began in the late afternoon and involved a procession from the top of the Mount of Olives down to the place of the resurrection, the bishop riding a donkey accompanied by children carrying branches.

From Jerusalem the celebration spread to Egypt, and by the fifth century it was celebrated in Constantinople. By the sixth century it became the custom for the procession to take place in the morning and it also spread to the West. Eamon Duffy, describes the Palm Sunday procession as 'the most elaborate and eloquent of the processions of the Sarum rite'.[2] The branches were from native trees and were distributed inside the church. The procession then moved outside following a painted cross without a figure on it and the procession moved around the churchyard, stopping at various points for a variety of dramatic actions, before re-entering the church by the west door and processing to the rood screen at the church crossing, where an anthem 'Ave rex noster' (Hail to our King) was sung.

Celebrations today

In preparing for a more public celebration of Palm Sunday, it might be worth remembering that, although the descriptions above might seem like ancient history to us, Holy Week is marked by processions throughout Spain, for example, and people who have spent Easter holidays in Spain may well have observed this and add this experience to the planning. The Holy Week procession culture in Spain is, indeed, so strong that communities will have posters printed advertising the times and routes of their processions. Also, whilst it would be tragic if flag-carrying were to descend into xenophobia, it is worth noting that the carrying of flags has re-entered British tradition at sports events and it is possible now to obtain beautiful flags and banners for use in worship and dance, which might serve this purpose very well. Communities in the north of England might also research the tradition of Whit Walks, which faded not so long ago, if they wish to be persuaded of the legitimacy of British religious processions!

Liturgy outside

It is suggested for this service that you take inspiration from tradition and celebrate the Commemoration of the Lord's Entry into Jerusalem outside. Where and how you do this will depend to some extent on your own local circumstances but the basic idea is for groups of worshippers to walk together, carrying branches, flags and anything else they wish to carry, and converge on one place where the dramatic liturgy will begin. In a group of rural parishes where the villages are fairly close together, it may be possible for worshippers to gather in each village and walk to the one where the service is to be held. In an urban parish, people might gather at various significant places; it would be good to meet where people naturally gather on a Sunday morning: a garden centre, a supermarket, a children's play area, a gym and so on. Check in advance with management, if it seems relevant, that they don't mind your meeting there. Perhaps you could give something away to passers-by as you gather: the little gold crosses you can get as table confetti for religious occasions, confirmation and first communion parties for example, is one idea. You can get these from party shops. Balloons are another possibility.

What needs to be prepared leading up to the service?

Gathering places

You will need to identify gathering places for the start of the processions and, if necessary, check with the relevant owners or managers that they don't mind groups of people gathering to pray and sing there.

Leaders and timings

A leader for each procession must be appointed, with clear instructions and a detailed route worked out. Timings will also need to be established for each route so that people arrive at the church as near together as possible.

Hazards and risk assessments

A risk assessment on the route's safety for a group of people walking together should be undertaken, so that the necessary instructions can be given to walkers by the leader of each group. Hazards should be identified so attention can be drawn to them: the needs of children and vulnerable adults should particularly be borne in mind. If there are going to be large numbers of people in the processions, you should tell the police.

Music

If you plan to sing at each of the gathering places, you will need to identify appropriate musicians. The best instruments to lead outdoor singing are brass but, if these are not available, outdoor singing is often best led just by a confident singer. If you feel that your congregation really will not cope with singing outside, then don't do it!

Service sheets

Print out the part of the service for each stopping place on separate cards. Have plenty so that they can be given to passers-by. Give each section a number in the top right-hand corner so that you can give out the correct sheet efficiently in each place.

Food steward

If you plan to make the first gathering into a substantial event, with breakfast or coffee, for example, this will need to be planned and arranged. Identify a person, different from the liturgical leader, who can do this for each party.

Branches

People should be encouraged to bring their own branches. For those people with gardens this should not be too difficult. In other circumstances you may need to identify appropriate places from which they can be cut. Some people may also like to bring flags and banners. For this service, reflecting the spontaneous and enthusiastic response to Jesus' journey towards Jerusalem, practically anything goes.

Dramatized readings

Most of the readings are dramatized. You will need to find people to play each part and provide them with a copy of the script. This is usually best planned in advance, though some congregations may be content to volunteer for parts quickly on the day. You will know what works best in your own community.

DRAMATIZED PALM GOSPELS FOR EACH OF THE THREE YEARS

YEAR A: MATTHEW 21.1-11

Narrator	When they had come near Jerusalem and had reached Bethphage, at the Mount of Olives, Jesus sent two disciples, saying to them,
Jesus	Go into the village ahead of you, and immediately you will find a donkey tied, and a colt with her; untie them and bring them to me. If anyone says anything to you, just say this, 'The Lord needs them.' And he will send them immediately.
Narrator	This took place to fulfil what had been spoken through the prophet, saying, 'Tell the daughter of Zion, Look, your king is coming to you, humble, and mounted on a donkey, and on a colt, the foal of a donkey.' The disciples went and did as Jesus had directed them; they brought the donkey and the colt, and put their cloaks on them, and he sat on them. A very large crowd spread their cloaks on the road, and others cut branches from the trees and spread them on the road. The crowds that went ahead of him and that followed were shouting,
Crowd	Hosanna to the Son of David! Blessed is the one who comes in the name of the Lord! Hosanna in the highest heaven!
Narrator	When he entered Jerusalem, the whole city was in turmoil, asking,
Crowd	Who is this?
Narrator	The crowds were saying,
Crowd	This is the prophet Jesus from Nazareth in Galilee.

YEAR B: MARK 11.1-11

Narrator	When they were approaching Jerusalem, at Bethphage and Bethany, near the Mount of Olives, he sent two of his disciples and said to them,
Jesus	Go into the village ahead of you, and immediately as you enter it, you will find tied there a colt that has never been ridden; untie it and bring it. If anyone says to you, 'Why are you doing this?' just say this, 'The Lord needs it and will send it back here immediately.'
Narrator	They went away and found a colt tied near a door, outside in the street. As they were untying it, some of the bystanders said to them,
Bystanders	What are you doing, untying the colt
Narrator	They told them what Jesus had said; and they allowed them to take it. Then they brought the colt to Jesus and threw their cloaks on it; and he sat on it. Many people spread their cloaks on the road, and others spread leafy branches that they had cut in the fields. Then those who went ahead and those who followed were shouting,
Crowd	Hosanna! Blessed is the one who comes in the name of the Lord! Blessed is the coming kingdom of our ancestor David! Hosanna in the highest heaven!
Narrator	Then he entered Jerusalem and went into the temple; and when he had looked around at everything, as it was already late, he went out to Bethany with the twelve.

YEAR C: LUKE 19.28-40

Narrator	After Jesus had said this, he went on ahead, going up to Jerusalem. When he had come near Bethphage and Bethany, at the place called the Mount of Olives, he sent two of the disciples, saying,
	Go into the village ahead of you, and as you enter it you will find tied there a colt that has never been ridden. Untie it and bring it here. If anyone asks you, 'Why are you untying it?' just say this, 'The Lord needs it.'
Narrator	So those who were sent departed and found it as he had told them. As they were untying the colt, its owners asked them,
Colt's owner	Why are you untying the colt?
Narrator	They said,
Two disciples	The Lord needs it
Narrator	Then they brought it to Jesus; and after throwing their cloaks on the colt, they set Jesus on it. As he rode along, people kept spreading their cloaks on the road. As he was now approaching the path down from the Mount of Olives, the whole multitude of the disciples began to praise God joyfully with a loud voice for all the deeds of power that they had seen, saying,
Crowd	Blessed is the king who comes in the name of the Lord! Peace in heaven, and glory in the highest heaven!
Narrator	Some of the Pharisees in the crowd said to him,
Pharisees	Teacher, order your disciples to stop.
Narrator	He answered, 'I tell you, if these were silent, the stones would shout out.'

Furniture and coins

For the Cleansing of the Temple reading you will need some tables (or at least some pieces of furniture) to be overturned as part of the drama of the scene. For the question about who should receive taxes, you need to be sure that a coin is available. A large coin, such as a British £2 piece would be helpful.

Palm crosses

Above all, you need to be sure that you have palm crosses available in the church to be distributed at the end of the service.

Structure, movement and flow	Words/text	Multisensory	Participation
THE GATHERING		People gather at each of the first gathering places. If it is appropriate, food or drinks might be shared. Breakfast could be eaten together. Branches and flags could be prepared and handed out.	Meeting, eating and drinking. Preparing and sharing branches, flags and whatever else is to be carried.

Greeting	Grace, mercy and peace from God our Father and the Lord Jesus Christ be with you **and also with you.** [T&S 470]		Spoken response
The Lord's Prayer	As our Saviour has taught us, so we pray **Our Father in heaven,** **hallowed be your name,** **your kingdom come,** **your will be done,** **on earth as in heaven.** **Give us today our daily bread.** **Forgive us our sins** **as we forgive those who sin** **against us.** **Lead us not into temptation** **but deliver us from evil.** **For the kingdom, the power,** **and the glory are yours** **now and for ever.** **Amen.** [CW 178]		Saying the Lord's Prayer
	The leader introduces the celebration using these or other appropriate words Dear brothers and sisters in Christ, during Lent we have been preparing by works of love and self-sacrifice for the celebration of our Lord's death and resurrection. Today we come together to begin this solemn celebration in union with the Church throughout the world. Christ enters his own city to complete his work as our Saviour, to suffer, to die, and to rise again. Let us go with him in faith and love, so that, united with him in his sufferings, we may share his risen life. [T&S 270]	Branches and flags	Holding up the branches and flags.

	The people hold up branches and say this prayer together **God our Saviour,** **whose Son Jesus Christ entered** **Jerusalem as Messiah to suffer** **and to die;** **let these branches be for us signs** **of his victory** **and grant that we who bear them** **in his name** **may ever hail him as our King,** **and follow him in the way that** **leads to eternal life;** **who is alive and reigns** **now and for ever. Amen.** [T&S 270 adapted]		
This could be used as a song. See for example the version by Carl Tuttle at 242 in *Mission Praise* (also available in a number of other books)	**Hosanna to the Son of David.** **Blessed is he who comes in the** **name of the Lord.** Behold your king comes to you, O Zion, meek and lowly, sitting upon an ass. Ride on in the cause of truth and for the sake of justice. Your throne is the throne of God, it endures for ever; and the sceptre of your kingdom is a righteous sceptre. You have loved righteousness and hated evil. Therefore God, your God, has anointed you with the oil of gladness above your fellows. **Hosanna to the Son of David.** **Blessed is he who comes in the** **name of the Lord.** [T&S 269]		
The Procession *The procession then moves off following an agreed route, to meet up with some groups that had started at other gathering points.*		Walking together and meeting.	Walking together and meeting.

93

On reaching the second meeting place, the people greet each other with the Peace and then the Palm Gospel is read. **The Peace**	Christ is our peace. He has reconciled us to God in one body by the cross. We meet in his name and share his peace. The peace of the Lord be always with you **and also with you.** [CW 290, 175]		
The Palm Gospel *A dramatized reading of the Gospel would be appropriate. (See tables above.)* **Song or hymn**	*When the Gospel is announced the reader says* Hear the Gospel of our Lord Jesus Christ according to N. **Glory to you, O Lord.** *At the end* This is the Gospel of the Lord. **Praise to you, O Christ.** *If it is appropriate to sing here, songs could include 'We have a King who rides a donkey' (NB be careful of the chorus – 'Jesus the king is risen' should obviously not be sung on Palm Sunday)', 'Majesty', 'All glory, laud and honour', 'Ride on, Ride on in majesty' and 'Make way, make way'.*	Branches and flags are waved throughout the reading.	Branches and flags. Hearing the reading. Singing.
Intercession	Let us pray: We give thanks for the joy and fellowship provided by the opportunity to follow in the Way of Christ; we pray for all for whom this is difficult, for those who are oppressed because of their faith. We give thanks for those who have the courage and honesty to work openly for justice and peace; and we pray for the city of Jerusalem, and for all who still make it a battleground.		

94

	We pray, Lord, that you will strengthen us when we are confident in our faith, and that you will be with us when we are weighed down by hardship, failure and sorrow and feel that you are far away: **Holy God, holy and strong, holy and immortal, have mercy upon us.** [T&S 273]		Responding to the prayers.
The Procession *The procession now continues to the church where the liturgy will continue.*	Let us go forth, praising Jesus our Messiah. [T&S 271]		
Questions	*What are your questions about the Gathering?*		
THE LITURGY OF THE WORD			
At the church. The people from all directions gather at the church gates or another similar place, which will represent the gates of Jerusalem.	*Songs may be sung, for example 'Give me joy (love) (peace) (hope) in my heart' and 'Hosanna, hosanna, hosanna in the highest', or others if not sung earlier.*	Waving flags and branches.	Singing.
		The people walk in procession up to the church, as noisily and joyfully as possible. Everyone should enter the churchyard and line the path, waving branches, and cheering. As the person representing Jesus enters the gates and walks into the church grounds, the branches are thrown on the ground in front of him. Flags continue to fly.	Waving branches and flags.

Dramatic Reading 1:	Narrator 1	Some tables are set up and some people take up their places behind the tables. The following dramatized account of the cleansing of the Temple is read.	Watching and taking part in the drama.
Jesus Cleanses the Temple *'Jesus' moves to a place in the church grounds where there is room for people to gather.*	Then Jesus entered the temple,		
	and drove out all who were selling and buying in the temple, and he overturned the tables of the money-changers and the seats of those who sold doves. He said to them,	Jesus turns over the tables and herds people from behind the tables.	
	Jesus 'It is written, "My house shall be called a house of prayer"; but you are making it a den of robbers.'		
	Narrator 1 The blind and the lame came to him in the temple, and he cured them. But when the chief priests and the scribes saw the amazing things that he did, and heard the children crying out in the temple,	People are brought to Jesus and he touches them.	
	Children 'Hosanna to the Son of David,'	Children shout and wave flags.	
	Narrator 1 They became angry and said to him,		
	Chief priests 'Do you hear what these are saying?'		
	Narrator 1 Jesus said to them,		
	Jesus 'Yes; have you never read, "Out of the mouths of infants and nursing babies you have prepared praise for yourself"?'		
	Matthew 21.12-16		

Dramatic Reading 2: ***The Question about Paying Taxes*** *'Jesus' and the crowd of worshippers move to another place in the church grounds where there is room for people to gather.*	**Narrator 2** Then the Pharisees went and plotted to entrap him in what he said. So they sent their disciples to him, along with the Herodians, saying, **Disciples of the Pharisees** 'Teacher, we know that you are sincere, and teach the way of God in accordance with truth, and show deference to no one; for you do not regard people with partiality. Tell us, then, what you think. Is it lawful to pay taxes to the emperor, or not?' **Narrator 2** But Jesus, aware of their malice, said, **Jesus** 'Why are you putting me to the test, you hypocrites? Show me the coin used for the tax.' **Narrator** And they brought him a denarius. Then he said to them, **Jesus** 'Whose head is this, and whose title?' **Disciples of the Pharisees** 'The emperor's.' **Narrator** Then he said to them, **Jesus** 'Give therefore to the emperor the things that are the emperor's, and to God the things that are God's.' **Narrator** When they heard this, they were amazed; and they left him and went away. *Matthew 22.15-22*	Disciples of the Pharisees' group approach Jesus. A member of the group gives 'Jesus' a coin. Pharisees' disciples rejoin the crowd, which now moves into the church.	
At the end of the drama, all make their way quietly into the church. *As the people gather in the church a hymn or song is sung.*	*'From heaven you came'* might be an appropriate song.	As people enter the church, they take up again the branches that had been cast down in front of Jesus.	

The Affirmation of Faith	We say together in faith **Holy, holy, holy** **is the Lord God almighty,** **who was, and is, and is to come.** We believe in God the Father, who created all things: **for by his will they were created** **and have their being.** We believe in God the Son, who was slain: **for with his blood,** **he purchased us for God,** **from every tribe and language,** **from every people and nation.** We believe in God the Holy Spirit: **the Spirit and the Bride say, 'Come!'** **Even so come, Lord Jesus!** **Amen.** *cf Revelation 4.8,11; 5.9; 22.17,20* [CW 148]		Saying the Affirmation of Faith.
Questions	*What are your questions about the Liturgy of the Word?*		
THE PRAYERS			

The Confession	God shows his love for us
	   in that, while we were still
	   sinners, Christ died for us.
	Let us then show our love for him
	by confessing our sins
	and as a sign of our penitence, we
	lay down our branches.
	
	[T&S 260 adapted]
	
	The leader should explain here where
	the branches are to be laid down.
	
	Lord Jesus Christ,
	we confess we have failed you as
	   did your first disciples.
	We ask for your mercy and your
	   help.
	
	When we take our ease
	rather than watch with you:
	Lord, forgive us.
	Christ have mercy.
	
	When we bestow a kiss of peace
	yet nurse enmity in our hearts:
	Lord, forgive us.
	Christ have mercy.
		As the confession is said, people come forward and lay down the branches in the place that has been chosen.	

	When we strike at those who hurt us rather than stretch out our hands to bless: Lord, forgive us. **Christ have mercy.** When we deny that we know you for fear of the world and its scorn: Lord, forgive us. **Christ have mercy.** [T&S 261] May God who loved the world so much that he sent his Son to be our Saviour forgive us our sins and make us holy to serve him in the world, through Jesus Christ our Lord. **Amen.** [CW 136]		
Hymn or song		Palm crosses are distributed to people during the singing.	Receiving palm crosses.
THE CONCLUSION			
The Distribution of Palm Crosses	We have laid down our branches as a sign of our penitence. Now, as we enter together the week in which we recall his suffering and death, we take up these palm crosses as a sign of our journey with Jesus: God our Saviour, whose Son Jesus Christ entered Jerusalem as Messiah to suffer and to die; let these palms be for us signs of his victory. May we ever hail him as our King, and follow him in the way that leads to eternal life; who is alive and reigns now and for ever. **Amen.** [T&S 270 adapted] Hosanna to the Son of David. **Blessed is he who comes in the name of the Lord.** [T&S 269]	People hold up the palm crosses.	Holding up the crosses.

Blessing	May the Father,
	who so loved the world that he
	  gave his only Son,
	bring you by faith to his eternal life.
	Amen.
	
	May Christ,
	who accepted the cup of sacrifice
	in obedience to the Father's will,
	keep you steadfast as you walk with
	  him the way of his cross.
	Amen.
	
	May the Spirit,
	who strengthens us to suffer with
	  Christ
	that we may share his glory,
	set your minds on life and peace.
	Amen.
	
	And the blessing …
	
	[T&S 277]		

The Dismissal *The ministers and people depart.*	Go in the peace of Christ. **Thanks be to God.** [T&S 277]		

Eight all-age worship ideas for Good Friday

The first four of these ideas would be suitable for use during the Ministry of the Word, or as the heart of a whole act of worship, in which case each might be preceded by a Gathering and followed by a liturgical Conclusion. The fifth idea might be used as an act of intercession. The sixth idea might be used penitentially or as a focus for intercession, and the two final ideas have been created to be used as acts of penitence and might be used during the penitential section of a service.

1. Dramatized readings

The events of Gethsemane and Good Friday are recounted through a series of four dramatized readings, each arranged for three voices and complemented by visual elements. The readings have been freely adapted from *The Message* by Eugene Peterson (see Resources, p. 240).

You will need:
- Twelve readers. Try to have a combination of adults and children in each group. One way of doing this would be to assign each script to a different family.
- A copy of the script for each reader.
- A large cross at the front of the church.
- Twelve objects to be brought up by the readers and placed at the foot of the cross: a green branch, a chalice, a sword; a blindfold, a cockerel (a silhouette cut from card), a torn tunic; a purple robe; a crown of thorns; three large nails; a sponge tied to a stick; a jar of wine; a notice with the words, 'The King of the Jews'.
- A projector and screen to display the title of each reading (optional).

The readings could follow one after another, or be interspersed with appropriate songs or prayers.

1: Father, not what I want

A: narrator

B: Jesus

C: narrator and Judas.

(The readers bring their objects and place them at the foot of the cross – the green branch, the chalice, the sword – then take up their positions to read.)

A After they had shared supper together, Jesus and his friends went out into the night. They came to a place called Gethsemane. Jesus told his disciples,

B 'Sit here while I pray.'

A He took Peter, James, and John with him. He was very distressed.

B 'The sadness in my heart is so deep it is almost crushing me. Stay here and keep watch with me.'

C Going a little farther on, he fell to the ground and prayed for a way out.

B 'Abba, Father, you can get me out of this. Take this cup of suffering away from me. [*Pause.*] But please, not what I want. What do you want?'

C He came back and found the three disciples sound asleep. He said to Peter,

B 'Simon, you went to sleep on me? Can't you stick by me even for an hour? Keep watch, all of you. Stay alert, and keep praying so that you don't fall into danger. There's a part of you that is eager and ready for anything. But another part of you is as lazy as an old dog sleeping by the fireside!'

A Jesus went back and prayed the same prayer. And again, they fell asleep. They just couldn't keep their eyes open.

C The third time, Jesus said,

B 'Still sleeping? Well, anyway, time's up. The moment has come. Here he is – my betrayer has arrived.'

A The words were no sooner out of his mouth when Judas, one of the twelve disciples,

showed up, and with him a gang of thugs sent by the religious leaders. They had swords and clubs.

C Judas had worked out a signal with them: 'The one I kiss, he's the man you want. Grab him! Make sure he doesn't get away.'

A He went straight to Jesus and said,

C 'Rabbi!'

A and kissed him.

C The others then grabbed Jesus and roughed him up.

A The disciples were all terrified and ran away.

2: Are you the Son of the God?

A: narrator, chief priest and servant girl

B: narrator, soldier and Peter

C: narrator and Jesus.

(The readers bring their objects and place them at the foot of the cross – the blindfold, the cockerel, the torn tunic – then take up their positions to read.)

A Jesus was taken to the Chief Priest. Peter followed at a safe distance and he mingled with the servants and warmed himself at the fire.

B The religious leaders looked high and low for evidence against Jesus. They wanted an excuse to have him put to death, but they found nothing; there were plenty of people willing to bring in false charges, but nothing added up. In the middle of it all, the Chief Priest stood up and spoke to Jesus.

A 'What do you have to say for yourself?'

C Jesus was silent.

A 'Are you the Messiah, the Son of the Blessed God?'

C 'Yes, I am, and you'll see it for yourself: the Son of Man, seated at the right hand of God, arriving on the clouds of heaven.'

B The Chief Priest lost his temper. He ripped his clothes and spoke to the other leaders:

A 'You heard the blasphemy! Are we going to stand for that?'

B They condemned him, one and all. The sentence: death.

A Some of them started spitting at him. They put a blindfold on him, and began slapping and punching him.

B 'Who hit you? Come on! If you're a prophet, prophesy!'

C While all this was going on, Peter was down in the courtyard. A servant girl came in. She stared at Peter.

A 'You were with Jesus of Nazareth.'

C Peter denied it:

B 'I don't know what you're talking about.'

C Just then, a cockerel crowed. Peter tried to slip away. The girl began telling the people standing around:

A 'He's one of them. He has to be. Look – he's got "Galilean" written all over him!'

C Now Peter got really nervous.

B He swore. 'Jesus of Nazareth? I never laid eyes on him.'

C The cockerel crowed a second time.

B And Peter remembered what Jesus had said: 'Before a cockerel crows twice, you'll deny me three times.'

C He collapsed in tears.

3: Crucify him!

A: narrator, soldier, member of crowd

B: narrator, Pilate, member of crowd

C: narrator, Jesus, member of crowd.

(The readers bring their objects and place them at the foot of the cross – the purple robe, the crown of thorns, the three large nails – then take up their positions to read.)

A The religious leaders presented Jesus to Pilate. Pilate asked him,

B 'Is this true, what you claim? Are you the King of the Jews?'

C 'If you say so.'

A The high priests let loose a barrage of accusations.

B 'Aren't you going to answer anything? That's quite a list of accusations.'

C Jesus said nothing.

B Pilate was impressed.

A It was the custom at Passover for Pilate to release a prisoner, anyone the people asked for. There was one criminal called Barabbas, locked up for murder and rioting. When a crowd gathered to ask for the usual favour, Pilate made a guess. But the religious leaders had worked them up.

B 'Do you want me to set free the King of the Jews?'

A,B,C 'We want Barabbas!'

B 'Then what do I do with this man you call King of the Jews?'

A,C 'Nail him to a cross!'

B 'But for what? What crime has he committed?'

A,C [*Louder:*] 'Crucify him!'

B 'Then I wash my hands of all responsibility for this man's death.'

A Pilate gave the crowd what they wanted. He set Barabbas free, and handed Jesus over for a beating and crucifixion.

C The soldiers dressed Jesus up in purple and made him a crown from branches with sharp thorns. They hit his head with a club, and spat on him, and pretended to worship him.

A 'Bravo, King of the Jews!'

C When they got bored with their game, they took off the purple cape and put his own clothes back on him. Then they marched him out to the place where they would kill him.

B There was a man walking by called Simon. He was from Cyrene. The soldiers made him carry the cross for Jesus.

A The soldiers led Jesus to a place called 'Golgotha', which means 'Skull Hill'. They offered him drugs to take away the pain, but Jesus refused. Then they nailed him to the cross. Jesus prayed.

C 'Father, forgive them. They don't understand what they're doing.'

4: It is finished

A: narrator, Jesus

B: narrator, member of the crowd, penitent criminal

C: narrator, member of the crowd, unrepentant criminal.

(The readers bring their objects and place them at the foot of the cross – the sponge tied to a stick, the jar of wine, the sign with the words 'The King of the Jews' – then take up their positions to read.)

A The soldiers divided up his clothes and threw dice to see who would get them. It was nine o'clock in the morning when they crucified him. The charge against him was written on a notice: 'The King of the Jews'. The soldiers, the people passing by and even the religious leaders, spat insults at him, making a great game of it.

B 'You said you were going to tear down the Temple and then rebuild it in three days.'

C 'Well, come on then – show us your stuff!'

B 'If you really are God's Son, why don't you jump down from that cross!'

C 'He saved others, but he can't save himself!'

A They crucified two criminals at the same time as Jesus, one to his right, the other to his left. One of them even joined in the mockery.

C 'Some Messiah you are! Save yourself! Save us!'

A But the other man silenced him.

B 'What? Have you no fear of God? We deserve this. But not him – he did nothing to deserve this. Jesus, will you remember me when you enter your kingdom?'

C And Jesus spoke.

A 'Today, you'll join me in paradise.'

B At the foot of the cross stood three women, Jesus' mother, his aunt, and Mary Magdalene. Jesus saw his mother, and also John – the disciple he loved – standing at her side.

A 'Lady, here is your son. John, here is your mother.'

C At noon the sky grew black, and the darkness lasted three hours. Then Jesus groaned out of the depth of his being.

A 'My God, my God, why have you abandoned me?'

C Some of the bystanders who heard him said,

B 'Listen, he's calling for Elijah.'

C Someone ran off, soaked a sponge in sour wine, put it on a stick, and gave it to him to drink.

B 'Let's see if Elijah comes to take him down.'

C But with a loud cry, Jesus gave his last breath.

A 'Father, I give my spirit into your hands.'

B At that moment the Temple curtain was torn in two – ripped right down the middle from top to bottom.

C When the Roman captain standing guard in front of him saw that Jesus had stopped breathing, he said, 'See – this has to be the Son of God!'

2. Group presentations

Members of the congregation move around the church to encounter a series of presentations based on the Good Friday story.

You will need:

- Four or five small groups willing to prepare in advance. Try to have a combination of adults and children in each group. Assign one of the following episodes to each group and ask them to devise a ten-minute presentation that helps members of the congregation engage with the events.

  Jesus is arrested.

  Jesus on trial.

  Jesus is mocked and beaten by the soldiers.

  Jesus is crucified.

  Jesus is buried in the tomb.

- A place in the church where each group can give its presentation.

If your congregation is large, divide into smaller groups. Repeat the presentations and have the people move around in rotation – it is not necessary to visit them in chronological order. Signal when it is time to move on by playing a piece of music, or by three hammer blows struck against a nail in a piece of wood.

Ten ways of telling the story:

- Dramatized reading
- Learning the Bible passage and telling the story from memory
- Acting out the scene
- A narrator reads from the Bible while others portray the events through mime
- A series of pictures drawn on a flipchart
- Projected images
- Puppets
- Godly play
- A 'television' news bulletin
- Narration with percussion and dance.

Ten ideas for responding to the story:

- Prayers written or drawn on a graffiti wall.
- Prayers expressed through modelling clay or play dough.
- 'Sorry' prayers written on red paper are shredded or torn, and the fragments scattered around a cross.
- Look at a painting together in twos and threes, and talk about what you see.
- Share a personal story that has helped you connect with the events.
- A meditation that involves tasting things, e.g. salt water (tears), wine vinegar (offered to Jesus on the cross).
- Planting seeds – cf. John 12.24.
- Poetry – reading or writing.
- Strips of red fabric are knotted to represent prayers and nailed to a cross.
- An object to take away, e.g. a nail, or a fragment of torn cloth.

3. D-I-Y Stations of the Cross

The congregation is divided into groups. Using craft materials and objects, each group creates a station based on a part of the Passion story that has been assigned to them.

Decide in advance how many stations you will need for the size of your congregation. Groups could be as small as two or as large as seven people.

Suggested stations:

Jesus is anointed at Bethany	John 12.1-11
Jesus rides into Jerusalem	Matthew 21.1-9
Jesus clears the Temple	Mark 11.15-18
Jesus washes the disciples' feet	John 13.3-8
The Last Supper	Mark 14.22-24

Jesus prays in the garden of Gethsemane	Luke 22.39-46
Jesus is arrested	Luke: 22.47-54
Peter denies knowing Jesus	Luke 22.54-62
Jesus is condemned to death	Matthew 27.20-26
Jesus takes up his cross	Matthew 27.26-31
Simon helps Jesus to carry the cross	Luke 23.26; Mark 15.21
Jesus meets the women of Jerusalem	Luke 23.27-31
Jesus is stripped and nailed to the cross	John 19.23-24; Luke 23.32-34
Jesus is mocked by the crowd	Luke 23.35-43
Jesus speaks to his mother from the cross	John 19.25-27
Jesus dies on the cross	Luke 23.44-49
Jesus is taken down and laid in the tomb	John 19.38-42

You will need:

- For each group: a place in the church to create the station; an instruction sheet (see text below); an A4 card with the title of the station and the Bible text printed on it; an A4 card with the title of the station and space for a written prayer.
- An assortment of craft materials: e.g. paper, card, pencils, marker pens, poster paint, mixing trays and paint brushes, modelling clay, glue sticks, adhesive tape, stapler, scissors, string, garden wire, drawing pins, lengths of wood, gold and silver foil, scrap fabric.
- An assortment of props and artefacts: e.g. lengths of fabric in various colours (red, purple, black, white, green), green branches, rope, coins, bread, wine, cup, plate, jugs and basins, towel, swords and spears, crown of thorns, hammer and large nails, crosses, dice, staff, sponge.
- Background music.

Text for the instruction sheet:

A *station* is somewhere to stop and wait for a while. *Stations of the Cross* are places where we can stop and think about Jesus' most important journey.

Work together to make a station in your corner of the church based on your part of the story.

You could create a sculpture or a picture using the craft materials.

You could gather objects from around the church.

You could find a way to include words from the Bible.

You could even include people in the scene.

Work together as quietly as you can.

Your station should be a place where people can pray about all that Jesus did, so write a prayer to help them. Place it next to your station.

Have your station ready by (*give a time*). Then we'll take 15 minutes to visit one another's stations. At the end we'll come back together for a final song and a prayer.

The activity can be incorporated into a service lasting one hour:

Opening song and explanation: 10 minutes;
Creating the stations in groups: 30 minutes;
Visiting the stations: 15 minutes;
Final song and blessing: 5 minutes.

Conclusion

May the Father,
who so loved the world that he gave his only Son,
bring you by faith to his eternal life.
Amen.

May Christ,
who accepted the cup of sacrifice
in obedience to the Father's will,
keep you steadfast as you walk with him the way of
    his cross.
Amen.

May the Spirit,
who strengthens us to suffer with Christ
that we may share his glory,
set your minds on life and peace.
Amen.

And the blessing …

[T&S 267]

If the congregation is large, let everyone visit the stations in their own time. It is not necessary to stop at every one, or even to visit them in the right order. Encourage the adults to help the children interpret what they see. A smaller congregation could move around the church together, with members of each group leading the prayers at their station.

4. D-I-Y Stations of the Cross – alternative approach

Instead of creating the stations within the service, they could be prepared in advance and brought to church. Invite families or church groups to take part and assign each one a different station. Alternatively, you could extend the invitation to include community groups such as local schools, members of an art club or photographic society, and so on.

5. Good Friday banners

Members of the congregation write or draw prayers on jagged paper shapes. These are then stuck on to a banner in the shape of a cross.

You will need:
- A banner made from a roll of black paper. Draw the outline of a cross in red pencil crayon. Leave space, top and bottom, to fold the paper over and construct a tunnel through which you can push a pair of dowel rods. Make the top dowel slightly longer than the width of the paper and tie a length of string to the two protruding ends. If your congregation is large, you might need to make more than one banner.
- Triangular shapes cut from red paper, at least one for every member of the congregation.
- Pens.
- Glue sticks.

Distribute the triangular paper shapes and the pens. Encourage everyone to write or draw a picture to represent their prayers. Remind the adults that they may need to help the younger children decide what to pray.

Invite everyone to glue their prayers onto the banner, keeping the shapes within the outline. It does not matter if some of the prayers overlap a little. Work with the banner spread out flat on the floor or on a large table. When all the shapes are stuck down, hang the banner where everyone can see it.

You could conclude by leading the congregation in spoken prayers of intercession that incorporate some of the ideas that have been expressed.

6. The sins of the world

This is suitable either as a focus for intercessions or for prayers of penitence.

Members of the congregation look through the newspapers for headlines and photographs that highlight the sin of the world. These are torn out and nailed to the cross.

You will need:
- A large wooden cross.
- Two or three hammers; nails – carpet tacks are best as they have a large, flat head.
- Recent newspapers, local and national.

Distribute the newspapers. Ask everyone to look for a headline or photograph that shows something of the effects of sin in the world. Remind the adults to help younger children choose an appropriate piece.

When everyone has found a good example, they should tear it out and pause to think:

Who is hurting here?

How does that make you feel?

How do you think it makes God feel?

Again, encourage the adults to help the children reflect on these questions. Allow three or four minutes for this.

Invite several people to tell the rest of the congregation about their choice. After seeing the headline or photograph, what do they want to say to God? Turn these thoughts into prayers. Thank God for sending Jesus to overcome the power of sin and death.

Finally, direct everyone to come forward and fix their fragment of newspaper to the cross by hammering a nail through it. Young children can participate if the adults start the nail off – but take care. When all the pieces are in place, stand the cross upright.

7. Hearts of stone

Suitable to use with the prayers of penitence. The congregation uses stones to make the shape of a cross. The people may also be sprinkled with water as a reminder of the promise in Ezekiel 36.25,26.

You will need:
- A large stone for each person – granite cobbles, available from a garden centre, are perfect for this activity.
- Water in the font if you are planning to include the sprinkling, and one or two ministers, and perhaps older children, to help with this.

Give everyone a stone. Introduce the Prayers of Penitence and ask all present to hold the stone in their hands as they recall their sins. After a period of silence – one minute is a long time for younger children – lead the congregation in this Kyrie confession from the Passiontide resources to be found in *Times and Seasons*.

Lord Jesus Christ,
we confess we have failed you as did your first
*   disciples.*
We ask for your mercy and your help.

When we take our ease
rather than watch with you:
Lord, forgive us.
Christ have mercy.

When we bestow a kiss of peace
yet nurse enmity in our hearts:
Lord, forgive us.
Christ have mercy.

When we strike at those who hurt us
rather than stretch out our hands to bless:
Lord, forgive us.
Christ have mercy.

When we deny that we know you
for fear of the world and its scorn:
Lord, forgive us.
Christ have mercy.

[T&S 261]

Absolution

Read Ezekiel 36.26 then ask all present to come forward and place their stone on the ground, working together to make the shape of a cross. As they do so, you could have an appropriate hymn played or sung by a soloist.

When people have returned to their seats, finish with an Absolution.

If you are including the sprinkling, read Ezekiel 36.25-26 before directing the congregation to come forward. After people have added their stone to the cross, they move to the font where the ministers simply dip their fingers into the water and flick a few drops over them. If the location of the font makes movement difficult, fill a basin with water from the font and carry it to a more convenient part of the church.

8. The hands of sinners

Suitable to use with the Prayers of Penitence. Members of the congregation make handprints on the cross as a reminder of our part in Jesus' death. This might work particularly well with Version 2 of Anthem 1 (see below), which is provided in the Good Friday Liturgy in *Times and Seasons*. It would work equally well with a Kyrie confession such as the one suggested above in the Hearts of Stone act of worship.

You will need:
- A large free-standing cross, preferably full size. Give it a coat of black or dark brown emulsion paint. Alternatively, cover the cross completely in dark paper.
- One or more trays of red poster paint, depending on the size of your congregation.
- Several washing-up bowls or buckets filled with water, soap and towels.

Invite everyone to come forward as the anthem is read and take it in turns to press one hand into the red paint, then to grasp the cross and leave a handprint behind. Encourage everyone to gather around the cross rather than returning to their seats. When the anthem is concluded, take a few moments in silence to reflect on the cross and the paint on your hands.

Version 2

VOICE 1

My people, what wrong have I done to you?
What good have I not done for you?
Listen to me.

VOICE 2

I am your Creator, Lord of the universe;
I have entrusted this world to you,
but you have created the means to destroy it.

VOICE 1

My people, what wrong have I done to you?
What good have I not done for you?
Listen to me.

VOICE 2

I made you in my image,
but you have degraded body and spirit
and marred the image of your God.
You have deserted me and turned your backs on me.

VOICE 1

My people, what wrong have I done to you?
What good have I not done for you?
Listen to me.

VOICE 2

I filled the earth with all that you need,
so that you might serve and care for one another,
as I have cared for you;
but you have cared only to serve your own wealth
*   and power.*

ALL

Holy God,
holy and strong,
holy and immortal,
have mercy upon us.

VOICE 1

My people, what wrong have I done to you?
What good have I not done for you?
Listen to me.

VOICE 2

I made my children of one blood
to live in families rejoicing in one another;
but you have embittered the races
*   and divided the nations.*

VOICE 1

My people, what wrong have I done to you?
What good have I not done for you?
Listen to me.

VOICE 2

I commanded you to love your neighbour as
*   yourself,*
to love and forgive even your enemies;
but you have made vengeance your rule and hate
*   your guide.*

VOICE 1

My people, what wrong have I done to you?
What good have I not done for you?
Listen to me.

VOICE 2

In the fullness of time I sent you my Son,
that in him you might know me,
and through him find life and peace;
but you put him to death on the cross.

ALL

Holy God,
holy and strong,
holy and immortal,
have mercy upon us.

VOICE 1

My people, what wrong have I done to you?
What good have I not done for you?
Listen to me.

VOICE 2

Through the living Christ, I called you into my
*   Church*
to be my servants to the world,
but you have grasped at privilege and forgotten my
*   will.*

VOICE 1

My people, what wrong have I done to you?
What good have I not done for you?
Listen to me.

VOICE 2

I have given you a heavenly gift and a share in the
*   Holy Spirit;*
I have given you the spiritual energies of the age to
*   come;*
but you have turned away
and crucified the Son of God afresh.

VOICE 1

My people, what wrong have I done to you?
What good have I not done for you?
Listen to me.

VOICE 2

I have consecrated you in the truth;
I have made you to be one
*   in the unity of the Father and the Son,*
*   by the power of the Spirit;*
but you have divided my Church and shrouded my
*   truth.*

ALL

Holy God,
holy and strong,
holy and immortal,
have mercy upon us.

[T&S 312–13]

Now direct people to wash their hands before
returning to their seats. It is better not to have
background music during this part of the prayers
– keep silent and listen to the splashing of the water.

Holy Week:
The Lenten tree pathway

A note about all the pathways in Holy Week

Holy Week is perhaps the most intense week of the year for Christians. This is the time when all our Lenten preparations come together and we walk the way of the cross with our Saviour. The material supplied for the pathways in Holy Week does not conform to the exact pattern used throughout Lent and which resumes during the Easter Season. Rather it provides for the nature of church life during Holy Week that tends to focus on worship together, especially on Good Friday, rather than meetings for study.

Within the Lenten tree pathway, however, we have provided for a session to explore the story of Palm Sunday.

The Lenten tree in groups

Adults

After Palm Sunday Symbol: Palms

Scripture passage: John 12.12-16 (Jesus' triumphal entry into Jerusalem)

Read out the passage, but try to make sure people can see it either in their own Bibles or on a specially printed sheet.

Allow a short silence for reflection on the reading

Comment

Allow anyone who wishes to offer a question that emerges from the reading to which they would like an answer. If possible, write them down and then use them in turn as discussion starters.

Symbol and reflection

A member of the group places a palm cross in the middle of the three candles.

Each member of the group is invited to reflect on what that palm cross means to them. Each person

could ask questions such as:

- The crowd on Palm Sunday has often been accused of being fickle: crying 'Hosanna' one day and 'Crucify' a few days later. Would I have been any less fickle?
- The ash used on Ash Wednesday is traditionally made from the previous year's palm crosses. How does that physical link across Lent help me appreciate the whole 'story'?
- A king riding on a donkey – what does that unusual combination say to us about Jesus?

Those who feel able are invited to share their thoughts with the rest of the group. Be aware that this may stir up some very personal thoughts that people may not want to share, so this part of the exercise should not be forced.

Silence is kept for further reflection.

Comment on palm leaves and crosses

The palm cross is a reminder of the day when Jesus rode into Jerusalem on a donkey and the crowds threw down their clothes – an Oriental custom still observed on occasions – as well as palm fronds, the symbol of triumph.

Jesus' entry into Jerusalem was significant for a number of reasons:

a) it was the fulfilment of a prophecy in Zechariah, who had foretold the arrival of the Messianic king in Jerusalem riding on a colt. The crowd hailed Jesus as 'the son of David', a loaded name used at a loaded time. The priestly establishment was understandably disturbed, as the palm was the national emblem of an independent Palestine. Waving palm branches was rather like waving Jewish flags.

b) it was also a kind of showdown with the authorities. Opposition to Jesus had been building, attempts on his life had been made, his popularity had grown alarmingly. Such was the situation some even wondered whether he would appear in Jerusalem at all – but he did, with flag-waving (palm-waving!) crowds.

c) there was another underlying significance, less obvious but crucial in God's salvation plan. It was Passover time and Jerusalem was bulging with visitors for the festival, at the heart of which was the symbolic killing of the Passover lamb. Into the festivities came a king riding on a donkey, a king who was in fact God's Passover Lamb.

In celebrating Palm Sunday, some churches like to have real palm branches in an attempt to recapture the ambience of the first Palm Sunday. But maybe the symbol of the cross made from palm is a way of combining all the strands of the Palm Sunday story – a king riding to his death. 'Ride on, ride on in majesty, in lowly pomp ride on to die.'[3]

Discussion

Ask: Out of this multi-stranded significant event, surprising word associations come into focus, for example, servant-king, dying-messiah … What do these (and possibly other) phrases mean to you?

We return to the Office of Prayer …

Response

A song may be sung or a quiet piece of music played.

Blessed are the merciful
for they will receive mercy.

Matthew 5.7

[DP 69]

Prayer

All present pick up a palm cross and as they do so are invited to reflect on the ways people give glory to God.

The leader then invites everyone to reflect on the ways they fail to honour Christ.

Music is played and everyone is invited to lay the palm cross back on the table.

When the music stops a short silence is kept.

All say this prayer
Teach us, good Lord, to serve you as you deserve;
to give and not to count the cost;
to fight and not to heed the wounds;
to toil and not to seek for rest;
to labour and not to seek for any reward,
save that of knowing that we do your will.

After Ignatius of Loyola (1556)

The Lord's Prayer is said.

The Conclusion

May God bless us and show us compassion and mercy.

Amen.

[DP 70]

All the pathways in outreach

There are likely to be visitors around at this time of the year and although the services need to observe the integrity that belongs to the liturgies, it is worth considering what opportunities there are to give attention to those who do not normally attend church. Symbolic engagement can be helpful here.

Maundy Thursday: Footwashing

In Holy Week, the footwashing is not only an important reminder of the nature of the king we serve but also of the kind of service we are meant to demonstrate in our love for one another in the body of Christ and also in our wider communities. It is therefore a ritual action that reminds the Church of her mission in the world to wash the feet of those who come to our doors. If you are brave enough to organize this outdoors in a public space, it will create a strong reaction. Invite people to join in. Provide towels for each person. It will be very moving for those who do join in. Provide a written explanation for all passers-by.

Good Friday

The Good Friday observances are often thought of as having their focus within the church community. However, you might want to consider ways of opening the church for prayer and quiet space during the day, especially after the three hours at the cross. Opportunities for the veneration of the cross are important as is the opportunity for prayer around the cross. A large floor cross could be placed in the church and candles provided so that people who wish to offer prayers can do so by placing a lit candle on the cross. Some churches organize an ecumenical procession of witness through the community, culminating in an act of worship.

You could also take your Stations of the Cross outside, especially if they have been produced by people from the congregation, adults or children. Find a place to display them where they will be seen by the whole neighbourhood.

Holy Saturday

This part of the journey is often overlooked, falling as it does between the events of Good Friday and the Easter Vigil. What is the distinctive mood and what are the key images that might help us? It is a day of absence and this absence is important. The stone is rolled across the tomb and there is a sense of emptiness and stillness. We have been left – abandoned it seems. Although we may know how the story ends, this part of it should not be skated over, so that we remember again the riskiness of exercising faith in the very place where all seems lost. Perhaps this day then is about those left behind, about those who are called to keep the faith in the darkest places. It might then be appropriate to provide opportunities for prayer for those whose faith is tested to its limits by circumstances. Prayer for those places where Christ seems most absent might also be important.

There is a fifteenth-century icon called *The Harrowing of Hell*, which has a black background and the figure of Christ in white in the centre. The icon demonstrates the dynamism of the work of Christ as he grasps Adam and Eve by the wrists and drags them up and out of their imprisonment in the dark. There is a reminder here that bringing resurrection life to others involves work and not just nice feelings. It is interesting to ask what the reactions of the figures being dragged out of hell might have been. All is quiet and then suddenly resurrection disturbs the peace! Many of us dislike change and perhaps this icon tells us (rather challengingly) how close the line is between our sense of security and comfort and a place of stultification or death. This icon could be an important focus for devotion in the home or in church on this day. Where do we need to wake up and start moving?

There is also a striking painting of the dead Christ, *The Body of the Dead Christ in the Tomb*, by Hans Holbein, which can help us during this season. The picture is shocking in its intimate portrayal of a dead body, including wounds and decaying flesh. It is important to ponder the reality of Christ's death if the resurrection is to take on its fullest meaning and this stark image emphasizes the power of God over death.

Literature can also be a helpful way in. In *The Amber Spyglass*, the third part of the trilogy *His Dark Materials*, Philip Pullman writes of Lyra and Will's journey to the world of the dead and the freeing of the souls. Pullman creates his own powerful vision of the world of the dead with echoes of Christian symbolism and classical mythology.[4] The death of Aslan and the period of time between Aslan's death and resurrection is well captured by C. S. Lewis in *The Lion the Witch and the Wardrobe*.[5] 'Funeral Blues', a poem by W. H. Auden,[6] captures the sense of finality and loss that death brings … and there are many other examples.

Holy Week:
The Head, hands and heart pathway

Practical inclusive ideas

A liturgy around the cross

Introduction

This liturgy is centred on the cross and includes meditations that focus the attention of the participants on the head of Christ; the hands of Christ; the feet of Christ and the wounded side of Christ. It could be used with an adult group that has been following the Head, hands and heart pathway in Lent, as a culmination of their journey together reflecting on these themes. The liturgy could be a way of marking the movement into Passiontide or alternatively could be used as part of the observances during Holy Week. You may need to adapt the opening words according to the time you use it.

Preparation

MAKE THE OUTLINE OF A CROSS ON THE GROUND

If the liturgy is used in a church, you might be able to make use of the building's cruciform shape.

Tape the outline of a cross on the floor using masking tape or similar. Light the lines of the cross at ground level, using small torches or candles and suspend a crown of thorns centrally over the cross, lit from above with spotlights if possible.

THE TWO LEADERS

There are two leaders who have different roles. Leader 1 presides over the liturgy and leads the participants through the meditations. Leader 2 has an important role to play in instructing the participants where to move and in leading the group into the meditative material through scriptural readings.

MUSIC

The soundtrack of *The Last Temptation of Christ* (suggested because of its rhythms and atmosphere rather than to make a theological statement) might be played as the group gathers.

You will need to be able to sing the Taizé chant 'Adoramus te Domine'. This is available in many books that publish music from Taizé, including *Music from Taizé, Volume 1*, where it can be found on page 44 of the Vocal Edition (Collins, London 1982).

THE MEDITATIONS, TO BE USED AT POINTS THROUGHOUT THE LITURGY

1. HEAD

We call to mind the cruel crown of thorns pressed into the brow of Christ;
The cruel words that twist spikes into the mind …
'Hail, King – if you are a King!'
If … if … if …
If only …
Insidious voices, more barbed than any thorn,
And each doubt, like a blow across the face,
leaves an ugly weal.
'Let this crown pass from me,
yet not my will, but yours!'
Christ surrounded; Christ hemmed in on every side.
The thorny thicket and the sacrificial lamb …
Good seed amongst the choking thorns,
thorns that crowd in and press out life.
As the lily among the thorns,
so is my love.
The King of Glory crowned for a while with pain –
a twisted diadem made by mocking hands.

And they plaited a crown of thorns …

Yet a while, and we shall see Jesus, crowned with glory and honour.

There are many kinds of crown –
crown of pain, crown of glory –
which one will you take hold of?

2. RIGHT HAND

We call to mind the reed in the hand of Christ.
A palm branch subverted perhaps?
Creation misused to mock its creator!

That it should come to this!
The king acclaimed a few days ago
now greeted with hoots of derision,
set round with brutal boot, with scorn and unbowed
    heads –
rejected for after all he is a most unkingly king.
The hand that held the sceptre, commanding heaven
    and earth,
is now the object of our mockery and scorn.

Yet a while, and all creation will be subject to his
    just and gentle rule.

There are many kinds of king.
Which one will you enthrone?

3. Left hand

We call to mind Christ's hand of blessing
extended to young and old, men and women.
The hand that touched, caressed, healed,
brought sight to the blind,
sent demons fleeing.
The hand extended over water, bread, wine,
with power over wind and weather,
with food to nourish all who came;
this hand that spangled heaven with stars
and this hand now is bound and stilled –
fastened to the earth,
to the wood of the cross.

Yet a while and this hand will reach out
to offer salvation to the world.

There is suffering and blessing in this hand.
Will you take hold of it and receive all that it offers?

4. Feet

We call to mind the feet of Christ:
the feet that walked alongside children, women and
    men.
Tired feet; dancing feet; running feet –
running to the tomb of Lazarus –
the feet that walked the way of the cross, bitter and
    slow.
And the people who came to see the crucifixion,
did they run eagerly or creep fearfully to the foot of
    the cross?
And the women, gathered again at the feet of the
    Lord,
this time weeping and heavy with sorrow;
powerless to touch the feet that now are bloody and
    torn.

Yet a while and we shall kneel again at the feet of
    Christ.
There are many of us now, kneeling in our hearts
    around these wounded feet.

Gift or burden –
what is it that you wish to lay there?

5. Side

We call to mind Christ's riven side –
blood and water
ebbing into the dust.
Here is the forgiving blood;
the baptismal water;
the cleansing and lifegiving stream.
Life and death; death and life –
the water and the wine,
our cup of salvation.
Yet a while and we shall see Christ
by whose wounds we are made whole.
Our wounds, the wounds of our church and our
    world are many.
Touching the wounds of Christ,
we seek to be washed in the water of life,
to be healed by the blood of the lamb that was slain
and to be sent out to minister life and healing
through our own brokenness and wholeness.

Meditations copyright © Diane J. Craven 2005

 The liturgy

THE GATHERING

Leader: *As we prepare for our worship, please
           come, find a space and stand around the
           edge of the cross.*

Bring the music to a sudden end and keep silence.

GREETING

Leader 1: *By his wounds we are healed.
          The Lord be with you*
          and also with you.

THE JOURNEY

Leader 1: *In the coming days the Church will recall
          again the story of our Lord's entry into
          Jerusalem, his passion and death and his
          glorious resurrection. In former times, those
          unable to make the journey to Jerusalem*

recalled his story in meditations as they walked a labyrinth. We gather now around the cross and we will recall the Passion of the Lord as we walk around this cross. We will stop five times to recall the sacrifice of Christ, thinking on the wounds Christ suffered for our sake.

Leader 2: *Please turn to your left as we slowly pace around the cross, singing the chant Adoramus te Domine – We adore you Lord.*

Hum *Adoramus te Domine*

As this is sung for the third time:

Leader 1: (Over the top of the chant)
We adore you, O Christ, and we bless you, because by your holy cross you have redeemed the world.

[T&S 314]

Leader 2: *Turn to face the cross. Place your hands on your head. With your fingers feel your head and face.*

Then Pilate took Jesus and had him flogged. And the soldiers wove a crown of thorns and put it on his head and they dressed him in a purple robe. They kept coming up to him, saying, 'Hail King of the Jews!' and striking him on the face.

LEADER 1: MEDITATION 1 – HEAD

Hum *'Adoramus te Domine'*

As this is sung for the third time:

Leader 1: (Over the top of the chant)
We adore you, O Christ, and we bless you because by your holy cross you have redeemed the world.

Leader 2: *Take your right hand, hold it, look at it, close your fingers together.*

They stripped him and put a scarlet robe on him, and after twisting some thorns into a crown.
They put it on his head. They put a reed into his right hand and knelt before him and mocked him, saying,
'Hail, King of the Jews!'
They spat on him, and took the reed and struck him on the head.

After mocking him, they stripped him of the robe
and put his own clothes on him,
then they led him away to crucify him.

LEADER 1: MEDITATION 2 – RIGHT HAND

Hum *'Adoramus te Domine'*

As this is sung for the third time:

Leader 1: (Over the top of the chant)
We adore you, O Christ, and we bless you because by your holy cross you have redeemed the world.

Leader 2: *Take your left hand. Hold it, feel your palm and your wrist.*

They brought Jesus to a place called Golgotha (which means place of a skull), they offered him drugged wine but he refused to take it. Then they fastened him to the cross. They shared out his clothes, casting lots to decide what each should have. It was nine o'clock in the morning when they crucified him.

LEADER 1: MEDITATION 3 – LEFT HAND

Hum *'Adoramus te Domine'*

As this is sung for the third time:

Leader 1: (Over the top of the chant)
We adore you, O Christ, and we bless you because by your holy cross you have redeemed the world.

Leader 2: *Look down at your feet. Feel the ground and the weight of your body going down into your feet.*

Meanwhile, standing near the cross of Jesus were his mother, and his mother's sister, Mary the wife of Cleopas, and Mary Magdalene. When Jesus saw his mother and the disciple whom he loved standing beside her, he said to his mother,
'Woman here is your son.'
Then he said to his disciple. 'Here is your mother.'
And from that hour the disciple took her into his own home.

LEADER 1: MEDITATION 4 – FEET

Hum *'Adoramus te Domine'*

As this is sung for the third time:

Leader 1: (Over the top of the chant)
*We adore you, O Christ, and we bless
you because by your holy cross you have
redeemed the world.*

Leader 2: *Place your hands on your right side, hold
them there and feel the movement of your
breath.*

*They asked Pilate to have the legs of the
crucified men broken and the bodies
removed. Then the soldiers came and
broke the legs of the first and of the other
who had been crucified with him. But
when they came to Jesus and saw that he
was already dead, they did not break his
legs. Instead, one of the soldiers pierced his
side with a spear, and at once blood and
water came out.*

LEADER 1: MEDITATION 5 – SIDE

Hum *'Adoramus te Domine'*

As this is sung for the third time:

Leader 1: (Over the top of the chant)
*We adore you, O Christ, and we bless
you because by your holy cross you have
redeemed the world.*

Leader 2: *Please step forward onto the cross.*

Leader 1: *Christ's body bore our sins on the tree.
We are the body of Christ.
We stand now on the cross.*

*Grant, Lord,
that we who have been baptized into the
death of your Son, our Saviour Jesus
Christ,
may continually put to death our evil
desires and be buried with him,
that through the grave and gate of death
we may pass to our joyful resurrection;
through his merits,
who died and was buried and rose again
for us,
your Son Jesus Christ our Lord.*
Amen.

[CW 399]

THE LORD'S PRAYER

Our Father in heaven …

THE CONCLUSION

Leader 1: *Christ is our peace.
He has reconciled us to God
in one body by the cross.
We meet in his name and share his peace.*

The peace of the Lord be always with you.
And also with you.

[CW 290]

*As we go,
let us offer one another a sign of peace,
God's seal on our prayers.*

Holy Week:
The Stations pathway

Practical inclusive ideas

A Good Friday Stations activity and service

This is an activity session and service all in one, based on the stations theme, which is designed for use on Good Friday or another day in Holy Week. Though primarily for children, adults will not be out of place if they join in and it would be good to encourage families to take part together.

You will need to create six stations around the church. It would be good to have the first in front of the holy table if possible. The last should be in a place that can represent Jesus' tomb.

Key personnel are:
- Storyteller to tell the story at each station. This could be one person or six, depending on the resources you have available.
- A worship leader, who holds the service together.
- A cook, who will provide hot cross bun dough ready risen, and take away raw hot cross buns to bake after they have been made at the beginning of the service, and bring them back cooked at the end. This person should also be asked to provide butter, knives, plates, etc.
- People to provide what it needed for each station and to set up the activities there beforehand. This could be six people or one or anything in between.
- Someone who is able to lead singing, if the worship leader is not able to do this.

What you will need at each station

STATION 1: THE LAST SUPPER

For the station: communion vessels: a chalice and paten, with a corporal to stand them on.

For the activity: Pre-risen hot cross bun dough divided into bun-sized lumps; knives for cutting crosses in the top; greased baking sheets; bowls with water for handwashing. Paper and pens to name the buns. A nearby oven, otherwise a car. At the end of

the service you will also need butter, knives, plates and other refreshments.

STATION 2: THE GARDEN OF GETHSEMANE

For the station: You may like to place this station where the Easter garden is to be made.

A few rocks, buckets containing greenery and flowers.

For the activity: Small saucers each with a block of damp florists' foam taped into it. The flowers and greenery from the station. A few pairs of scissors.

STATION 3: THE TRIAL OF JESUS

For the station: A picture or model of a cockerel, a whip, a purple robe (piece of cloth) and a crown of thorns.

For the activity: Flexible sticky twigs gathered from gardens and parks. Soft florists' wire. Scissors. You may find a florist's shop has suitable sticks or material if you don't want to look for your own,

STATION 4: JESUS TAKES UP HIS CROSS

For the station: a cross large enough to need a team of children to carry it, and some nails and a hammer.

For the activity: You will need to remember to choose people who can carry the big cross and the hammer and the nails.

STATION 5A: JESUS IS CRUCIFIED

For the station: Set up the cross that you have carried so that it stands safely against a wall.

For the activity: Make crosses. If you have appropriate pieces of wood, plenty of adult help and an appropriate space in which to work, you would do this by nailing together pieces of wood. Otherwise they can be made by tying wood together. Let each person make a cross. Then when everyone has finished, tidy away the materials and gather at the foot of the cross.

STATION 5B: JESUS DIES ON THE CROSS

For the station: An appropriate place at which to stand the cross up safely. The means to make it stand safely if necessary. Try this all out beforehand. A large white sheet to remind you of the body of Jesus upon the cross. You may also like to have a sign saying 'The King of the Jews' to attach to the cross. You may want to have it written in Hebrew, Latin and Greek if this is appropriate.

For the activity: Wood for making the individual crosses (90 cm lengths cut into 60 cm and 30 cm lengths), with two small nails for fixing. An assortment of hammers and places to hammer. If you do not wish to use hammers and nails, you will need string and scissors to tie the wood together.

STATION 6: JESUS IS BURIED

For the station: The sheet carried from the last station

The service and activity

If you can possibly gather in front of the holy table, this would be ideal because the event starts by recalling the Last Supper.

In the name of the Father,
and of the Son,
and of the Holy Spirit.
Amen.

Peace to you, and peace to the people of (name of community).

Jesus told his disciples, 'If any want to become my followers, let them deny themselves and take up their cross and follow me. For those who want to save their life will lose it, and those who lose their life for my sake will find it.'

Matthew 16.24,25

On this sad day we are going to try to do what Jesus said. We shall make a little journey round the church. We shall each make a cross to carry with us to remind us of Jesus' words and we shall be able to take them home, to remind us of this journey as we travel through the year.

First we need to learn some words and a song that we shall use on the journey:

RESPONSE

We adore you, O Christ, and we bless you
because by your holy cross you have redeemed the world.

[T&S 239]

SONG

'Jesus remember me, when you come into your kingdom' (see Resources, p. 241).

STATION 1: THE LAST SUPPER

Have the communion vessels on the holy table and tell the story of the Last Supper briefly, using the vessels. At the end of the telling conclude with the response:

We adore you, O Christ, and we bless you
because by your holy cross you have redeemed the world.

Jesus shared bread with friends on that night. On Good Friday we have special bread to eat that helps to remind us of this whole story.

Hot cross buns are good reminders because the bread reminds us of Jesus' body, broken for us; the cross on top reminds us of the cross on which he was crucified and the spices that we put in remind us that, after Jesus died, his friends put spices on his body before they buried it.

There is time now for each of us to make a hot cross bun to bake and have at the end of the service.

Give out dough and let each person make a bun and mark it with a cross, using a knife. Put each bun on a baking tray and put a scrap of paper under it with the maker's name on.

When all the hot cross buns have been made and people have washed their hands, finish your time at this station by singing 'Jesus, remember me, when you come into your kingdom'.

STATION 2: THE GARDEN OF GETHSEMANE

You may like to place this station where the Easter garden is to be made.

Mark the station by placing greenery and flowers there in buckets, together with small saucers containing damp oasis.

Tell the story of the arrest of Jesus in the garden of Gethsemane. At the end of the telling, conclude with the response:

We adore you, O Christ, and we bless you
because by your holy cross you have redeemed the world.

Invite people now to make their own little 'garden' by using the greenery and flowers in the buckets to make small flower arrangements that can be put into the garden that will be made ready to mark Easter day.

When all the gardens have been made, finish your time at this station by singing 'Jesus, remember me, when you come into your kingdom', then move on to:

STATION 3: THE TRIAL OF JESUS

Make the station using reminders of incidents during Jesus' trial: a cockerel to remind us of Peter's denial, a whip to remind us of the cruel way in which Jesus was treated, and a purple robe and a crown of thorns.

Tell the story of Jesus' trial. At the end of the telling conclude with the response:

We adore you, O Christ, and we bless you
because by your holy cross you have redeemed the world.

An appropriate activity at this station would be to make crowns of thorns. Don't use really dangerous thorny twigs. A collection of bendy sticks that have blown off the trees over the winter will do fine. Bind them together with soft, florists' wire.

When the crowns of thorns are finished, conclude your time at this station by singing 'Jesus, remember me, when you come into your kingdom' then move on to:

STATION 4: JESUS TAKES UP HIS CROSS

For this station you will need a large cross, and some nails and a hammer.

Tell the story of Jesus taking up his cross and walking through the streets to the place where he was to be crucified. At the end of the telling conclude with the response:

We adore you, O Christ, and we bless you
because by your holy cross you have redeemed the world.

The activity for this station is to take up the cross and, with the hammer and nails, carry it to the next station. If the cross is really large, you will need a number of people to carry it. Once it has been picked up and the procession is arranged sing 'Jesus, remember me, when you come into your kingdom' then move on to:

STATION 5A: JESUS IS CRUCIFIED

Set up the cross that you have carried so that it stands safely against a wall.

Tell how Jesus was nailed to the cross. You could put a large piece of fabric (for example a white sheet) onto the cross to remind us of the body of Jesus.

For the activity here, make crosses as described above.

STATION 5B: JESUS DIES ON THE CROSS

Tell how Jesus died on the cross. Take down the large sheet and use two people to carry it carefully rolled up to:

STATION 6: JESUS IS BURIED

If you have a large memorial tomb in your church, you might use this as the burial place, or you could use the space under the holy table. Walk in silence to the burial place. Gently lay the sheet into the place. Ask everyone to kneel down, then say

We adore you, O Christ, and we bless you
because by your holy cross you have redeemed the world.

After this sing 'Jesus remember me when you come into your kingdom'.

Ask someone to read this Good Friday Collect:

Eternal God,
in the cross of Jesus
we see the cost of our sin
and the depth of your love:
in humble hope and fear
may we place at his feet
all that we have and all that we are,
through Jesus Christ our Lord.
Amen.

[T&S 307]

Say the Lord's Prayer together.

You may like to sing a song here. 'Were you there when the crucified my Lord?', or 'There is a green hill far away', would be appropriate, but any other appropriate song would be suitable.

THE BLESSING

May Jesus of the upper room,
Jesus of the cross,
Jesus of the tomb,
Jesus the giver of new life,
bless you and keep you always.
Amen.

Move away from the burial place now. If you have a refreshment area in the church, go there. If not, choose a suitable place to gather to eat. The hot cross buns that were made at the beginning of the service should now be baked, so people can help themselves to their bun, butter it and eat it. It might be good to supply drinks also.

EASTER

Seasonal introduction

Holy Saturday and Easter Eve

This is the night ...

Holy Saturday is much neglected rather as if we don't quite know what to do with a day in which, apparently, nothing happens. It is one of life's waiting places, and important because of that. Perhaps this day points up for us just how much waiting has gone on in this whole journey. Jesus waiting for his time to come; the Pharisees looking for the chance to catch Jesus out; the authorities waiting for the ripe time to arrest Jesus; Judas waiting to betray him; the disciples waiting in the garden; the waiting at the foot of the cross; the waiting by the tomb ... Michael Perham writes:

We must not be afraid of the long unspectacular waiting of which much of life is made up, nor must we be too urgent for the coming of every Easter in our lives, lest we fail to learn from the silence before the first alleluia breaks forth. Think of Jesus, in the place of the departed, waiting for his salvation to come. Let the waiting teach us through its long silences the infinite patience of God.[1]

Easter Eve gives us another kind of space in which to explore our responses to the death of Christ. In this still waiting place, it is as if our life flashes in front of our eyes. In the ancient ritual of Easter Eve, the gathered people hear again the story 'Of man's first disobedience and the fruit of that forbidden tree ... '[2]; the story of the results of sin; the story of God's relationship with his people; the story of being brought through the waters; and the story of the cost of bringing the people of God home. In the darkness a single pinpoint of light pierces the gloom. The paschal candle, fragile and yet undimmed, reminds us of the darkness both within and without – a darkness that has overshadowed the events we have witnessed in the preceding week. It reminds us of the fragility of our faithfulness to our baptismal calling and the steadfastness of God's light and love. The Exsultet itself has a similar sense of both fragility and power – a single voice in the darkness but a voice that holds the story in a song that reaches into the

darkest corners of the building. These words are for now and for what is not yet: This is the night – the night when new life begins to stir. Can these bones live? Maybe, just maybe, it is possible ... it is perhaps the water imagery of the readings in this liturgy – the waters of creation, the flood and the Passover – and the gathering of the assembled company around the font, that remind us most powerfully that we ourselves have been brought through the waters. Now we are called again to live as the community of the baptized – those who have looked on death and lived.

Easter

Dawn surely comes after the long night and we celebrate the day of resurrection with ... the chocfest that is the commercial side of an ancient festival. The shelves of any supermarket are positively groaning under the weight of beribboned chocolate eggs. Why eggs? Some of our Easter customs have their roots in pagan festivities to mark the return of Spring. Eostre – from which we derive the word Easter – was the Norse goddess of spring and rebirth. Much of the symbolism associated with pagan practices at the spring solstice had to do with fertility and the natural cycles of death and rebirth. When Christians celebrate, the egg can be attributed with a variety of symbolic overtones: it is a symbol of new life; it is fragile and yet strong; it is the place where human life begins; some people have suggested that it resembles the stone at the entrance to the tomb. Coincidentally, paralleling Jesus' words in John 12 about the seed that dies to produce a hundred-fold is a pagan symbolic story of a corn king who dies and is reborn.

In the Church, the life from death imagery inspires the tradition of the Easter garden and liturgies around the Easter garden are an important way of enabling people to work with these potent ideas. Some churches have a wooden cross as a focal point in their Good Friday observances that is then decorated with flowers brought by members of the congregation on Easter Day. If the journey through Lent and

Holy Week and the waiting of Holy Saturday have been painstakingly travelled then Easter Day takes its meaning from them. The joy of resurrection is possible only because Christ endured death and conquered it.

The colours of the season are interesting in this regard: white is both a colour and a non-colour. Here it can become for us a colour that is an empty space where the effects of an encounter with the risen Lord are to be written; a space where new life takes shape. The Gospels provide us with a series of these encounters that serve as models for our own. Jesus appears to the disbelieving, to the doubter, to the denier. However, we should not forget that first of all he appears to the women, who are then charged with the task of telling the good news. Resurrection is not cosy – it breaks through barriers, challenges preconceptions and changes things. It happens when we least expect it and we don't always recognize it. Perhaps now is the time in our communities to consider where the life of God is breaking through and to give thanks. It is perhaps also the time to consider where resurrection life is being contained or controlled and to let the reality of Christ's 'bursting from the tomb'[3] challenge us to change – not least in those church annual reports and meetings! The task, then, is to find the places where resurrection life is taking shape and to support it by prayer and service.

Pentecost

Now to the festival of fire – to the warmth and energy of the flames of the Spirit and the red altar frontals that remind us of both blood and passion. The imagery of Pentecost and of the work of the Holy Spirit is conflicting: fire and water; oil and rushing wind, a force that is energizing and terrifying at the same time; people filled with the Spirit who yet look as if they are drunk; strangers speaking to us in our own language. This is a time when the Church looks outwards and considers again its mission in the world. But first we are each required to consider our own vocation and ministry. Many churches use this time in the church year for exactly this purpose, to identify and affirm the callings of the people of God and to anoint them for ministry. Some particular thought needs to be given to the ways in which this can be done in a multi-age context so that the giftings and ministries of children and young people are fully recognized alongside those of adults. We should also pray for people in our midst who

exercise particular ministries for the benefit of the whole community, not forgetting the lowliest.

Our journey through Lent, Holy Week and Easter should have changed us. Our energies may now find a focus in a different place. The colour red that marks this season is perhaps the thing that takes us back to the start of this journey. It is the twin themes of passion and of blood associated most of all with this colour that show us the lengths to which love can and does go so that the lost can be found. That love is now the message that the Church is called to carry forward.

Easter:
Stand-alone seasonal material

The Easter Liturgy

The Easter Liturgy is for Christians in the West the paradigm service from which all other liturgies derive. Its whole purpose is that we engage with the risen Christ and so enter into the basic truth and experience of our faith – that Jesus Christ is our risen Lord. Because of the importance of this liturgy there has been an understandable temptation to treat it with a misplaced reverence, as if the presence of children will somehow undermine its great value. Nothing could be further from the truth. To take no heed of their presence is to ignore the great gifts that children can bring to this extraordinary act of worship.

In reality, the Easter Liturgy can be given even more life when we take account of the gift of exuberant joy, about which adults have so much to learn from children. However, careful thought needs to be given to the way these ceremonies are conducted so that they make real connections with the realities of the lives of the participants, whatever their age.

The Easter Liturgy has four key elements:
- *The Service of Light* is a proclamation that Christ is risen from the dead and is the light of the world, overcoming all the powers of darkness, even death itself. This should be celebrated with as much sensory richness as possible. The Easter Candle, which symbolizes the risen Christ, is lit from the new fire and processed around the church. From it the individual candles of the worshippers are lit, reminding us that we are filled with the light of Christ.
- *The Vigil* tells the story of salvation, using readings and psalms.
- *The Baptismal Liturgy* makes the link between the events of the resurrection of Christ and the life of the Church and Christians today, reminding us that our baptism is about our entry into the risen life of Christ.
- *The Liturgy of the Eucharist* reminds us that the risen Christ revealed himself through the breaking of bread (Luke 24.30-31), and that the Eucharist stands at the heart of the Easter experience.

Times and Seasons presents us with three possible 'shapes' or patterns for the Easter Liturgy. Each has its own merits, and each can be adapted to an all-age context, though different treatment will be needed for each.

Patterns A and B offer different ways of dealing with the Service of Light and the Vigil Readings which retell the story of salvation. Both begin with the lighting of the New Fire. After that, they follow different routes through the Service of Light and the Vigil Readings as follows:

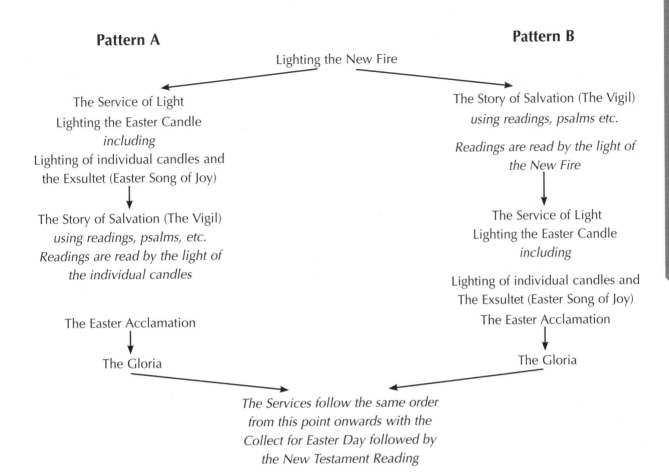

Pattern A

The Service of Light
Lighting the Easter Candle
including
Lighting of individual candles and
the Exsultet (Easter Song of Joy)

The Story of Salvation (The Vigil)
*using readings, psalms, etc.
Readings are read by the light of
the individual candles*

The Easter Acclamation

The Gloria

Lighting the New Fire

Pattern B

The Story of Salvation (The Vigil)
using readings, psalms etc.

*Readings are read by the light of
the New Fire*

The Service of Light
Lighting the Easter Candle
including

Lighting of individual candles and
The Exsultet (Easter Song of Joy)
The Easter Acclamation

The Gloria

*The Services follow the same order
from this point onwards with the
Collect for Easter Day followed by
the New Testament Reading*

Pattern C

Pattern C offers the opportunity for an informal dawn Eucharist at some place of local significance. There is no worked-out order for this service but it is left to the creative imagination of the local church to devise an appropriate act of worship. Directions are to be found on pages 398–400 of *Times and Seasons*.

In this volume we offer two fully worked-out services:

1. Service on the Eve of Easter (Saturday evening) incorporating the possibility of a community bonfire;

2. Service that lasts throughout the night but also incorporates the possibility of a dawn Eucharist.

These are by no means the only possible ways in which the Easter Liturgy can be expressed but they are sufficiently different to show the range of possibilities open to us.

A Service for Saturday evening

An Easter service with a community bonfire

This service has a strong mission focus and begins with a community bonfire and uses fireworks after the Easter Acclamation. It is a service to which all the community can be invited and assumes a large element of the service will be conducted outdoors. This service would be a major outreach event and needs appropriate planning for it to work well.

This service follows the structure of Pattern A because the nature of a community bonfire induces excitement from the moment the fire is lit. It is therefore more appropriate to choose a liturgical structure that reflects this, which is Pattern A.

This service should not start until it is dark.

Once the Easter Acclamation (Alleluia! Christ is risen …) has been made, those in the congregation with ribbons or something to wave could be encouraged to use them every time 'Alleluia' is used.

Structure, movement and flow	Words/Text	Multisensory	Participation
Before the service	*If this is a celebration for all the community, a brief explanation might be helpful before any ceremonies begin.*		A large bonfire is prepared somewhere near the main place of worship. Groups within the community could be asked to help to build it. Publicity/ Invitations could be produced inviting everyone to this great celebration of the Church.
THE SERVICE OF LIGHT			
Lighting the new fire	*Everyone gathers around the unlit bonfire.* *The congregation may ask* **Why is this night so special?** *The president says* Dear brothers and sisters in Christ, on this most holy night, when our Lord Jesus Christ passed from death to life, the Church invites her children throughout the world to come together in vigil and prayer. This is the Passover of the Lord. We remember his death and resurrection by hearing his word and celebrating his mysteries, confident that we shall share his victory over death and live with him for ever in God. *Once the fire is burning strongly a minister says* Blessed are you, Lord God of all creation, to you be glory and praise for ever.	The bonfire is lit.	A number of people could help with the lighting of the fire, though precautions should be taken to avoid any accidents.

	Your steadfast love extends to the heavens and your faithfulness never ceases. Illuminate our hearts with your wisdom and strengthen our lives with your word, for you are the fountain of life; in your light we see true light. Blessed be God, Father, Son and Holy Spirit. **Blessed be God for ever.** [T&S 334]		
Marking the Easter Candle	*If the Easter Candle is to be marked, instructions can be followed from pages 408–409 of* Times and Seasons. *The president says* Christ yesterday and today, the beginning and the end, Alpha and Omega, all time belongs to him, and all ages; to him be glory and power, through every age and for ever. **Amen.** *Nails or incense studs may be inserted into the Easter Candle.* *The president concludes* By his holy and glorious wounds may Christ our Lord guard and keep us. **Amen**. [T&S 335]		The Candle could have been marked during some group activity before the service. Representatives from different community groups could be involved in the marking of the Candle, a representative from each group inserting either a nail or an incense stud.

Lighting the Easter Candle	*The president lights the Easter Candle, saying* May the light of Christ, rising in glory, banish all darkness from our hearts and minds. *The bearer of the candle raises it and says or sings* The light of Christ. **Thanks be to God.** [T&S 335] *The bearer may do this three times, each time louder than the one before.*		(Sung) Response
Presentation of Candidates	*If there are candidates for baptism and/or confirmation, they are presented at this point. (See CI p. 111.)*		If there are candidates, they should be seated near the place from which any Vigil readings will be read.
Lighting of congregational candles	*A song or chant such as 'Lord Jesus Christ, your light shines within us' from Taizé may be sung.*		The minister carrying the candle moves around the congregation ensuring that everyone's candle is lit.
The Exsultet (Optional)	*The minister carrying the candle returns to the place from which the Vigil readings are to be read and places the candle in a stand.* *The Exsultet (the Easter Hymn of Praise) may be used in this or another form from pp. 410ff of* Times and Seasons. Choirs of angels, stars and planets: **all God's people sing and dance.** All creation, Church of God: **all God's people sing and dance.** We praise you Lord of life and death: we glorify your name: **all God's people sing and dance.** This is the night you set us free, bringing us home in love; holy night, when you led your people through the fearsome sea: **all God's people sing and dance.**		(Sung) Response or Easter Hymn of Praise.

	This is the night you brought your Son through the doors of death; O holy night, when death takes flight and hope is born again: **all God's people sing and dance.** This is the night our tears of sadness turn to shouts of joy; holy night, when the choirs of earth sing the songs of heaven: **all God's people sing and dance.** This is the night when Christ our Light makes the darkness bright: **all God's people sing and dance.** Christ is the life that knows no end. Christ is the love that burns within. Christ is the peace that floods the world. Christ is the Lord who reigns on high. **All God's people sing and dance. Amen.** [T&S 413] *If it would be more appropriate to sing a hymn, you could use 'Darkness is gone' by John Bell of the Iona Community or the Taizé chant 'Christus resurrexit'.*		
Easter Acclamation	*The minister says* Alleluia. Christ is risen. **He is risen indeed. Alleluia, Alleluia, Alleluia.** [T&S 338]		Bells are rung, cymbals clashed, instruments played, ribbons waved, all accompanied by shouting, stamping and fireworks. It is important that the natural excitement of the bonfire and the fireworks should be allowed to subside naturally. The temptation to move on quickly to the Vigil readings should be avoided. Instead, people should be allowed to enjoy the bonfire. Games may be played, songs may be sung, etc.

THE VIGIL			
A hymn or song may be sung to announce the beginning of the Vigil	*The president may introduce the Vigil using these or other appropriate words* As we await the risen Christ, let us hear the record of God's saving deeds in history, recalling how he saved his people in ages past and in the fullness of time sent his Son to be our Redeemer; and let us pray that through this Easter celebration God may bring to perfection in each of us the saving work he has begun. [T&S 338] *Any of the readings suggested on pages 375–97 of* Times and Seasons *may be used.* *This history of salvation may be told using poetry, song, activity, testimony as well as the set Scripture readings.*	Lights are taken from the Easter Candle to illuminate the Bible from which the Vigil readings will be taken	The congregation is encouraged to gather for the telling of the story of salvation. This may be done using Scripture readings, poetry, testimony, activity, etc. It is important to be relaxed and be aware that many of the gathering may wish to do other things around the fire while the formalities of the Vigil proceed.
Gloria in Excelsis	*is used, or an appropriate Easter hymn, during which all the candles in the church are lit.*		Singing Led by the Easter Candle, the whole congregation processes into church singing the Gloria or another suitable hymn of praise. All the candles in the church are lit from the Easter Candle while the members of the congregation go to their seats. We need to be relaxed about the fact that many may prefer to gather outside around the bonfire rather than go into church for the rest of the service. This could be accounted for in the planning so that someone might direct the thoughts and activities of those who stay behind.

The Collect	Let us pray that we may reign with the risen Christ in glory.		
	[T&S 339]		
	A period of silent prayer is kept.		
	God of glory, by the raising of your Son you have broken the chains of death and hell: fill your Church with faith and hope; for a new day has dawned and the way to life stands open in our Saviour Jesus Christ. **Amen.**		
	[CW: Additional Collects Easter Day]		
	Lights are switched on and the people's candles extinguished.		

The service continues with the Liturgy of the Word – see p. 138.

An all-night service with sleepover

This service might have as its target group the teenagers of the church and community, though there is no reason why it should not attract people of all ages. Again, it begins with the lighting of a bonfire, which is used informally throughout the night as the place of storytelling. The stories are interspersed with activity, prayer and song. It leads into sleep, or at least a pause, before the Service of Light, which ideally coincides with dawn.

The dawn start for the Service of Light provides the opportunity for anyone to join at this point and so offers a Dawn Eucharist for the whole of the Church community regardless of whether they have attended the Vigil of Readings held on the previous evening.

This service follows the structure of Pattern B because this lends itself more easily to the relaxed storytelling structure necessary to make this service work.

This service should not start until dusk on the Saturday evening. Given that this is an all-night event, it may even start quite late on the Saturday night.

Structure, movement and flow	Words/text	Multisensory	Participation
Before the service			A large bonfire is prepared somewhere near the main place of worship. Seats are arranged around the bonfire so that the storytellers can be heard.

Lighting the fire *by which the readings are read*	*Before the bonfire is lit a reader from the congregation says* In the beginning when God created the heavens and the earth, the earth was a formless void and darkness covered the face of the deep, while a wind from God swept over the face of the waters. Then God said, 'Let there be light'; and there was light. *Genesis 1.1*		The people are gathered together around the bonfire.
		The bonfire is lit by a number of people, taking care that all who do so are acting safely.	The bonfire is lit by authorized members of the congregation.
	As the fire begins to take hold the president says Blessed are you, Lord God of all creation, to you be glory and praise for ever. Your steadfast love extends to the heavens and your faithfulness never ceases. Illuminate our hearts with your wisdom and strengthen our lives with your word, for you are the fountain of life; in your light we see true light. Blessed be God, Father, Son and Holy Spirit. **Blessed be God for ever.** [T&S 354]		
THE VIGIL			
Introduction	*The congregation may ask* **Why is this night so special?** *The president may introduce the Vigil using these or other appropriate words* This is the night in which our Lord Jesus Christ passed over from death to life. The Church invites her members, dispersed throughout the world, to gather in vigil and prayer. For this is the Passover of the Lord, in which through word and sacrament we share in his victory over death. *If there are candidates for baptism and/or confirmation they are presented at this point. (See CI p. 111.)*		Baptism and/or confirmation candidates should have special seats near the place where the stories will be told.

The Vigil Readings	*The congregation may ask* **What did God do to save his people?**		The story of God's love throughout history is told around the bonfire, which becomes the storytelling place.
	The president says As we await the risen Christ, let us hear the record of God's saving deeds in history, recalling how he saved his people in ages past and in the fullness of time sent his Son to be our Redeemer. Let us pray that through this Easter celebration God may bring to perfection in each of us the saving work he has begun.		Scripture reading may be used or members of the congregation could be encouraged to 'tell a story' in their own words. Stories from the Bible may also be read from books where they have been paraphrased or retold.
	[T&S 354]		After each reading or story there may be some activity, prayer, song or anything that enables the congregation to engage with the part of the story being told.
	Any of the readings suggested on pages 375–97 of Times and Seasons *(with or without the accompanying psalms and prayers) or other suitable passages of Scripture may be used.*		Activities might include the marking of the Easter Candle, tending the fire throughout the night, preparation of drama to be used in the service after dawn, the making of bread for the Eucharist, even the making of the Easter Candle itself.

			Each story is told by the light of the fire. People may go to other places for the related activity, particularly if a church hall is available. If possible the worship space should not be used during the Vigil.
			For those staying overnight there needs to be an opportunity for eating and drinking. If possible, relate this to specific readings (e.g. Exodus 12.1-24)
			The activity after this reading might be the preparation of supper before 'bed', which would then bring the evening element of the service to a close.
			Obviously some might wish to stay up for longer, or even all night, talking around the bonfire. This should not be discouraged provided there is sufficient supervision.

After sleep	*If possible, the beginning of this part of the service should be timed so that the Easter Acclamation coincides with the rising of the sun.*
	
	The president blesses the rekindled bonfire from which the Easter Candle is to be lit, saying
	Eternal God,
	who made this most holy night
	to shine with the brightness of your
	   one true light:
	set us aflame with the fire of your
	   love,
	and bring us to the radiance of your
	   heavenly glory;
	through Jesus Christ our Lord.
	Amen.
	
	[T&S 355]
			The people gather around the fire.
			
			The bonfire, which will have died down overnight, is rekindled.

Reading	Exodus 14.10-31; 15.20-21 Crossing the Red Sea		This reading and the canticle of Moses and Miriam could have been dramatized as one of the activities of the previous evening.
Canticle	Exodus 15.1b-13,17-18 *Canticle response:* **This is my God and I will praise him.** *Silence*	This could be sung in one of its many forms, for example the version by Peter Moger in *Music for Common Worship 1*, pp. 354–7 (see Resources, p. 241).	Singing

	Christ our Passover is sacrificed for us.
	Therefore let us keep the feast.
	
	Let us pray that God will give
	    freedom to his enslaved people.
	
	Blessed are you, Lord, God of our
	    salvation.
	You heard the agony of your people
	as they cried out from their slavery,
	and you gave them Moses
	to lead them to a land flowing with
	    milk and honey.
	Hear the cry of the enslaved and the
	    homeless today
	and lead us through the turbulent sea
	    of life
	to our true home with you,
	O Lord, our Maker and Redeemer.
	Amen.
	
	[T&S 382]		

THE SERVICE OF LIGHT			
Lighting the Easter Candle	Christ yesterday and today, the beginning and the end, Alpha and Omega, all time belongs to him, and all ages; to him be glory and power, through every age and for ever. **Amen.** *If the Easter Candle has not yet been marked, it may be marked here. See pages 408–409 of* Times and Seasons *for notes on marking the Easter Candle.*		

	Nails or incense studs may be inserted into the Easter Candle. By his holy and glorious wounds may Christ our Lord guard and keep us. **Amen.** [T&S 355] *The president lights the Easter Candle, saying* May the light of Christ, rising in glory, banish all darkness from our hearts and minds. [T&S 356] *The minister bearing the candle enters the place of worship, followed by the other ministers, and they pause just inside the entrance.* *The minister bearing the candle raises it and says or sings* The light of Christ. **Thanks be to God.** [T&S 357]		
Procession inside the building	*The procession moves into the building and then stops. The versicle and response are repeated, and the candles of those around are lit from the Easter Candle.* *The procession continues to the centre of the building and stops once more. The versicle and response are again repeated.* *The Easter Candle is placed on a stand in the midst of the building.*		
Exsultet (Optional)	*The Exsultet (The Easter Hymn of Praise) may be used in this or another form from pages 410–417 of Times and Seasons.* Choirs of angels, stars and planets: **all God's people sing and dance.** All creation, Church of God: **all God's people sing and dance.**		(Sung) Response

	We praise you Lord of life and death: we glorify your name: **all God's people sing and dance.** This is the night you set us free, bringing us home in love; holy night, when you led your people through the fearsome sea: **all God's people sing and dance.** This is the night you brought your Son through the doors of death; O holy night, when death takes flight and hope is born again: **all God's people sing and dance.** This is the night our tears of sadness turn to shouts of joy; holy night, when the choirs of earth sing the songs of heaven: **all God's people sing and dance.** This is the night when Christ our Light makes the darkness bright: **all God's people sing and dance.** Christ is the life that knows no end. Christ is the love that burns within. Christ is the peace that floods the world. Christ is the Lord who reigns on high. **All God's people sing and dance. Amen.** [T&S 413]		
Easter Acclamation	*The minister says* Alleluia. Christ is risen. **He is risen indeed. Alleluia, alleluia, alleluia.** [T&S 360]		In a perfect world, this acclamation coincides with the rising of the sun. Bells are rung, cymbals clashed, instruments played, ribbons waved, all accompanied by shouting, stamping, etc.
Gloria in Excelsis	*is used, or an appropriate Easter hymn is sung, during which all the other candles in the church are lit.*		

The Collect	Let us pray that we may reign with the risen Christ in glory.		
	A period of silent prayer is kept.		
	God of glory, by the raising of your Son you have broken the chains of death and hell: fill your Church with faith and hope; for a new day has dawned, and the way to life stands open in our Saviour Jesus Christ. **Amen.**		
	[T&S 360] *Lights are switched on and the people's candles extinguished.*		

The service continues with the Liturgy of the Word – see below.

The Easter Liturgy from the Liturgy of the Word onwards

Both the previous services follow the same pattern from here.

The Easter Liturgy is *the* baptismal event of the whole year and, if possible, a baptism should be included or at the very least the church should be encouraged to reaffirm together their baptismal commitment. For the purposes of simplicity and space the service here allows only for the renewal of our baptismal commitment. If a baptism and/or confirmation is to be included in this service, there are indications throughout about how and where this might happen and references to where the appropriate texts might be found.

Structure, movement and flow	Words/text	Multisensory	Participation
THE LITURGY OF THE WORD			
New Testament Reading *Romans 6.3-11*	*At the end the reader may say* This is the word of the Lord. **Thanks be to God.** Alleluia. Christ is risen. **He is risen indeed. Alleluia.**		It is possible to omit this and, given the number of readings up to this point, this might be wise.
Hymn or song			Singing.
The Gospel Reading	*This acclamation may herald the reading of the Gospel* Jesus Christ is risen from the dead. **Alleluia.** He has defeated the powers of death. **Alleluia.** Jesus turns our sorrow into dancing. **Alleluia.** He has the words of eternal life. **Alleluia.**		Ribbons could be waved through this acclamation.

	When the Gospel is announced the reader says Hear the Gospel of our Lord Jesus Christ according to *N*. **Glory to you, O Lord.** *At the end* This is the Gospel of the Lord. **Praise to you, O Christ.** [T&S 361]	The Gospel could be read from the Easter Candle or in the middle of the congregation. People with ribbons and/or incense could accompany any movement.	
Sermon	*This may also include drama, testimony, etc.*		If this is part of the all-night event, this could have been prepared by one of the groups the night before.
Questions	*What are your questions about the Liturgy of the Word?*		
THE LITURGY OF INITIATION			
Hymn or song	*The ministers and any candidates for baptism and/or confirmation move to the place of baptism.*	The Easter Candle leads the procession to the place of baptism.	Singing. If there are no candidates for baptism, everyone might gather around the font.
	The congregation may ask **Why are we gathered here at this place of baptism?** *The minister addresses the candidates and those who wish to reaffirm their baptismal vows* As we celebrate the resurrection of our Lord Jesus Christ from the dead, we remember that through the paschal mystery we have died and been buried with him in baptism. In baptism, God calls us out of darkness into his marvellous light. To follow Christ means dying to sin and rising to new life with him. Therefore I ask: Do you turn to Christ as Saviour? **I turn to Christ.** Do you repent of the sins that separate us from God and neighbour? **I repent of them.** Do you renounce the deceit and corruption of evil? **I renounce them.** [T&S 356 adapted]		Question and answer.

Signing with the cross	*If there are candidates for baptism, the signing of the cross takes place here (see CI p. 68)*		
Prayer over the water	*The president pours water into the font.* Praise God who made heaven and earth, **who keeps his promise for ever.** Let us give thanks to the Lord our God. **It is right to give thanks and praise.** Almighty God, whose Son Jesus Christ was baptized in the river Jordan, we thank you for the gift of water to cleanse us and revive us. Saving God, **give us life.** We thank you that through the waters of the Red Sea you led your people out of slavery to freedom in the Promised Land. Saving God, **give us life.** We thank you that through the deep waters of death you brought your Son, and raised him to life in triumph. Saving God, **give us life.** Bless this water, that your servants who are washed in it may be made one with Christ in his death and in his resurrection, to be cleansed and delivered from all sin. Saving God, **give us life.** Send your Holy Spirit upon them, bring them to new birth in the household of faith, and raise them with Christ to full and eternal life; for all might, majesty, authority, and power are yours, now and for ever. Amen. Saving God, **give us life.** [T&S 362]	As the prayer over the water is said the song 'Spirit of the living God, fall afresh on me' may be sung quietly in the background. An additional verse as printed below might be added: **Spirit of our risen Lord, bless this water now.** **Spirit of our risen Lord, bless this water now.** **Wash us; cleanse us; free us; fill us.** **Spirit of our risen Lord, bless this water now.**	The 'Saving God' of the response could be led by the candidates or by different members of the congregation.

Profession of Faith	*The people reaffirm their Profession of Faith together with any candidates for baptism.*		
	Let us declare our faith in God, Father, Son and Holy Spirit.		
	Do you believe and trust in God the Father, source of all being and life, the one for whom we exist? **We believe and trust in him.**		
	Do you believe and trust in God the Son, who took our human nature, died for us and rose again? **We believe and trust in him.**		
	Do you believe and trust in God the Holy Spirit, who gives life to the people of God and makes Christ known in the world? **We believe and trust in him.**		
	This is the faith of the Church. **This is our faith. We believe and trust in one God, Father, Son and Holy Spirit. Amen.**		
	[CW 144]		
The Baptism	*If there is to be a baptism, it takes place here.*		
Affirmation	*The minister may then say to those in the congregation who wish to reaffirm their commitment to Christ* I call upon those who are affirming their baptismal faith to renew their commitment to Jesus Christ.		
	I answer the call of God my creator. I trust in Jesus Christ as my Saviour. I seek new life from the Holy Spirit.		
	[CI 203]		
	Hymns or songs may be sung as the waters of baptism are sprinkled over the people. Alternatively, all members of the congregation may be invited to renew their commitment to Christ by going to the water and making the sign of the cross with it on their forehead.		Singing. Getting wet.

	At the end the president says Almighty God, we thank you for our fellowship in the household of faith with all who have been baptized into your name. Keep us faithful to our baptism, and so make us ready for that day when the whole creation shall be made perfect in your Son, our Saviour Jesus Christ. **Amen.** [CI 203] May Christ dwell in your hearts through faith, that you may be rooted and grounded in love and bring forth the fruit of the Spirit. **Amen.** [T&S 365]		
Confirmation	*If there is a confirmation, it takes place here (CI pp. 118–119)*		
Welcoming the newly baptized and confirmed	*If there have been baptisms or confirmations, they are welcomed at this point.* [CW 361]		
Questions	*What are your questions about the Liturgy of Initiation?*		
THE LITURGY OF THE EUCHARIST			
The Peace	The risen Christ came and stood among his disciples and said, 'Peace be with you.' Then were they glad when they saw the Lord. Alleluia. Alleluia. The peace of the risen Christ be always with you **and also with you. Alleluia.** [T&S 367] *These words may be added* Let us offer one another a sign of peace. *All may exchange a sign of peace, greeting one another with these words:* 'Christ is risen.'	Human contact.	Ribbons could be waved. Movement in sharing the peace.

A hymn or a song			Singing.
Preparation of the Table	*The gifts of the people may be gathered and presented.* *The table is prepared and bread and wine are placed upon it.* *At the preparation of the table this prayer may be said* Be present, be present, Lord Jesus Christ, our risen high priest; make yourself known in the breaking of bread. **Amen.** [T&S 367]		The bread and wine could have been made as part of any activities during the Vigil. Sharing in the prayer.
Taking of the Bread and Wine	*The president takes the bread and wine.*		
The Eucharistic Prayer	*The president uses one of the authorized Eucharistic Prayers with an appropriate proper preface.*		*See the notes on how to use a Eucharistic Prayer in an all-age context.*
The Lord's Prayer	Rejoicing in God's new creation, let us pray with confidence as our Saviour has taught us. *The Lord's Prayer is said.* [T&S 368]		
The Breaking of the Bread	*The president breaks the consecrated bread.* Jesus says, I am the bread of life, whoever eats this bread will live for ever. **Lord, our hearts hunger for you; give us this bread always.** *The Agnus Dei may be used as the bread is broken.*		
The Giving of Communion	*The president invites the people to communion, saying* Alleluia. Christ our Passover is sacrificed for us. **Therefore let us keep the feast. Alleluia.** [T&S 369] *During the distribution hymns and anthems may be sung.*		Ribbons could be waved. Singing.

Post-Communion Prayer	The president may say this or another suitable prayer
	God of Life,
	who for our redemption gave your
	    only-begotten Son to the death of
	    the cross,
	and by his glorious resurrection
	have delivered us from the power of
	    our enemy:
	grant us so to die daily to sin,
	that we may evermore live with him
	    in the joy of his risen life;
	through Jesus Christ our Lord.
	Amen.
	
	[T&S 369]		

Questions	*What are your questions about the Liturgy of the Eucharist?*		
THE DISMISSAL			

The Blessing	Alleluia. Christ is risen.
	He is risen indeed. Alleluia.
	
	God the Son,
	    who in bursting from the grave has
	    won a glorious victory,
	give you joy as you share the Easter
	    faith.
	Amen.
	And the blessing …
	
	[T&S 370]
			Ribbons could be waved.

Giving the Lighted Candle	*If there have been baptisms and/or confirmations, the lighted candle is given at this point. See IS, p. 133.*		

The Dismissal	With the risen life of Christ within
	    you,
	go in the peace of Christ. Alleluia,
	    alleluia.
	Thanks be to God. Alleluia, alleluia.
	
	[T&S 371]
			Ribbons could be waved.

The Eucharist on Easter Day

The tomb, the cross and the flowers: an Easter morning Gathering Rite

PREPARATION

THE TOMB

Give the church porch or part of the entrance hall the feeling of a tomb. Do this by hanging it with dark fabric. You could ask people for old dark coloured curtains, or very dark coloured bed sheets. Alternatively, you could buy from a garden centre the black fleece or plastic that is used for putting under pebbles or shredded bark to suppress weeds. If you are using the church porch, you can leave stonework uncovered but cover any notice boards and drape the dark fabric over windows and the doors, so that people have to pass through it into the dark space. If you are using a larger entrance hall, you could erect the outside of a small frame tent, and then drape this with dark fabric to hide its shape and still give the feel of passing into and through a dark place. You will also need to remember to have people on hand at the service to help anyone with mobility or visual difficulties through this space. This act of support and service is, however, part of the rite. You might also have spices laid in this area. You could burn incense in a bowl on top of lit charcoal but, if you do this, make sure that it is well out of reach so that no one touches it by accident and gets burnt. (It would also need to be well away from any fabric.) Lavender, cloves or pot pourri might serve equally well.

THE CROSS AND THE FLOWERS

For the ordinary worshipper in a medieval church, the focal point inside the building was usually a large cross on top of a screen across the chancel arch. During the twentieth century, the holy table has often been brought forward to the front of the nave, demanding the re-creation of a visual focus here, rather than letting the eye simply drift into the depths of the now unused chancel.

In an old church with a tall, but very plain chancel arch, having a cross suspended at the height of the medieval rood fits the scale of the building perfectly, and can enhance the celebration of the church's year. A lightweight, temporary cross can be used and its decoration changed according to the season.

The main requirement is two suitable pulleys, of the kind used in old-fashioned suspended clothes airers. A good hardware shop can often supply what is needed, with pulleys that can be screwed securely into wood or masonry. The diameter of the cord must be matched carefully to the pulley, so that it cannot jump off and become wedged. A large diameter cord is easier on the hands than something too thin, and provides a useful margin of safety. Note that, when the cross is raised, and the cord holding the cross

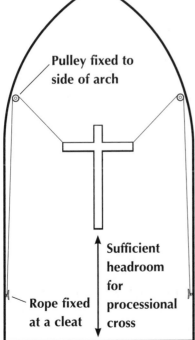

How to suspend a cross.

Pulley fixed to side of arch

Sufficient headroom for processional cross

Rope fixed at a cleat

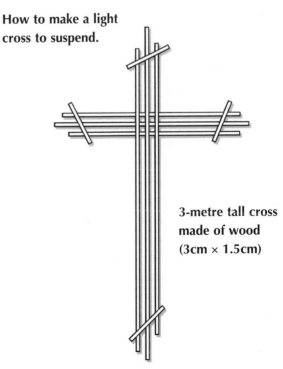

How to make a light cross to suspend.

3-metre tall cross made of wood (3cm × 1.5cm)

145

may be an angle of around 45°, the cross will appear to weigh twice as much as it did on the ground, and the strain on the pulley is also increased.

An open cross, painted black, provides the basis for several different designs. The cross is decorated as it stands, suspended from the ropes, at ground level. Only when the display is complete is it hoisted into position. It is useful to check the final position before flowers are in place, and mark the positions on the ropes to which they should be hauled by wrapping a short piece of coloured tape around the rope at the appropriate place. Watering is best done with a pump-action waterer with a long stem, as used for hanging baskets.

With a clear east window behind, semi-transparent, gauzy materials can be particularly effective. As an alternative to flowers, a long looped length of butter muslin, representing the shroud in which Jesus' body had been wrapped, can be effective. This could be left throughout the Easter season, and then replaced by a mixture of red, orange and yellow for Pentecost.

An alternative to having flowers is to have a large cross made of plywood, in which a silhouette of the risen Christ is cut.

If you don't have a suitable place to suspend the cross, or feel that this is not safe, it might be made to stand up somewhere in the church building, in which case it will need to be reasonably solid. It might be good to transform the cross that was used for Good Friday services.

You then need to provide a means of decorating the cross with fresh flowers so that they do not instantly wither. During Lent, gather up 500 ml water bottles (the kind people buy with their packed lunch). Cut off the neck of each bottle so you are left with little plastic tubes. To prepare the cross for decoration, attach these tubes to the cross in various places. You can do this either by using a drawing pin or a panel pin towards the top of the bottle. Make sure they are sufficiently well fastened to bear the weight of the water you will add. To decorate the cross people will put flowers and leaves into the water-filled bottles. You can then hide the plastic bottles by winding yellow or gold net or some other light fabric around the cross. It can be attached by tucking it behind the bottle, though you may prefer to make it more secure using panel pins. You could ask people to bring flowers with them on Easter morning, but it would be sensible to have some available for those who have not received this message. You do not need to spend vast amounts of money for this: daffodils work well

for this sort of decoration, and are usually available around Easter time. It may be possible for people with gardens to bring some branches with spring blossom: forsythia, flowering currant and some kinds of viburnum flower around Easter (depending when Easter falls) and the bright green, newly opened leaves of trees and bushes also look fresh and bright.

Set up the cross with the bottles attached and the fabric added. Have about 2 cm of water in the bottom of each bottle so it is not too heavy. As people arrive, greet them outside if possible. Invite them to select and help themselves to some flowers and then enter the dark 'tomb'. Remember to have people available to help them if necessary. On entering the church, invite them to decorate the cross with their flowers. There will not be space for everyone to do this at once so have other preparatory activities for people to do at the same time. People might cut for themselves a half-metre length of gold ribbon from a roll to wave each time 'Alleluia' is said or sung. Service sheets and candles can be distributed. People might choose an instrument to shake. Everyone should gather in the area near the door from the 'tomb' rather than sitting in the body of the church.

Preparatory notes

Which pathway?

There are elements of all the pathways in this service: the use of the cross for decoration is reminiscent of the Lenten tree ideas; the movement to different points around the building has echoes of stations and the use of the sensory relates to Head, hands and heart.

What needs to be prepared leading up to the service?

There is a good deal of preparation to be done for this service and it may be necessary for it to be carried out quite quickly. If there is an Easter Vigil on Saturday evening or early on Sunday, the immediate preparation for this service cannot happen until after that. Therefore, gather everything you will need carefully and store it all together in one place so that you can get hold of it quickly when you start the preparation.

You will need:
- Black or dark fabric to make the church porch dark (see suggestions in the description above).
- A way to hang the dark material: pins, sticky tack, gaffer tape would all come in useful.
- A cross.

- Flowers. (If you can arrange for people to supply these from their gardens that would be cost effective. Most people will have some spring blossoms or new leaves available if they have some bushes in their garden. The exception will be in years when Easter is unusually early.)
- Tubes made from used, small, drinks bottles (plastic).
- Drawing pins or the equivalent to attach these to the cross.
- Materials for suspending the cross if this is your intention.
- The Easter Candle.
- Bells and other musical instruments. If you don't have access to musical instruments, saucepans beaten with wooden spoons make a superb alternative.
- Ribbon, to be cut into pieces about half a metre long for people to wave, and pairs of scissors if you intend people to cut their own from longer pieces.
- A bowl (or other vessel) of water placed in the Easter garden.

- A means of sprinkling people with water (either 'the real thing', an 'aspergillum' or a piece of conifer or yew, or sprigs of rosemary, which work just as well really).

WHAT NEEDS TO HAPPEN BEFORE THE SERVICE?

Prepare your tomb entrance.

Make sure you have flowers.

Make sure the cross is ready and prepared.

Make sure there is a bowl of water in the Easter garden and a stone to roll away from the entrance

Ensure ribbon is available if you are planning to use it, and bells and other instruments.

WHAT NEEDS TO BE MADE READY IMMEDIATELY BEFORE THE SERVICE?

Have helpers available to assist people through the dark porch if necessary.

Make sure the flower arranging material is ready and available and there are ribbons and scissors available also.

Structure, movement and flow	Words/text	Multisensory	Participation
THE GATHERING			
When the service begins, the ministers enter through the porch 'tomb' and stand at the entrance.	*The president says* Christ yesterday and today, **the beginning and the end,** Alpha and Omega, all time belongs to him, and all ages; **to him be glory and power,** **through every age and for ever.** **Amen.** *A minister brings in the lit Easter Candle and proclaims* Alleluia. Christ is risen. **He is risen indeed.** **Alleluia, alleluia, alleluia.**	Flags and ribbons may be waved.	Said response. Flags and ribbons, bells and other instruments.

Verses of an Easter hymn of praise are sung as the minister carrying the Easter Candle leads the way to the Easter Garden. All gather there.	*The president says* This is the day when our Lord Jesus Christ was raised gloriously from the dead, crushing the power of sin and destroying the sting of death. Throughout the world Christians celebrate the awesome power of God as Christ calls us out of darkness to share in his marvellous light. May we, and all Christ's people, shine as lights in the world to the glory of God the Father. *The minister holding the candle says or sings* The light of Christ. **Thanks be to God.** [T&S 418]	Bells can be rung and other percussion instruments sounded. A fanfare might be played.	
At the Easter garden	*The minister holding the candle says or sings* The light of Christ. **Thanks be to God.** Alleluia. Christ is risen. **He is risen indeed. Alleluia.**	Flags and ribbons are waved.	Flags and ribbons for Alleluias.
	A reader says The angel said to the women, 'Do not be afraid; I know that you are looking for Jesus who was crucified. He is not here; for he has been raised, as he said.' *Matthew 28.5,6* [T&S 418–19]	The stone may be rolled away from the tomb; figures may be placed at the tomb and a candle may be lit and placed in the Easter garden.	

Prayers of Penitence	*The president says* Jesus Christ, risen Master and triumphant Lord, we come to you in sorrow for our sins, and confess to you our weakness and unbelief. Like Mary at the empty tomb, we fail to grasp the wonder of your presence. Lord, have mercy. **Lord, have mercy.** Like the disciples behind locked doors, we are afraid to be seen as your followers. Christ, have mercy. **Christ, have mercy.** Like Thomas in the upper room, we are slow to believe. Lord, have mercy. **Lord, have mercy.** [T&S 429]		
The Absolution *The president prays over a vessel of water that is lifted out of the Easter garden.*	God our Father, your gift of water brings life and freshness to the earth; in baptism it is a sign of the washing away of our sins and the gift of life eternal. Sanctify this water, we pray. Renew the living spring of your life within us, that we may be free from sin and filled with your saving health; through Christ our Lord. **Amen.** May the God of love and power forgive you and free you from your sins, heal and strengthen you by his Spirit, and raise you to new life in Christ our Lord. **Amen.**	The president and people are sprinkled with the water. The president says the Absolution and the water container is replaced in the Easter garden.	Being sprinkled with water.
	[T&S 430] Alleluia. Christ is risen. **He is risen indeed. Alleluia.**	Flags and ribbons are waved.	Waving flags and ribbons.

	The minister holding the candle says or sings The light of Christ. **Thanks be to God.**	Hymns and songs are sung as the members of the congregation come to the minister holding the Easter Candle and light their own candles. The light may be passed around if there are lots of people present.	Lighting candles.
The Empty Cross			
More verses of the Easter hymn of praise may be sung as the Easter Candle leads a procession to the place where the decorated cross is to be set up.	*A minister says* Alleluia. Christ is risen. **He is risen indeed. Alleluia.**	The cross is brought and placed in position.	Seeing the decorated cross.
Gloria in Excelsis	*The Gloria in Excelsis is said or sung.*	Bells and other instruments may play. Flags and ribbons may be waved.	Sounding bells and waving flags and ribbons.
The Collect	Let us pray that we may reign with the risen Christ in glory. *A period of silent prayer is kept.* God of glory, by the raising of your Son you have broken the chains of death and hell: fill your Church with faith and hope; for a new day has dawned and the way to life stands open in our Saviour Jesus Christ. **Amen.** [T&S 405]		
Questions	*What are your questions about the Gathering?*		
THE LITURGY OF THE WORD			
Readings	*Acts 10.34-43 is read.*		Listening to the reading.
		A psalm or Easter hymn is sung while members of the congregation process to their seats and the ministers to their usual places in the church.	

Gospel Reading	This acclamation may herald the	Flags and ribbons at	Waving flags and
The Gospel book is carried to the place where the Gospel is to be read.	Gospel Reading.	each Alleluia.	ribbons.
	Jesus Christ is risen from the dead **Alleluia.** He has defeated the powers of death. **Alleluia.** Jesus turns our sorrow into dancing. **Alleluia.** He has the words of eternal life. **Alleluia.**		
	[T&S 431]		Hearing the Gospel.
	When the Gospel is announced the reader says		
	Hear the Gospel of our Lord Jesus Christ according to N. **Glory to you, O Lord.**		
	At the end This is the Gospel of the Lord. **Praise to you, O Christ.**	At the end of the Gospel, the members of the congregation extinguish their candles.	
The Sermon		While the sermon is preached, some people should quietly remove the black drapes from porch and fold them up.	
The Nicene Creed	The Nicene Creed is said.		Saying the Creed.
Questions	What are your questions about the Liturgy of the Word?		
THE LITURGY OF THE SACRAMENT			
The Peace	The risen Christ came and stood among his disciples and said, 'Peace be with you.' Then were they glad when they saw the Lord. Alleluia.		Waving flags and ribbons. Sharing the Peace.
	Alleluia! The peace of the risen Christ be always with you **and also with you. Alleluia.**	Flags and ribbons may be waved.	
	[T&S 367]		
Preparation of the Table A hymn or song is sung.	The gifts of the people may be gathered and presented.		

Taking of the Bread and Wine	*The table is prepared and bread and wine are placed upon it.*
	
	This prayer may be said at the preparation of the table
	Lord of life,
	with unbounded joy we offer you
	    our sacrifice of praise.
	As we are fed with the bread of
	    heaven
	may we know your resurrection
	    power;
	through Christ our risen Lord.
	Amen.
	
	The president takes the bread and wine.
	
	[T&S 367]		

The Eucharistic Prayer	*An authorized Eucharistic Prayer is used with this short preface*
	
	But chiefly are we bound to praise
	    you
	because you raised him gloriously
	    from the dead.
	For he is the true paschal lamb who
	    was offered for us,
	and has taken away the sin of the
	    world.
	By his death he has destroyed death,
	and by rising to life again he has
	    restored to us everlasting life.
	
	[T&S 368]		

The Lord's Prayer	*The Lord's Prayer is said.*		Saying the Lord's Prayer.

Breaking of the Bread	Jesus says, I am the bread of life, whoever eats this bread will live for
	    ever.
	Lord, our hearts hunger for you;
	give us this bread always.
	
	The president invites the people to communion, saying
	Alleluia. Christ our passover is
	    sacrificed for us.
	Therefore let us keep the feast.
	    Alleluia.
		
		Flag and ribbons may be waved.
			Receiving communion.
			
			Waving flags and ribbons.

Prayer after Communion	God of Life, who for our redemption gave your only-begotten Son to the death of the cross, and by his glorious resurrection have delivered us from the power of our enemy: grant us so to die daily to sin, that we may evermore live with him in the joy of his risen life; through Jesus Christ our Lord. **Amen.** [T&S 369]		
A hymn or song is sung			
THE DISMISSAL	Alleluia. Christ is risen. **He is risen indeed. Alleluia!** God the Father, by whose love Christ was raised from the dead, open to you who believe the gates of everlasting life. **Amen.** God the Son, who in bursting from the grave has won a glorious victory, give you joy as you share the Easter faith. **Amen.** God the Holy Spirit, who filled the disciples with the life of the risen Lord, empower you and fill you with Christ's peace. **Amen.** And the blessing … *A minister says* With the risen life of Christ within you, go in the peace of Christ. Alleluia, alleluia. **Thanks be to God. Alleluia, alleluia.** [T&S 370–71] *The ministers and the people depart.*	Flags and ribbons may be waved. Flags and ribbons may be waved.	Waving flags and ribbons.
Questions	*What are your questions about the Liturgy of the Sacrament and the Dismissal?*		

A service for Ascension Day

A Gathering Rite, Liturgy of the Word and Conclusion

After the Gathering Rite this service parallels in structure that of Ash Wednesday. The focus is the making of the sign of the cross, not in ash, but in celebratory glitter. Penitence is replaced by praise and shame replaced by confidence in our ascended Lord.

Instruments, etc. need to be gathered together and distributed before the service begins. The making of banners and instruments could have formed part of activities leading up to the celebration of the Ascension.

The glitter can be purchased at almost any cosmetics outlet. Mixing it with a little oil gives it a thicker consistency more appropriate for the making of the sign of the cross.

Structure, movement and flow	Words/text	Multisensory	Participation
THE GATHERING			
	At the entry of the ministers God has gone up with a shout, the Lord with the sound of a trumpet. *Psalm 47.5*	This may be accompanied by a short burst of instruments, especially an organ if there is one, trumpets, rattles, shakers, the waving of banners, banging of saucepans, rattling of keys, shaking of ribbons, or any other celebratory noise.	Response and noise making!
Hymn or song			Singing.
The Greeting	Grace, mercy and peace from God our Father and the Lord Jesus Christ be with you **and also with you.** [T&S 470] *The president introduces the service using these, or other suitable words. It may be in the following question and answer format.* **Why are we meeting today?** Dear brothers and sisters in Christ, for forty days we have been celebrating with joyful hearts the resurrection of our Lord Jesus Christ, his bursting from the tomb and his defeat of the power of sin and death. He appeared to his disciples many times and told them about the kingdom of God.		Question and answer encourages sense of participation.

	Why is this day special?		
	Today we recall how he left this earth and returned to his Father, ascending into heaven to take his throne over all dominions and powers. Trusting in his reign over all creation, and submitting to his kingly yet loving rule, let us hear the story of his parting. [T&S 470 adapted]		
The Ascension Reading	A reading from the Acts of the Apostles (1.4-11) While staying with them, he ordered them not to leave Jerusalem, but to wait there for the promise of the Father. 'This', he said, 'is what you have heard from me; for John baptized with water, but you will be baptized with the Holy Spirit not many days from now.' So when they had come together, they asked him, 'Lord, is this the time when you will restore the kingdom to Israel?' He replied, 'It is not for you to know the times or periods that the Father has set by his own authority. But you will receive power when the Holy Spirit has come upon you; and you will be my witnesses in Jerusalem, in all Judea and Samaria, and to the ends of the earth.' When he had said this, as they were watching, he was lifted up, and a cloud took him out of their sight. While he was going and they were gazing up towards heaven, suddenly two men in white robes stood by them. They said, 'Men of Galilee, why do you stand looking up towards heaven? This Jesus, who has been taken up from you into heaven, will come in the same way as you saw him go into heaven.' *At the end the reader says* Alleluia. Christ is risen. **He is risen indeed. Alleluia.** *A minister says* Seeing we have a great high priest who has passed through the heaven, Jesus the Son of God, let us offer him the praise worthy of his name. [T&S 471]	This reading could be read over suitable music. This may be recorded or an improvisation by instrumentalists.	This reading should *not* be read by the person leading this part of the service. It could be read with congregational involvement as in the *Dramatised Bible*.

Extended Praise	*This could be two or three praise songs strung together interspersed with various acclamations affirming Christ's majesty. See NP pp. 223–9 for examples.*	This may be accompanied by instruments and noise, as at the opening Acclamation. Confetti could be thrown by the congregation or 'sprayed' into the air by dropping it in front of strong fans or blowers. Once the praise has begun, incense could be burnt in a large bowl at the front of the worship space.	Joyful and exuberant singing. During the extended praise anyone could be free to go and place more incense in the bowl.
	The worship should calm with the final song, which could be of a quieter, yet worshipful, nature leading eventually into silence.		
The Collect	*The president introduces a period of silent prayer with the words* Let us pray that our risen and ascended Lord will lead us to eternal life. *Silence may be kept.* Risen Christ, you have raised our human nature to the throne of heaven: help us to seek and serve you, that we may join you at the Father's side, where you reign with the Spirit in glory, now and for ever. **Amen.** [T&S 472]		The president encourages the congregation into personal prayer.
THE LITURGY OF THE WORD			
Hymn or song	*During this hymn/song the Gospel reader moves to the Easter Candle, from where the Gospel will be read.*		Singing. If possible the congregation gathers around the Easter Candle for the Gospel Reading

Gospel Reading	*This acclamation may herald the Gospel Reading.* Alleluia. **Alleluia.** God has highly exalted Jesus Christ. **Alleluia.** At the name of Jesus every knee shall bow. **Alleluia.** Let every tongue confess that Jesus Christ is Lord. **Alleluia.** **Glory to God the Father.** *cf Philippians 2.9-11* *When the Gospel is announced the reader says* Hear the Gospel of our Lord Jesus Christ according to *N*. **Glory to you, O Lord.** *At the end* This is the Gospel of the Lord. **Praise to you, O Christ.** [T&S 474]		
Sermon			
A hymn or song			Singing.
Litany of Praise	Christ has gone up on high. **Alleluia.** God raised Christ from the dead. **Alleluia.** And enthroned him at his right hand in the heavenly realms. **Alleluia.** God put all things in subjection beneath his feet **Alleluia.** And gave him as head over all things to the Church. **Alleluia.** We died, and our life lies hidden with Christ in God. **Alleluia.** We set our minds on things above. **Alleluia.**		During this Litany any banners could be waved.

	When Christ, who is our life, is revealed, we too will be revealed with him in glory. **Alleluia.** Christ has gone up on high. **Alleluia.** [NP 229 adapted]		
Affirmation of Faith	Let us affirm our faith in Jesus Christ the Son of God. **Though he was divine,** **he did not cling to equality with God,** **but made himself nothing.** **Taking the form of a slave,** **he was born in human likeness.** **He humbled himself** **and was obedient to death,** **even the death of the cross.** **Therefore God has raised him on high,** **and given him the name above every name:** **that at the name of Jesus** **every knee should bow,** **and every voice proclaim that Jesus Christ is Lord,** **to the glory of God the Father.** **Amen.** *cf Philippians 2.6-11* [CW 147]		
Signing with the Cross	Christ is the reflection of God's glory and the exact imprint of God's very being. *Hebrews 1.3* *As the cross is made on each person, these or other words may be used, or the act may be performed with no words* I sign you with the cross, the sign of Christ. Proclaim God's glory: and may the Son of God be glorified through you. *Based on John 11.4*	People are invited to come forward to have the sign of the cross made on their forehead in glitter mixed with oil. This may be accompanied by brief laying on of hands.	The president invites people to come forward and makes the sign of the cross on the forehead of the first person to come forward. The glitter is then handed to that person who then imposes the glitter cross on the next person, and so on. The final person makes the sign of the cross on the president.

		Throughout the glittering, appropriate songs may be sung.	Everyone should be included regardless of age.
	At the end of the 'glittering' the president says this prayer The love of the Lord Jesus draw you to himself; the power of the Lord Jesus strengthen you in his service; the joy of the Lord Jesus fill your hearts; this day and always. **Amen.**		
The Peace	*The peace may be exchanged in song as people greet each other, singing for example 'Peace to you' by Graham Kendrick* *(or)* Jesus says: 'Peace I leave with you; my peace I give to you. If you love me, rejoice because I am going to the Father'. Alleluia. The peace of the Lord be always with you **and also with you.** Let us offer one another a sign of peace. *All may exchange a sign of peace.* [T&S 477]	Human contact.	Movement – sharing the Peace.
If the service is eucharistic, it continues with the Preparation of the Table. *If it is a Service of the Word, the Lord's Prayer should be said at the end of the glittering and the service continues with the Conclusion below or with prayers of Intercession and then the Conclusion.*			

The Conclusion

If the service is eucharistic, this follows after the post-communion prayers. *If it is a Service of the Word, it follows immediately after either the Peace or Prayers of Intercessions*			
THE DISMISSAL	*An exuberant hymn of praise may be sung.*		Singing.
Reading	A reading from the Acts of the Apostles (1.12-14) Then the disciples returned to Jerusalem from the mount called Olivet, which is near Jerusalem, a sabbath day's journey away. When they had entered the city, they went		

	to the room upstairs where they were staying. They were constantly devoting themselves to prayer, together with certain women, including Mary the mother of Jesus, as well as his brothers. *No responses are used at the end of the reading.* *Silence is kept.*	A small gong, cymbal or bell or something similar may be sounded to indicate silence.	
Responsory	As we wait in silence, **make us ready for your coming Spirit.** As we listen to your word, **make us ready for your coming Spirit.** As we worship you in majesty, **make us ready for your coming Spirit.** As we long for your refreshing, **make us ready for your coming Spirit.** As we long for your renewing, **make us ready for your coming Spirit.** As we long for your equipping, **make us ready for your coming Spirit.** As we long for your empowering, **make us ready for your coming Spirit.** [T&S 480] *Silence may be kept after which a short, reflective hymn, song or chant may be sung.* May the Spirit, who set the Church on fire upon the day of Pentecost, bring the world alive with the love of the risen Christ. And the blessing … **Amen.**	Silence moves carefully into singing.	Each of these could be led by a different member of the congregation. Singing. Going out.

	A minister says Waiting expectantly for the promised Holy Spirit, go in peace to love and serve the Lord. Alleluia, alleluia. **In the name of Christ. Alleluia, alleluia.** *or* Waiting expectantly for the promised Holy Spirit, go in the peace of Christ. Alleluia, alleluia. **Thanks be to God. Alleluia, alleluia.** *The ministers and people depart.* [T&S 481 adapted]		

A Eucharist for Pentecost

Preparatory notes

What needs to be prepared leading up to the service?

The service sheet. It is helpful to produce a special service sheet for an occasion like this, so that the liturgy is accessible to all who are literate. You can add short instructions about the liturgical actions as well, such as 'We now carefully place our stones in the water as part of our prayer of confession.' You can add illustrations to the sheet – these can be reproductions of children's line drawings created beforehand, or line drawings designed to be coloured in during the service. Do not be afraid to supplement the liturgy with additional low-key colouring or craft activities like this, in which children can participate while the service goes on. A very young or restless child will be much happier and will still be engaged with the 'feel' of the service and with the liturgical actions, including walking forward to receive a blessing.

Look at your church building. Are there any temporary changes you could make that would make this service feel inclusive and special? If you have chairs, you could arrange them in a different pattern – perhaps around a central space where a nave altar, the 'pools of water' and the oasis for the 'intercession flames' could be sited.

The Gathering. This requires the use of three candles or indoor sparklers. Sparklers are very dramatic, but more difficult to handle safely. Make sure that

they are the indoor variety, not the kind used on 5 November. Party shops will advise you on safety issues. If you use candles, they could be different colours or have different designs on them (you can paint on candles with acrylic paint quite safely) or it is now possible to buy candles that burn with different coloured flames. The three candles could also be in different kinds of stand or holder, or held by three people who process them to different areas of the building at the end of the call to worship. Consider what will enhance the worship in your context and choose accordingly.

The Confession and Absolution. Two possible liturgical actions are offered here: at the Absolution, worshippers retrieve a glass nugget or plastic jewel from a 'pool' area – doing it slowly, savouring the wetness on their hands as a sign of the Spirit's renewing power. Or, if you judge that people will be too likely to flick water and distract each other, the second option might be more suitable: worshippers place a plain pebble into the water during the Confession, and see it 'renewed' in colour by the water. (Do remind people to *place* their stone, not drop it or throw it into the water. Pebbles can be purchased from garden centres; they will need to be washed before using in worship.) The 'pool' could be anything from a washing-up bowl or bowls, an elegant metal bowl, to a display of 'pools' including an indoor fountain. (This is not as complicated to arrange as you might think – many garden centres sell small pump units for indoor water features for less than £20; You could use a child's moulded sandpit tray. If you add a fabric drape to cover the edges and some candles in appropriate holders, your indoor fountain can look and sound wonderful. Be careful to follow the manufacturer's instructions on the use of the pump unit, as electricity and water are not a good mix! You may like to add an additional circuit breaker for added security. You should have a number of smaller 'pools' adjacent to the one with the fountain, for people to place or retrieve their glass nugget/stone, as it is not advisable to have people putting their hands into the water where the pump is in operation. If you are looking to create a whole water scene, try buying lengths of net – four or five metres – in white, pale blue, dark blue, etc. It is fairly inexpensive and yet wonderfully stiff and frothy, so you can bunch it up into shapes like flowing water.)

**Gold card
10–12 cm tall
6–8 cm wide**

**Red card
5–7 cm tall
4 cm wide**

**Stick a green
garden stick to
the gold card**

**Stick the red card on top of
the gold card and green stick
to make an inner flame**

The Prayers of Intercession. The suggested liturgical action for the Intercessions involves card flames: make a large flame shape of gold 'mirror' card (10–12 cm tall, 6–8 cm wide approximately) and a smaller flame shape of red metallic sticky-backed foil (5–7 cm tall, 4–6 cm wide; see also page 244). For the best effect, use the finest materials you can find and ask a sure-fingered creative adult to cut out the flame shapes. Hold a small, green, garden stick against the front of the gold card shape. Secure

it by sticking the red metallic flame shape over it. The stick is now sandwiched between the two flame shapes and so held securely in place. Make a 'flame' for each member of the congregation. You can vary the length of the sticks. Place some florists' foam for dried flower arrangements in a suitable place where all the congregation can see it. You can disguise the base of the blocks of foam with orange, red or gold fabrics. Blocks of dry florists' foam are very light, so fix them in some way so that they will not easily tip over. You need roughly one block of foam per 30 flames. Give a moment during or at the conclusion of the Intercessions when people can bring their flame and push it into the foam as a sign of their prayer. The final display of card flames can be very beautiful as it catches the light.

The Talk requires two pictures – one of the baptism of Christ and one of the day of Pentecost. Try to get images that are worth looking at in their own right, rather than ones that are just conventional illustrations. Piero della Francesca's *Baptism of Christ* (1448–50) and El Greco's *The Pentecost* (1596–1600) would work well; so would some of the creative line drawings designed for service sheets. Avoid humorous images that would work against the tone of the talk. You could incorporate the images into displays of fabrics, flowers, etc. that would be present from the beginning of the Eucharist, or you could hold them up at the appropriate point in the talk. Visibility is a key issue: each image will probably need to be at least A2 size. Images can be downloaded from the Internet and either enlarged by colour photocopying or projected (be aware of copyright issues and leave time to contact the relevant gallery or web site). Another option is to print a small image (about half the size of a postcard) for each member of the congregation. Small images can be distributed with the service sheet and they have the added advantage that they can be taken home. The talk also requires symbols to evoke a dove, water and fire. If you have decorated the church with these three symbols, then simply indicate the relevant display at that point in the talk. If you have created a pool or pools for use in the Confession, for instance, point to these and perhaps dip your hand in the water. If your context does not permit the use of the more ambitious displays suggested in this outline, you could use the hand gesture described for the final responses to symbolize the dove, pour some water into a bowl for water, and light a candle for fire.

The Closing Responses do not require any special materials, but do take time to practise the gestures so that you can teach them to the congregation confidently.

 Resources for the service

1. Reading from the Acts of the Apostles
- Actions of apostles;
- Words of onlookers.

When the day of Pentecost had come, they were all together in one place. And suddenly from heaven there came a sound like the rush of a violent wind, and it filled the entire house where they were sitting. Divided tongues, as of fire,

(Light the sparklers)

appeared among them, and a tongue rested on each of them. All of them were filled with the Holy Spirit and began to speak in other languages,

(Turn to one another)

as the Spirit gave them ability.

Now there were devout Jews from every nation under heaven living in Jerusalem. And at this sound the crowd gathered and was bewildered, because each one heard them speaking in the native language of each. Amazed and astonished, they asked,

'Are not all these who are speaking Galileans? And how is it that we hear, each of us, in our own native language? Parthians, Medes, Elamites, and residents of Mesopotamia, Judea and Cappadocia, Pontus and Asia, Phrygia and Pamphylia, Egypt and the parts of Libya belonging to Cyrene, and visitors from Rome, both Jews and proselytes, Cretans and Arabs – in our own languages we hear them speaking about God's deeds of power.'

All were amazed and perplexed, saying to one another,

'What does this mean?'

But others sneered and said,

'They are filled with new wine.'

(Acts 2.1-13)

2. The Talk: The Dove, the Water and the Fire

HINTS FOR USING THIS STORY:
- Learn the script as if it were a dramatic monologue. You need to know it well enough to be able to tell it without holding any notes or reminders; this will help you make contact with the congregation and make it much easier to point to the visual symbols. By all means change parts of the script to make it suitable for your context, but work these changes out beforehand and learn them – don't simply rely on your native 'gift of the gab' because it is likely that the story will then become too wordy and you will be too focused on projecting yourself as the storyteller.
- Become immersed in the story so that you are listening and responding to it yourself even as you tell it.
- Do not be afraid of pauses and moments of silence; these are very important, particularly as you indicate the different visual symbols. Children and adults will take their cue from you – if you are still and centred on the present moment of the story, they mostly will be too.
- Above all, avoid the 'pantomime' approach to all-age preaching that involves jokey and knowing asides addressed to the adults at the expense of the dignity of children. Mercifully, using visual symbols and narratives gives very little scope for this.
- You could ask children to present the different visual symbols, for example, to pour the water, or hold up an image – but do it only if you feel it will add to the worship, do not do it on the assumption that this will make the children feel 'involved'. Your aim should be to involve them in the mystery of Pentecost, not in the practical difficulties of 'upfront' ministry. If they are going to take part, rehearse them beforehand so that they can play their part with dignity, skill and independence in the way that you would hope an adult participant would be able to.
- Begin your talk with the same prayer you would use when you begin a sermon. This signals that the story is part of the Ministry of the Word, not five minutes' light entertainment.

The Talk

The Holy Spirit is God. The Holy Spirit goes where he chooses, he is invisible, and although we can't see him, he is real.

The Holy Spirit is God coming near to us. (Bring your two hands gently together in a handshake.)

(Either: hold up a model dove, or point to the display showing a dove or make the dove hand gesture as described for the closing responses) *God … being gentle.*

(Either: pour some water, or point to the display involving water) *God … giving life.* (Either: light a candle, or point to fiery display/candles used in call to worship/hold up card flame to be used in the intercessions) *God … firing us up.*

(Indicate a picture of Jesus' baptism.) *This is Jesus, on the day he was baptized. Do you see John the Baptist pouring water on Jesus' head? John didn't want to baptize Jesus at first, because he felt that Jesus didn't need to be baptized. He said, 'I baptize people because they are sorry for the wrong things they have done, but you have done nothing wrong. You are God's chosen one – I should be baptized by you!' 'Please baptize me', Jesus said, 'for God wants me to do this.' And so John baptized him, and then he saw the Holy Spirit fly like a dove* (make the 'dove action' described for the closing responses) *and settle on Jesus. God came gently, like a dove, and a voice said, 'This is my special son, I am very pleased with him.' It was a very gentle moment, because a dove is a very gentle bird, but God came near.* (Bring your hands gently together in a handshake.) *It was the start of all that Jesus did and taught.*

(Indicate or stand near the display of water, or the water you poured out earlier.) *Some years later, Jesus went to the Temple to worship. It was a special festival and the Temple was crowded with people. It was part of the Jewish Harvest, and the priest was thanking God for the gift of water: water to drink, and water to make the crops grow for food; water that gives life. In the middle of the prayers, Jesus stood up and called out with a loud voice, 'If anyone is thirsty, let them come to me and drink. Whoever believes in me – it will be as if water bubbles up inside them.' This story is written in John's Gospel, and John explains that Jesus was talking about the Holy Spirit living in his followers. The followers of Jesus will be filled up with life like a spring of water, because God will come near* (bring hands together in a handshake) *and give them life.*

After Jesus had returned to be with God the Father, and his followers couldn't see him any more, although they knew that he was near, something amazing happened. (Show Pentecost picture or ask people to look at the small image.) *All the followers of Jesus were together, praying. Suddenly, they heard a sound like a rushing wind, and something like a flame appeared over each of their heads. It was the Holy Spirit coming very near.* (Bring your hands gently together in a handshake.) *They felt brave, and full of life and they wanted to tell other people the story of Jesus – and so they rushed out into the streets and started to shout about how great God is. God came near,* (bring hands together in a handshake) *this time in a fiery way, like little flames. The followers of Jesus felt fired up, because the fiery wildness of God had come close to them. They went out and began to travel all over the world to tell people the story of Jesus. We call the day this happened 'the day of Pentecost' and we celebrate it as the birthday of the Church. The Holy Spirit is God coming near to us.* (Bring your hands together in a handshake.)

(Indicate dove) *God being gentle.*

(Indicate water) *God giving life.*

(Indicate flame) *God firing us up.*

1. **Hands together, both palms facing you, fingers together and pointing upwards.**

2. **Cross hands then bring the thumbs together to form the dove's head and body.**

3. **Rippling the fingers looks like the dove's wings moving to make it fly.**

4. **Dove at rest.**

Structure, movement and flow	Words/text	Multisensory	Participation
THE GATHERING			
A hymn or song is sung			Singing.
The Greeting	The Lord be with you **and also with you.** Alleluia. Christ is risen. **He is risen indeed. Alleluia.**		

	Holy Spirit,
	you came as tongues of flame to
	    your disciples gathered together.
	
	As we wait in silence,
	fill us with your Spirit.
	
	Joy bubbled up in the disciples, like
	    water flowing from a spring.
	
	As we long for your refreshing,
	fill us with your Spirit.
	
	You brought wisdom, strength and
	    courage with the gentleness of a
	    dove.
	
	As we long for your equipping,
	fill us with your Spirit.
		An indoor sparkler or candle is lit.
		
		An indoor sparkler or candle is lit.
		
		An indoor sparkler or candle is lit.
			Response and seeing the sparklers or candles.

The Pentecost Reading	A reading from the Acts of the Apostles (2.1-13) *At the end of the reading the narrator* *says* The Lord is here. **His Spirit is with us.**	Use a dramatic reading of this passage, such as that provided in the introduction above.	Participation or listening to the dramatized reading.
A song or hymn is sung			

The Confession	The Holy Spirit has come to us to
	    remind us of all that Jesus said
	    and did.
	Let us confess the ways in which we
	    have not lived as his followers.
	Lord, you awaken our coldness to
	    the fire of your love.
	Lord, have mercy.
	Lord, have mercy.
	
	You speak to us about our sins with a
	    gentle voice.
	Christ, have mercy.
	Christ, have mercy.
		If you are going to use stones and place them in the water, invite people to do so at this point. Emphasize that we place our stones carefully and quietly, as part of our prayers of confession, asking God to make us clean. Allow as much time as it takes – savour the moment.	Use of the stones and the water.

	You bring us to the living water to revive us. Lord, have mercy. **Lord, have mercy.**	You could have some instrumental music or quiet singing at this point, although silence would also be effective.	
The Absolution	May the Father of all mercies cleanse you from your sins, and restore you in his image to the praise and glory of his name, Through Jesus Christ our Lord. **Amen.** [CW 135]		
Gloria in Excelsis	*The Gloria may be said or sung, or another version, perhaps from Taizé or the Peruvian Gloria may be used.*		Singing.
The Collect	Holy Spirit, sent by the Father, ignite in us your holy fire; strengthen your children with the gift of faith, revive your Church with the breath of love, and renew the face of the earth, through Jesus Christ our Lord. **Amen.** [T&S 494]		
Questions	*What are your questions about the Gathering section of the service?*		
THE LITURGY OF THE WORD			
The Gospel	Alleluia, alleluia. Come, Holy Spirit, fill the hearts of your faithful people and kindle in them the fire of your love. **Alleluia.** *When the Gospel is announced the reader says* Hear the Gospel of our Lord Jesus Christ according to John. *(John 7.37-39)* **Glory to you, O Lord.** *At the end* This is the Gospel of the Lord. **Praise to you, O Christ.** [T&S 496]		
Sermon	The Dove, the Water and the Fire *(see separate text)*		

Affirmation of Faith	Let us declare our faith in God. **We believe in God the Father, from whom every family in heaven and on earth is named.** **We believe in God the Son, who lives in our hearts through faith, and fills us with his love.** **We believe in the Holy Spirit, who strengthens us with power from on high.** **We believe in one God; Father, Son and Holy Spirit. Amen.** [CW 148]		
Prayers of Intercession	We hold our card flames and pause for a moment in quietness. Think of someone who needs your prayers today. It might be someone you know well, or someone you have only heard about on the news. Hold your flame and think of them and quietly ask God to help them. (*Pause*). Now think of a country that needs your prayers. Hold your flame and think of them and quietly ask God to help them. (*Pause*) Now think of Christians all over the world celebrating Pentecost today. Hold your flame and think of them and quietly thank God for them. (*Pause*) When you are ready, come and push your flame into the florists' foam as a sign of your prayer.	Each member of the congregation has a cardboard flame on a stick, to hold during the biddings. After the biddings people may come forward and place their flames in the florist's foam at the front of the church. Appropriate music might be played or a song or hymn might be sung.	Holding the flames and then putting them into the florists' foam.
Questions	*What are your questions about the Liturgy of the Word?*		
LITURGY OF THE SACRAMENT			
The Peace	The fruit of the Spirit is love, joy, peace. If we live in the Spirit, let us walk in the Spirit. The peace of the Lord be always with you **and also with you.** [T&S 486]		

Offertory hymn or song			
Preparation of the Table			
Taking of the Bread and Wine	With this bread that we bring **we shall remember Jesus.** With this wine that we bring **we shall remember Jesus.** Bread for his body, wine for his blood, gifts from God to his table we bring. **We shall remember Jesus.** [CW 292]	The gifts of the people may be gathered and presented. The table is prepared and bread and wine are placed upon it. This or another prayer at the Preparation of the Table may be said. The president takes the bread and wine.	
The Eucharistic Prayer	*The president uses one of the authorized Eucharistic Prayers.*		
The Lord's Prayer	**Our Father in heaven, hallowed be your name, your kingdom come, your will be done, on earth as in heaven. Give us today our daily bread. Forgive us our sins as we forgive those who sin against us. Lead us not into temptation but deliver us from evil. For the kingdom, the power, and the glory are yours now and for ever. Amen.**		
Breaking of the Bread	*The president breaks the consecrated bread.* We break this bread to share in the body of Christ. **Though we are many, we are one body,** **because we all share in one bread.** [CW 179]		
Giving of Communion	*The president says* Alleluia. Christ our passover is sacrificed for us. **Therefore let us keep the feast. Alleluia.**		
			People receive communion.

Prayer after Communion	Faithful God, who fulfilled the promises of Easter by sending us your Holy Spirit and opening to every race and nation the way of life eternal: open our lips by your Spirit, that every tongue may tell of your glory; through Jesus Christ our Lord. **Amen.** [T&S 500]		
THE CONCLUSION		The ministers and the congregation go to gather at the Paschal Candle.	
	When all the candles are lit the president says For fifty days we have celebrated the victory of our Lord Jesus Christ over the powers of sin and death. We have proclaimed God's mighty acts and we have prayed that the power that was at work when God raised Jesus from the dead might be at work in us. As part of God's Church here in *N*, I call upon you to live out what you proclaim. Empowered by the Holy Spirit will you dare to walk into God's future trusting him to be your guide? **By the Spirit's power, we will. Send us out.** Will you dare to embrace each other and grow together in love? **We will. Holy Spirit, rest on us.** Will you dare to share your riches in common and minister to each other in need? **By the Spirit's power, we will. Send us out.**	Make dove shape. Flap dove's wings gently, lifting your arms so that the dove flies. Make dove shape. Flap dove's wings gently, and bring to rest on chest. Make dove shape. Flap dove's wings gently, lifting your arms so that the dove flies.	

	Will you dare to pray for each other until your hearts beat with the longings of God? **We will. Holy Spirit, rest on us.**	Make dove shape. Flap dove's wings gently, and bring to rest on chest.	
	Will you dare to carry the light of Christ into the world's dark places? **By the Spirit's power, we will. Send us out.**	Make dove shape. Flap dove's wings gently, lifting your arms so that the dove flies.	
	If there are no other services on this feast the Paschal Candle may be extinguished in silence. [T&S 501 adapted]		
	The president says The Lord is here. **His Spirit is with us.** Today we have remembered the coming of God's power on the disciples and we invite that same Spirit to drive us out into the wild places of the world. *Weather permitting, the ministers and people process out of church, or to the back of church. A hymn may be sung.* *The president blesses the people, saying* May the Spirit, who set the Church on fire upon the day of Pentecost, bring the world alive with the love of the risen Christ. **Amen.** And the blessing … *A minister says* Filled with the Spirit's power, go in the light and peace of Christ. Alleluia, alleluia. **Thanks be to God. Alleluia, alleluia.** [T&S 502]		
Questions	*What are your questions about the Conclusion?*		

Practical inclusive ideas for all the pathways in Eastertide

LENTEN TREE

HEAD, HANDS AND HEART

STATIONS OF THE CROSS

Eastertide: A journey for fifty days

Since the introduction of the *Common Worship* calendar in 1997, one of the most significant changes has been that, in seasonal time, Sundays are described as being of a season, rather than being after a festival. This underlines the fact that the great festivals are not just one-off peaks in the Christian year. Rather they mark the beginnings of times in which we can explore central theological themes through worship.

Eastertide is one such season – a great fifty days – running from Easter Day to Ascension Day (forty days in celebration of the resurrection) and a further ten days (in anticipation of the gift of the Holy Spirit) from Ascension to Pentecost. The *Common Worship* lectionary readings make it clear that this whole season is a time to reflect on what it means to live in the light of the resurrection. The inclusion of a reading from the Acts of the Apostles as the first reading in the Principal Service Lectionary underlines this: reflecting on the stories of Christians who lived in the immediate post-Easter period can help us live as 'Easter people'.

Times and Seasons provides a range of worship resources for the Easter season. These are largely alternative texts for slotting into a Eucharist or Service of the Word: penitential material, acclamations, intercessions, Eucharistic prefaces and texts for the dismissal. In addition, though, there is a vast array of material for the 'Easter Liturgy' – including a fully worked-out service that might include the lighting of the Paschal Candle, Vigil readings, baptism (or at least renewal of baptismal vows), and First Eucharist of Easter. This Easter Liturgy is full of symbolic riches – riches that deserve to be revisited and explored throughout the Easter season. One possible approach to this is to take one of the major themes of the Easter Liturgy on each of the Sundays of Eastertide, for example,

Light
- Light features strongly in the Easter Liturgy. Traditionally the service begins in darkness and the darkness is dispelled by the lighting of the Easter Candle – a sign of the risen Christ present with us to eternity.
- The early Christians turned east (the direction of sunrise) to make their promises in baptism, and many congregations still do so as they affirm their faith by saying the Creed.

Water
- The Exodus of the Israelites through the Red Sea is seen by many as prefiguring the resurrection – a movement from slavery to freedom.
- Easter is the major baptismal season. The use of water in worship enables everyone to reaffirm their baptismal promises.

Joy
- At the heart of the Easter Gospel is the joy of the apostles: joy that is ours, too, as we affirm our risen Lord among us.
- The *Gloria in Excelsis* reappears at the Easter Liturgy after its absence in Lent and the Easter Liturgy includes the *Easter Song of Praise* (or *Exsultet*).

Word
- The Vigil readings at the Easter Liturgy tell the story of salvation from the creation of the world to Jesus' rising from the dead.
- It's significant that the disciples on the road to Emmaus met Jesus first in the unfolding of these Scriptures.

The breaking of bread
- On arrival at Emmaus, the disciples recognized the risen Jesus in the breaking of the bread. Other resurrection appearances, too, include Jesus sharing food with his disciples.
- Eucharistic celebration takes on an added dimension in Eastertide as we recall that it is our risen Lord who meets us in the sacrament.

Each other
- The risen Christ appeared in the upper room as the disciples were together and proclaimed 'peace' to them.

- The one absentee from their fellowship when Christ appeared was Thomas, who was unable to witness that first appearance.
- Jesus promised that where two or three of his disciples were gathered together he would be there in their midst and that he would dwell in the hearts through faith.

Each of these themes provides a possible focus for worship on the second to the sixth Sundays of Easter. On the seventh Sunday (the Sunday after Ascension Day), the readings anticipate the gift of the Holy Spirit. This is an opportunity either to begin to look forward to Pentecost or to celebrate the Ascension.

Using the lectionary

- Eastertide is a 'closed season' as far as the lectionary is concerned. However, there is an enormous range of choice within the readings provided.
- The readings from Acts are mandatory. Old Testament readings are provided for the whole season, but, if these are used, then the reading from Acts must be the second reading.
- A Gospel reading must be included if the service is eucharistic.
- The following table shows a possible route through Eastertide, taking some of the major themes from the Easter Liturgy and returning to one of them on each of the Sundays.

A Scheme for Eastertide in Year A

Sunday	Theme	Year A readings
Second Sunday of Easter	Water Waters of the Red Sea	**Exodus 14.10-31; 15.20,21** Acts 2.14a,22-32 1 Peter 1.3-9 John 20.19-31
Third Sunday of Easter	Joy 'Sing aloud, O daughter of Zion'	**Zephaniah 3.14-20** Acts 2.14a,36-41 1 Peter 1.17-23 Luke 24.13-35
Fourth Sunday of Easter	Breaking of bread/Eucharist 'they devoted themselves … to the breaking of bread'	Genesis 7 **Acts 2.42-47** 1 Peter 2.19-25 John 10.1-10

Fifth Sunday of Easter	Light 'God called you out of darkness …'	Genesis 8.1-19 Acts 7.55-60 1 Peter 2.2-10 **John 14.1-14**
Sixth Sunday of Easter	Word 'If you love me you will keep my commandments'	Genesis 8.20 – 9.17 Acts 17.22-31 1 Peter 3.13-22 John 14.15-21
Seventh Sunday of Easter (after Ascension)	Meeting Jesus in each other	Ezekiel 36.24-28 Acts 1.6-14 1 Peter 4.12-14; 5.6-11 John 17.1-11
Pentecost	The gift of the Spirit	Numbers 11.24-30 Acts 2.1-21 *or* 1 Corinthians 12.3b-13 John 7.37-39 or 20.19-23

A Scheme for Eastertide in Year B

Sunday	Theme	Year B readings
Second Sunday of Easter	Water Waters of the Red Sea	**Exodus 14.10-31; 15.20,21** Acts 4.32-35 1 John 1.1 – 2.2 John 20.19-31
Third Sunday of Easter	Joy 'Sing aloud, O daughter of Zion'	**Zephaniah 3.14-20** Acts 3.12-19 1 John 3.1-7 Luke 24.36b-48
Fourth Sunday of Easter	Light The rainbow after the flood	**Genesis 7.1-5,11-18; 8.6-18; 9.8-13** Acts 4.5-12 1 John 3.16-24 John 10.11-18
Fifth Sunday of Easter	Breaking of Bread/Eucharist 'Abide in me'	Baruch 3.9-15,32 – 4.4 *or* Genesis 22.1-18 Acts 8.26-40 1 John 4.7-21 **John 15.1-8**
Sixth Sunday of Easter	Word 'My word shall not return to me empty'	**Isaiah 55.1-11** Acts 10.44-48 1 John 5.1-6 John 15.9-17

| Seventh Sunday of Easter (after Ascension) | Meeting Jesus in each other

'Whoever has the Son has life'

Unpacking Ascension as the festival of 'the nearness of Jesus' | Ezekiel 36.24-28
Acts 1.15-17,21-26
1 John 5.9-13
John 17.6-19 |
| Pentecost | The gift of the Spirit | Ezekiel 37.1-14
Acts 2.1-21
Romans 8.22-38
John 15.26-27;
16.4b-15 |

| Seventh Sunday of Easter (after Ascension) | Meeting Jesus in each other | Ezekiel 36.24-28
Acts 16.16-34
Revelation 22.12-14,16-17,20-21
John 17.20-26 |
| Pentecost | The gift of the Spirit | Genesis 11.1-9 *or*
Acts 2.1-21
Romans 8.22-38
John 15.26-27;
16.4b-15 |

A Scheme for Eastertide in Year C

Sunday	Theme	Year C readings
Second Sunday of Easter	Water Waters of the Red Sea	**Exodus 14.10-31;** **15.20,21** Acts 5.27-32 Revelation 1.4-8 John 20.19-31
Third Sunday of Easter	Joy 'Sing aloud, O daughter of Zion'	**Zephaniah 3.14-20** Acts 9.1-6 [7-20] Revelation 5.11-14 John 21.1-19
Fourth Sunday of Easter	Breaking of Bread/Eucharist 'they will hunger and thirst no more'	Genesis 7.1-5,11-18; 8.6-18; 9.8-13 Acts 9.36-43 Revelation 7.9-17 John 10.22-30
Fifth Sunday of Easter	Word 'I give you a new commandment'	Baruch 3.9-15,32 – 4.4 *or* Genesis 22.1-18 Acts 11.1-18 Revelation 21.1-6 John 13.31-35
Sixth Sunday of Easter	Light 'the Lord God will be their light'	Ezekiel 37.1-14 Acts 16.9-15 Revelation 21.10,22–22.5 John 14.23-29 *or* John 5.1-9

A journey of fifty days: Eastertide liturgies

The purpose of *Times and Seasons* is to provide resources to help create a distinctive feel for each season of the year, notably different from ordinary time. We suggest that each season should be markedly different in its:

- liturgical content
- liturgical colour
- music
- atmosphere
- overall tone.

While Eastertide is the most important of all seasons for the Church, hitherto there has been little distinctive material to mark it. That is one of the reasons why the new service of The Stations of the Resurrection in *Times and Seasons* has been so widely welcomed. Additionally, though, by using some of the themes that are both explicit and implicit in the Easter Liturgy, we can make special each of the Sunday services through the Easter season. *Times and Seasons* already incorporates two new services for Ascension and Pentecost, giving each its own distinctive liturgy rather than simply suggesting the change of the odd prayer, reading and or hymn.

Over the seven weeks of Easter, we proclaim the resurrection constantly and focus our hearts on meeting with the risen Jesus in our worship. The hymns of Easter Day should be sung throughout the season; the alleluias should be heard for the full 50 days; the majesty of Easter should be maintained until the Feast of Pentecost. And, as we discovered above, distinctive themes appear each year through the lectionary.

Here we offer at least a fully worked-out Gathering Rite (the beginning of the service lasting up to the Collect of the day) for each of these themes using material drawn from *Times and Seasons*. This simply replaces the ordinary Gathering of *Common Worship*

Eucharist Order 1. In some cases we offer even more, and each can be adapted to suit either a eucharistic service or a Service of the Word. By using these we can make Easter special for more than just one day.

These suggestions form the Practical Inclusive Ideas for all the pathways during Eastertide.

A Gathering Rite and a fully worked-out Service of the Word: The risen Jesus meets us in the waters of baptism

Structure, movement and flow	Words/text	Multisensory	Participation
PREPARATION			
Greeting	Alleluia. Christ is risen. **He is risen indeed. Alleluia.** [T&S 419]		
	The president introduces the liturgy.		
Hymn or song	*During this hymn, the ministers (and the people, if possible, move to the font.)* *(The hymn should, if possible, make reference to the Exodus or at least make a link between resurrection and water. A suggestion is 'Come, ye faithful, raise the strain'.)*	Music (starts here and continues) Music continues seamlessly under the following words, leading directly into the *Kyrie*.	Singing. Movement to font.
Prayers of Penitence	In baptism we died with Christ, so that as Christ was raised from the dead, we might walk in newness of life. Let us receive new life in him as we confess our sins in penitence and faith. *cf Romans 6.4* [T&S 428]	(Font is large and visible.)	

	Like Mary at the empty tomb, we fail to grasp the wonder of your presence. (*sung*) Kyrie eleison: **Kyrie eleison**. Christe eleison: **Christe eleison**. Kyrie eleison: **Kyrie eleison**. Like the disciples behind locked doors, we are afraid to be seen as your followers. (*sung*) Kyrie eleison: **Kyrie eleison**. Christe eleison: **Christe eleison**. Kyrie eleison: **Kyrie eleison**. Like Thomas in the upper room, we are slow to believe. (*sung*) Kyrie eleison: **Kyrie eleison**. Christe eleison: **Christe eleison**. Kyrie eleison: **Kyrie eleison**. [T&S 429 adapted]	While the music continues in the background, the president pours a large quantity of water into the font. Water is clearly visible and audible. The president moves among the congregation, sprinkling them with water from the font. This needs to be a big, visible action, either with an aspergillum or with big branches	The three introductory sentences are led by three different voices (voice-over music).	
	(*Suggested musical setting: John Bell/ Iona.*) *The president prays* God our Father, your gift of water brings life and freshness to the earth; in baptism it is a sign of the washing away of our sins and the gift of life eternal. Sanctify this water, we pray. Renew the living spring of your life within us, that we may be free from sin and filled with your saving health; through Christ our Lord. **Amen.** *A song (e.g. 'River, wash over me') is sung.*	Music continues to this point. People get wet!	People move to places – a 'journey'.	
	The president concludes with this Absolution May the God of love and power forgive you and free you from your sins, heal and strengthen you by his Spirit, and raise you to new life in Christ our Lord. **Amen.** [T&S 430]			

Praise	Jesus Christ is risen from the dead **Alleluia.** He has defeated the powers of death **Alleluia.** Jesus turns our sorrow into dancing. **Alleluia.** He has the words of eternal life. **Alleluia.** [T&S 431]	Might be sung.	Led by members of the congregation (voices from around the building).
Collect	Let us pray. *Silence is kept.* Risen Christ, for whom no door is locked, no entrance barred: open the doors of our hearts, that we may seek the good of others and walk the joyful road of sacrifice and peace, to the praise of God the Father. **Amen.** [CW Additional Collects Easter 2]		
Questions	*What are your questions about the Preparation?*		
LITURGY OF THE WORD			
First reading	*Exodus 14.10-31; 15.20-21* *The passage is read from the Dramatised Bible, using the Praise dialogue as a refrain throughout the narrative.* Jesus Christ is risen from the dead. **Alleluia.** He has defeated the powers of death. **Alleluia.** Jesus turns our sorrow into dancing. **Alleluia.** He has the words of eternal life. **Alleluia.** [T&S 431]	Another possibility is to use film, showing a clip that tells the story of the Exodus. Music follows …	Congregation shares in telling of the Exodus story, and in the Praise dialogue.
Gospel Acclamation	*This Gospel Acclamation is sung (e.g. to Christopher Walker and Fintan O'Carroll's Celtic Alleluia).*		Congregation stands to 'meet the risen Jesus' in the Gospel.

	Alleluia. Alleluia. Alleluia. **Alleluia. Alleluia. Alleluia.** Jesus said, 'All who see the Son and believe in him may have eternal life; and I will raise them up on the last day'. Alleluia. Alleluia. Alleluia. **Alleluia. Alleluia. Alleluia.** [T&S 431 adapted]	The Gospel reader, with cross and lights (and perhaps incense) moves to centre nave. The congregation faces the reader.	
Second reading	*John 20.19-23* When it was evening of that day, the first day of the week, and the doors of the house where the disciples had met were locked for fear of the Jews, Jesus came and stood among them and said, 'Peace be with you!' After he said this, he showed them his hands and his side. Then the disciples rejoiced when they saw the Lord. Jesus said to them, 'Peace be with you! As the Father has sent me, so I send you.' When he had said this, he breathed on them and said to them, 'Receive the Holy Spirit. If you forgive the sins of any, they are forgiven them; if you retain the sins of any, they are retained.'		
Talk	*The talk must make an effective link between the word (predominantly Exodus) and the liturgical action that is to follow, talking about the significance of baptism and the promises made in baptism.*	The talk should have multisensory component.	Should have high participatory value. A recently-baptized person might be asked to reflect on the experience.
Re-affirmation of Baptismal Faith	*Song (e.g. 'Do not be afraid, for I have redeemed you')* *The minister then says to those in the congregation who wish to re-affirm their commitment to Christ* I call upon those who are affirming their baptismal faith to renew their commitment to Jesus Christ. *They respond* **I answer the call of God my creator.** **I trust in Jesus Christ as my Saviour.** **I seek new life from the Holy Spirit.** [CI 203]	During this song a number of people fill bowls with water taken from the font and go to stations around the congregation, enabling people to sign themselves with the cross more easily. Music to continue up to the Lord's Prayer (below).	

	The president says (voice-over) Almighty God, we thank you for our fellowship in the household of faith with all who have been baptized in your name. Keep us faithful to our baptism, and so make us ready for that day when the whole creation shall be made perfect in your Son, our Saviour Jesus Christ. **Amen.** [CI 203] May Christ dwell in your hearts through faith, that you may be rooted and grounded in love and bring forth the fruit of the Spirit. **Amen.** [CI 205]	All members of the congregation are invited to renew their commitment to Christ by going to the water and making the sign of the cross with it on their forehead.	Making the sign of the cross.
Questions	*What are your questions about the Liturgy of the Word and the Re-affirmation of baptismal faith?*		
PRAYERS			
Prayers of Intercession	*The minister explains that members of the congregation are invited to place stones in the bowls according to the prayers they wish to offer. One bowl may be designated for the world, one for the Church, one for those recently baptized/confirmed/ admitted to communion (as appropriate), one for those in special need, one for the departed, etc.*	The bowl carriers (see above) take their bowls of water to a number of places around the church building. The action (and sound) of plain stones in water. Quiet music continues.	Movement. Placing of stones.

	The minister concludes the prayers
	Heavenly Father,
	you have delivered us from the
	    power of darkness
	and brought us into the kingdom of
	    your Son:
	grant that, as his death has recalled
	    us to life,
	so his continual presence in us may
	    raise us to eternal joy;
	through Christ our Lord.
	Amen.
	
	[T&S 432]		

The Lord's Prayer	Rejoicing in God's new creation, as our Saviour taught us, so we pray [DP 268] **Our Father in heaven …**	Music leads into Lord's Prayer (said or sung)	Singing or speaking.
Questions	*What are your questions about the* *Prayers?*		
CONCLUSION			
Hymn	*An Easter hymn is sung. It should be* *long enough to allow movement to* *the font but not over-long.* *It should be an effective sending-* *out' hymn (e.g. 'Good Christians all,* *rejoice and sing!' or 'Thine be the* *glory').*	Singing.	During this hymn, everyone moves to the font – or as near as possible.
Acclamation	Alleluia. Christ is risen. **He is risen indeed. Alleluia, alleluia,** **alleluia.**		
	Praise the God and Father of our Lord Jesus Christ. **He has given us new life and hope** **by raising Jesus from the dead.** God has claimed us as his own. **He has brought us out of darkness.** **He has made us light to the world.** Alleluia. Christ is risen. **He is risen indeed. Alleluia.** [T&S 407]		

Dismissal Gospel	Hear the Gospel of our Lord Jesus Christ according to John. **Glory to you, O Lord.** Jesus said, 'I am the resurrection and the life. Those who believe in me, even though they die, will live, and everyone who lives and believes in me will never die.' *John 11.25-26* This is the Gospel of the Lord. **Praise to you, O Christ.** [T&S 439]		The congregation turns to face the reader of the Gospel
Blessing	Alleluia! Christ is risen. **He is risen indeed.** **Alleluia!** God the Father, by whose love Christ was raised from the dead, open to you who believe the gates of everlasting life. **Amen.** God the Son, who in bursting from the grave has won a glorious victory, give you joy as you share the Easter faith. **Amen.** God the Holy Spirit, who filled the disciples with the life of the risen Lord, empower you and fill you with Christ's peace. **Amen.** [T&S 440]		Each of the versicles might be led by a different voice.
Dismissal	We are raised to new life with Christ. Go in his peace. Alleluia, alleluia. **Thanks be to God. Alleluia, alleluia.** [T&S 440]		All turn to face the door.
Questions	*What are your questions about the Conclusion?*		

A Gathering Rite for the Second Sunday of Easter: The risen Jesus meets us in the joy of the resurrection

Structure, movement and flow	Words/text	Multisensory	Participation
THE GATHERING			
Acclamation	Alleluia. Christ is risen. **He is risen indeed. Alleluia.**		
Hymn	*An Easter hymn of praise is sung.*	The ministers move to their places. If there is a procession it could be led by the Easter Candle.	Visual and sung.
The Greeting	*The president greets the congregation, after which we respond* **And also with you.** Alleluia. Christ is risen. **He is risen indeed. Alleluia.**		
Thanksgiving for the Resurrection	*The president says* Let us bless the Father, the Son, and the Holy Spirit. Let us praise and exalt him for ever. Blessing and honour and glory and power be to him who sits upon the throne and to the Lamb for ever and ever. Amen.	The president could stand by the Easter Candle for this thanksgiving.	Alternatively, if size and architecture allow, the whole congregation could begin at the back, process in behind the candle and gather around the Easter Candle for the whole of the Gathering.

	Great and marvellous are your works, Lord God the almighty; just and true are your ways, King of saints; all glorious your gifts, Spirit of life.		Each of these three verses could be spoken by different sections of the congregation.
	Blessing and honour and glory and wisdom and thanksgiving and honour and power and might be to our God for ever and ever. Amen.		
	O give thanks to the Lord, for he is gracious: **for his mercy endures for ever.**		These responses could be led by different people gathered around the Easter candle or by members of the congregation from their places.
	He has loved us from all eternity: **for his mercy endures for ever.**		
	And remembered us when we were in trouble: **for his mercy endures for ever.**		
	For us and for our salvation he came down from heaven: **for his mercy endures for ever.**		
	He became incarnate of the Holy Spirit and the Virgin Mary and was made man: **for his mercy endures for ever.**		
	By his cross and passion he has redeemed the world: **for his mercy endures for ever.**		
	And has washed us from our sins in his own blood: **for his mercy endures for ever.**		
	On the third day he rose again: **for his mercy endures for ever.**		
	And has given us the victory: **for his mercy endures for ever.**	Incense could be placed on hot charcoal in a large bowl near the Easter Candle.	
	He ascended into heaven: **for his mercy endures for ever.**		
	And opened wide for us the everlasting doors: **for his mercy endures for ever.**		

	He is seated at the right hand of the Father: **for his mercy endures for ever.** And ever lives to make intercession for us: **for his mercy endures for ever.** **Glory to the Father and to the Son and to the Holy Spirit; as it was in the beginning is now and shall be for ever. Amen.** *The president says* Blessing and honour and thanksgiving and praise more than we can utter, more than we can conceive, be to you, O most adorable Trinity, Father, Son, and Holy Spirit, by all angels, all people, all creation, for ever and ever. **Amen. Alleluia.** Alleluia! Christ is risen. **He is risen indeed. Alleluia!** [T&S 421–3 adapted]		
Gloria in Excelsis	*The Gloria is sung as the incense fills the worship area. A metrical version could be sung to a well-known Easter hymn tune such as 'Maccabeus'.*		If the whole congregation has gathered around the Easter Candle, all move to their places during the Gloria or after the Collect.
The Collect			
The service continues with the Liturgy of the Word.			

A Gathering Rite for a Eucharist or a Service of the Word: The risen Jesus meets us in the light of the resurrection

Structure, movement and flow	Words/text	Multisensory	Participation
THE GATHERING			
A hymn or song	*The ministers enter led by the Easter Candle followed by three pairs of people, each pair carrying one smaller, lit candle.* *Sing all but the last verse of the hymn.* *We stop singing before the final verse, though the music continues quietly.*		The idea of having pairs removes the difficulties of reading a text while also carrying an object. If possible each pair should consist of an adult and a child. The child carries the candle and always stands in front of the adult, who reads all the text. The bearer of the Easter Candle moves to a central point at the front, if possible in an elevated position, with the text reader behind or to the side. The three bearers of the smaller candles are spread across the front of the worship area.
The Greeting	Alleluia. Christ is risen. **He is risen indeed. Alleluia.**		
Acclamation	*The first reader for a smaller candle says* Blessed are you, Sovereign God, conqueror of death: your light invades the places of darkness, and restores sight to the blind. **Blessed be God for ever.** *The second reader for a smaller candle says* In the resurrection of Jesus a new world is created where light and life burst forth. **Blessed be God for ever.**		

	The third reader for a smaller candle says A new humanity is clothed with your love and sings with hope of a beauty still to come. **Blessed be God for ever.** *The reader for the Easter Candle says* Joy of those who walk in darkness, destroyer of death, hope of resurrection: Blessed are you, Father, Son and Holy Spirit. **Blessed be God for ever.** *We continue with the final verse of the hymn/song.*		
Prayers of Penitence	Christ our passover lamb has been sacrificed for us. Let us therefore rejoice by putting away all malice and evil and confessing our sins with a sincere and true heart. *1 Corinthians 5.7,8* [T&S 428] *Silence for reflection.* Like Mary at the empty tomb, we fail to grasp the wonder of your presence. *The reader extinguishes the small candle.* Lord, have mercy. **Lord, have mercy.** Like the disciples behind locked doors, we are afraid to be seen as your followers. *The reader extinguishes the small candle.* Christ, have mercy. **Christ, have mercy.**	The bearers of the small candles together with their readers move to different points around the congregation. Each of the three introduces one of the following penitential Kyries. The Kyries may be sung.	This could be said by a member of the congregation from his or her seat.

	Like Thomas in the upper room, we are slow to believe. *The reader extinguishes the small candle.* Lord, have mercy. **Lord, have mercy.** *The president pronounces the Absolution* May the God of love and power forgive you and free you from your sins, heal and strengthen you by his Spirit, and raise you to new life in Christ our Lord. **Amen.** [T&S 429–430]		
Gloria in Excelsis or a hymn of praise	*This begins as soon as the Amen of the Absolution is said, with no introduction.*	As soon as the singing begins the small candles go to the Easter Candle and are relit. Having relit the smaller candles, the Easter Candle surrounded by the three smaller ones (without accompanying readers, who return to their places) moves to the middle of the congregation.	
The Collect	*The president says the Collect of the Day.*	After the Collect has been said the Paschal Candle is placed in its stand and the smaller candles are placed around its base.	
The service continues with the Liturgy of the Word.			

 The risen Jesus meets us in the breaking of the bread

Structure, movement and flow	Words/Text	Multisensory	Participation
THE GATHERING			
Acclamation	Alleluia. Christ is risen. **He is risen indeed. Alleluia.**		

Hymn	An Easter hymn of praise is sung	The ministers move to their places. If there is a procession it should be led by the bread and wine, which are placed near the Easter Candle. It is more appropriate if real bread or matzo is used and if the wine is in a bottle or a transparent flagon.	Visual and sung.
The Greeting	The president greets the congregation, after which we respond **And also with you.** Alleluia. Christ is risen. **He is risen indeed. Alleluia.**		
Presentation of bread and wine	The bread is held up and the bearer says I am the bread of life, anyone who comes to me shall not hunger. **Alleluia. Lord, give us this bread always.** The wine is held up and the bearer says Anyone who believes in me shall never thirst. **Alleluia. Lord, give us this bread always.** Both bearers say together Anyone who eats my flesh and drinks my blood has eternal life, and I will raise them up on the last day. **Alleluia. Lord, give us this bread always.**		
Prayers of Penitence	**We meet to eat your bread of life.** **We meet to drink your cup of salvation.** **Forgive us when our lives deny life and hope.** The bearer of the bread says God our Father, we are sorry for the times when we have used your gifts carelessly, and acted ungratefully.	The 'Lord, have mercy … ' could be sung, in which case the music begins during the pause for reflection.	

	Pause for reflection. *The bearer of the wine says* We belong to a people who are full and satisfied, but ignore the cry of the hungry. Lord, have mercy. **Lord, have mercy.** *The bearer of the bread says* We are thoughtless and do not care enough for the world you have made. Christ, have mercy. **Christ, have mercy.** *The bearer of the wine says* We store up goods for ourselves alone, as if there were no God, no heaven, no resurrection. Lord, have mercy. **Lord, have mercy.** [NP 84 adapted] *The president pronounces the Absolution.*		
Gloria in Excelsis	*The Gloria or a song of praise is sung.*		
The Collect of the Day		The musical theme of the Gloria could continue as the president says the collect.	

The service continues with the Liturgy of the Word.

The bread and wine used in this part of the service should be the bread and wine used for the Eucharist of that day.

 A Gathering Rite and fully worked-out Eucharist that might be used on Easter 6 (Years A and B) and Easter 5 (Year C): The risen Jesus meets us in the Word

Structure, movement and flow	Words/Text	Multisensory	Participation
Before the Service		Two people are invited to carry in the Easter Candle (which leads the procession) and a big Bible or Gospel book.	The markings on the candle and a 'cover' for the Bible could have been prepared by members of the congregation.

THE GATHERING		Visual: once the ministers have entered the worship area the Bible is lifted high and the bearer leads the response.	
	Your word is a lantern to our feet **and a light upon our path.**		Everyone shares in the opening response.
Entrance hymn	*An Easter hymn is sung.*	Visual – ministers enter with candle and Bible held high in procession.	Singing.
Greeting	*The president says* Grace, mercy and peace from God our Father and the Lord Jesus Christ be with you **and also with you.** [T&S 470] Alleluia. Christ is risen. **He is risen indeed. Alleluia.**	Architecture permitting, the procession could stop in the middle of the congregation – people could be encouraged to gather around the Bible.	
Prayer	Blessed are you, Lord our God. How sweet are your words to the taste, sweeter than honey to the mouth. **Blessed be God (for ever).** How precious are your commands for our life, more than the finest gold in our hands. **Blessed be God (for ever).** How marvellous is your will for the world, unending is your love for the nations. **Blessed be God (for ever).** Our voices shall sing of your promises and our lips declare your praise. Blessed be God Father, Son and Holy Spirit. **Blessed be God for ever.** [DP 304 adapted]	The person or people carrying the Bible hold/s it up high and someone next to it leads the following prayer/acclamation.	

Praise	Glory to God in the highest *(or an Easter hymn) is sung. If a version of the Gloria is used, perhaps use a metrical version or a form that is different from the one used in ordinary time.*		Congregational singing.

Collect	*The president introduces a period of silent prayer with the words 'Let us pray' or a more specific bidding.*
	
	The Collect is said
	Risen Christ,
	by the lakeside you renewed your
	  call to your disciples:
	help your Church to obey your
	  command
	and draw the nations to the fire of
	  your love,
	to the glory of God the Father.
	Amen.
	
	[CW: Additional Collects Easter 6]		

Questions	*What are your questions about the Gathering?*		
LITURGY OF THE WORD			
Reading	*One of the readings from the Acts of the Apostles.* *At the end the reader says* This is the word of the Lord. **Thanks be to God.**	The congregation sits down – movement.	This could be read dramatically with congregational participation.
Gradual hymn		The reader picks up the Bible and carries it to the middle of the congregation.	Singing. The whole congregation moves to gather round the Bible for the reading.
Gospel Reading	*The Gospel is announced with the following proclamation* Jesus Christ is risen from the dead. **Alleluia.** He has defeated the powers of death. **Alleluia.** Jesus turns our sorrow into dancing. **Alleluia.** He has the words of eternal life. **Alleluia.** [T&S 340]		Each phrase could be led by members of the congregation. The congregation as a whole participates in the Alleluias.

	Hear the Gospel of our Lord Jesus Christ according to John. **Glory to you, O Lord.** *The Gospel for the day is read* This is the Gospel of the Lord. **Praise to you, O Christ.**		At the end of the reading the congregation returns to places – movement
Sharing	*Instead of a sermon, people could be encouraged to share their favourite Bible passages or stories – or they could be given a list from which to choose.*		
Affirmation of Faith	Let us declare our faith in the resurrection of our Lord Jesus Christ. **Christ died for our sins in accordance with the Scriptures; he was buried; he was raised to life on the third day in accordance with the Scriptures; afterwards he appeared to his followers, and to all the apostles: this we have received, and this we believe. Amen.** *cf 1 Corinthians 15.3-7* [CW 147]	Congregation stands – movement.	The congregation joins in the affirmation of faith.
Questions	*What are your questions about the Liturgy of the Word?*		
PRAYERS			
Prayers of Intercession	*The minister introduces the active prayer* *A chant such as 'O Lord hear my prayer' may be sung.* *When everyone has placed their prayer cards around the Bible, the minister concludes with a short prayer.*	*Drawing, writing, moving*	Through the service the Bible is placed in a prominent position. The congregation may be given cards on which they write or draw subjects for prayer. When they are ready they bring them forward and place them around the Bible.
Questions	*What are your questions about the Prayers?*		

LITURGY OF THE SACRAMENT			
The Peace	God calls us to life. **In his word is our life.** God calls us to peace. **In his word is our peace.** The peace of the risen Lord be with you **and also with you.**	The congregation stands – movement.	The congregation shares in the response.
Hymn			Singing.
Preparation of the Table		Visual – the table may be prepared from scratch with different people bringing in the Altar cloth, candles, corporal, paten, chalice, bread, wine, water, etc.	
The Eucharistic Prayer	*An authorized Eucharistic Prayer is used.*	Visual – actions of the president. By using real bread and glass chalices the congregation can see the eucharistic elements.	The congregation shares in the responses through the prayer. Members of the congregation might learn their own manual action to be used through the prayer.
The Lord's Prayer	Trusting in God's word, let us pray as our Saviour taught us **Our Father …**		The congregation says the prayer.
Breaking of the Bread	The word of God in Scripture has been broken open for us. (Now) … *the president breaks the bread …* We break this bread to share in the body of Christ. **Though we are many, we are one body,** **because we all share in one bread.** [CW 179]	Visual – bread is broken dramatically.	The congregation shares in the response.
Giving of Communion	God's holy gifts for God's holy people. **Jesus Christ is holy,** **Jesus Christ is Lord,** **to the glory of God the Father.** [CW 180]		The congregation shares in the response.

During the Administration	*Songs may be sung.*		Singing.
			The congregation moves to receive communion or a blessing.
			People could be given a paperback copy of one of the Gospels as they return from communion – or a card with a verse on it such as 'Your word is a lantern to our feet and a light upon our path.'
DISMISSAL			
Post-Communion Prayers	*Silence is kept.* **Almighty God,** **we thank you for the gift of your** **holy word.** **May it be a lantern to our feet,** **a light upon our paths,** **and a strength to our lives.** **Take us and use us** **to love and serve all people** **in the power of the Holy Spirit** **and in the name of your Son,** **Jesus Christ our Lord.** **Amen.** [CW 47]		The congregation says the prayer.
Hymn		The ministers move to the door from where the Dismissal Gospel is to be read. The procession may be led by the Easter Candle and the large Bible, which is held high.	The congregation follows and everyone gathers at the exit.

Acclamation	The Word of life which was from the
	     beginning
	 we proclaim to you.
	
	 The darkness is passing away
	 and the true light is already shining;
	 the Word of life which was from the
	     beginning.
	
	 That which we heard, which we saw
	     with our eyes,
	 and touched with our hands,
	 we proclaim to you.
			Members of the congregation could lead the responses and the congregation as a whole shares in the responses.

	For our fellowship is with the Father, and with his Son, Jesus Christ our Lord. **The Word of life, which was from the beginning,** **we proclaim to you.** [CW 47]		
Dismissal Gospel	Hear the Gospel of our Lord Jesus Christ according to John. **Glory to you, O Lord.** Jesus said to the Jews who had believed in him, 'If you continue in my word, you are truly my disciples; and you will know the truth, and the truth will make you free.' *John 8.31-32* This is the Gospel of the Lord. **Praise to you, O Christ.**		Dramatic reading of the Dismissal Gospel with congregational participation.
Blessing	Alleluia. Christ is risen. **He is risen indeed. Alleluia.** May the risen Christ, the Word of God, fill you with boldness to proclaim the gospel; and the blessing …		
Dismissal	Blessed are those who hear the word of God and obey it. Go in the peace of the risen Christ. **Thanks be to God.**		Ministers and congregation leave.
Questions	*What are your questions about the Liturgy of the Sacrament and the Dismissal?*		

 A Gathering Rite for the Seventh Sunday of Easter: The risen Jesus meets us in each other

Structure, movement and flow	Words/Text	Multisensory	Participation
THE GATHERING			
	If possible, the congregation gathers in a room other than the church. If this is not possible, the congregation might gather at the back of the worship area or at the very least people should be encouraged to face the back as the ministers enter.		

	The ministers are led by the Easter Candle which stands as much as is possible in the middle of the gathered people. *Someone in the congregation shouts* Alleluia. Christ is risen. **He is risen indeed. Alleluia.**		
A hymn or a song	*This should be a song emphasizing our togetherness in Christ.*		
The Greeting	*The president says* Grace, mercy and peace from God our Father and the Lord Jesus Christ be with you **and also with you.** [T&S 470] Alleluia. Christ is risen. **He is risen indeed. Alleluia.** *The president may introduce the service*		
The Peace	*The president says* The risen Christ came and stood among his disciples and said, 'Peace be with you.' Then were they glad when they saw the Lord. Alleluia. *John 20.19,20* [T&S 435] The peace of the Lord be always with you **and also with you. Alleluia.**	As the peace is shared a song such as 'Peace is flowing like a river' could be sung.	We greet each other and as much time as possible is allowed for the Peace to be shared.
Prayers of Penitence	*Once people are holding hands a member of the congregation introduces the prayers of penitence, saying* Trusting in God's love for us, and our love for one another, let us dare to call to mind our sins against him, against each other, and against our world.		If possible, members of the congregation hold hands in a large circle or as much as can be approximated given the architecture of the particular building.

	Individuals are encouraged to speak out a word or phrase that speaks of our sin. Words such as Selfishness Arrogance Self-importance *We say together* **Father,** **we have sinned against heaven and against you.** **We are not worthy to be called your children.** **We turn to you again.** **Have mercy on us,** **bring us back to yourself** **as those who once were dead** **but now have life through Christ our Lord.** **Amen.** *cf Luke 15* [CW 127] *The president pronounces the Absolution.*		
		If a song was sung during the sharing of the Peace, it is sung briefly once again after the Absolution.	The Absolution could be marked by each person squeezing the hand of those whose hands they are holding.
Praise	Alleluia. Christ is risen. **He is risen indeed.** **Alleluia, alleluia, alleluia.** Praise the God and Father of our Lord Jesus Christ. **He has given us new life and hope** **by raising Jesus from the dead.** God has claimed us as his own. **He has brought us out of darkness.** **He has made us light to the world.** Alleluia. Christ is risen. **He is risen indeed. Alleluia.** [T&S 407] *We move straight into a hymn or song.*		These acclamations may be led by members of the congregation. During the singing the whole assembly processes into church led by the Easter Candle, which is placed in its usual place at the front of the church.
The Collect of the Day			
The service continues with the Liturgy of the Word.			

Easter:
The Lenten tree pathway

The Lenten tree in groups

Children

There is a session for each of the weeks of Eastertide. The opening part of the session is drawn from Prayer during the Day in Eastertide from *Common Worship: Daily Prayer*. This provides an opportunity for the children to become familiar with some significant liturgical texts used in the familiar setting of their group. This material is suitable for use either on Sunday or during the week. The material provided will last for between 45 minutes and an hour.

Opening part of the meeting (common to every session)

Before the meeting begins, place three small candles and a basket of little Easter eggs (the ones that are about the size of blackbirds' eggs) on a table in the middle of the space where the children gather.

PREPARATION

Make sure there is someone at the door to greet each child on arrival. Ask if they have had a good week and if there is anything special they want to share this week. When individual children are ready to sit down, direct them to join a circle where the leader greets them too and encourages them to join in the discussion of the circle.

OPENING PRAYER

When everyone has arrived, light the first candle.

Let us say thank you to God that Jesus rose from the dead.

Light the second candle.

Let us say thank you to God that the disciples believed and shared the good news.

Light the third candle.

Let us say thank you to God for all the wonderful things we see and hear every day of our lives.

Let us say our opening prayers:
O God, make speed to save us.
O Lord, make haste to help us.

If I climb up to heaven you are there:
If I make the grave my bed, you are there also.

Psalm139.7

[DP 76]

THE WORD OF GOD

PSALM 114

Everyone says the refrain together. The alternate lines of the psalm might be said by two groups or by the leader and then everyone else.

Refrain:
Tremble O earth at the presence of the Lord.

When Israel came out of Egypt,
the house of Jacob from a people of a strange tongue,
Judah became his sanctuary,
Israel his dominion.
The sea saw that, and fled;
Jordan was driven back.
The mountains skipped like rams,
the little hills like young sheep.
What ailed you, O sea, that you fled?
O Jordan, that you were driven back?
You mountains that you skipped like rams,
you little hills like young sheep?
Tremble, O earth at the presence of the Lord,
at the presence of the God of Jacob,
Who turns the hard rock into a pool of water,
the flint-stone into a springing well.
Tremble, O earth, at the presence of the Lord.

[CW 732]

You could sing here a short song that you all know.

PRAYER

Say this prayer together:
Christ yesterday and today,
the beginning and the end,

Alpha and Omega,
all time belongs to you,
and all ages:
to you be glory and power,
through every age and for ever.
Amen.

[DP 79]

Different material for each week

ON OR AFTER EASTER DAY – SYMBOLS: A PICTURE OF THE EMPTY TOMB

THE WORD OF GOD IN THE STORY OF THE RESURRECTION OF JESUS

A member of the group places the picture of the empty tomb between the three candles.

Read or tell the Easter Day Gospel story for whichever lectionary year you happen to be in:

> Year A: Matthew 28.1-10
>
> Year B: Mark 16.1-8
>
> Year C: Luke 24.1-12

In any year, an alternative Gospel is John 20.1-18.

SYMBOLS AND REFLECTION

Think about the story together. You may like to use the four questions used in the Godly Play method of thinking about sacred stories:

> I wonder which part of the story you liked best?
>
> I wonder what was the most important part of the story?
>
> I wonder if there is any part of the story that is about you, or I wonder where you are in the story?
>
> I wonder if there is any part of the story we could leave out and still have all the story we need?

When you have finished wondering together, you could take the container of Easter eggs out of the middle of the circle and invite the children to pass it round and give one to their neighbour, saying 'Alleluia, Christ is risen' as they do so. You should demonstrate with the first child.

ART, CRAFT AND OTHER ACTIVITIES

Invite children to choose what they do to respond to the story. Allow a free choice and make sure you have plenty of paper, paint, clay and so on for them so that they can each choose their own activity.

Invite them to use the ash and sackcloth also if they would like to.

FINAL PRAYER

We all say this Easter prayer together. Use this prayer every week so that, by the end of Easter, the children will know it.

God of glory,
by the raising of your Son
you have broken the chains of death and hell:
fill your Church with faith and hope;
for a new day has dawned
and the way to life stands open
in our Saviour Jesus Christ.
Amen.

[T&S 405]

The Lord's Prayer is said.

THE CONCLUSION

May the risen Christ give us his peace.
Alleluia. Amen.

ON OR AFTER THE SECOND SUNDAY OF EASTER – SYMBOL: A PICTURE OF JESUS AND ST THOMAS

Possibly the best picture to use, which is easily available on the Internet, is Caravaggio's *The Incredulity of St Thomas*. If you feel it is too graphic, there are many others.

A member of the group places the picture the middle of the three candles.

THE WORD OF GOD

Read or tell the Gospel story John 20.19-31. If you feel it is too long, start at verse 24.

SYMBOLS AND REFLECTION

Think about the story together (see suggestions above).

When you have finished wondering together, move straight to the activity time.

ON OR AFTER THE THIRD SUNDAY OF EASTER – SYMBOL: BREAD OR BREAD AND FISH (*DEPENDING ON THE YEAR*)

A member of the group places bread or bread and fish in the middle of the three candles.

THE WORD OF GOD IN THE GOSPEL STORY FOR THE THIRD SUNDAY OF EASTER IN WHICHEVER LECTIONARY YEAR IT IS

Year A: Luke 24.13-35

Year B: Luke 24.36b-48

Year C: John 21.1-19

Think about the story together (see Session 1 for suggestions).

When you have finished wondering together, you could pass the bread around the circle and invite everyone to take a piece and eat it. (Remember to check about food sensitivities before you do this and make sure you have wheat/gluten-free bread available if required.)

Then follow the pattern of Session 1 above.

ON OR AFTER THE FOURTH SUNDAY OF EASTER – SYMBOL: SHEEP

A member of the group places some model or toy sheep in the middle of the three candles. Make sure you have enough for everyone.

THE WORD OF GOD IN THE GOSPEL STORY FOR THE FOURTH SUNDAY OF EASTER IN WHICHEVER LECTIONARY YEAR IT IS.

Year A: John 10.1-10

Year B: John 10.11-18

Year C: John 10.22-30

Think about the story together (see suggestions in Session 1).

Invite each person to take one of the sheep from the table and to hold it, look at it and think of times when they have been lost or afraid and they have been found and made safe.

ON OR AFTER THE FIFTH SUNDAY OF EASTER – SYMBOL: YEAR A, A PATHWAY; YEAR B, A VINE; YEAR C, PICTURE OF A PERSON CARING FOR SOMEONE IN NEED

A member of the group places the picture in the centre of the three candles.

THE WORD OF GOD IN THE GOSPEL STORY FOR THE FIFTH SUNDAY OF EASTER IN THE LECTIONARY FOR THE RELEVANT YEAR

Year A: John 14.1-14

Year B: John 15.1-8

Year C: John 13.31-35

Think about the story together (see suggestions in Session 1).

ART, CRAFT AND OTHER ACTIVITIES

Invite children to choose what they do to respond to the story. Allow a free choice and make sure you have plenty of paper, paint, clay and so on for them so that they can each choose their own activity. Make the figures you have used available.

Then follow the pattern of Session 1 above.

ON OR AFTER THE SIXTH SUNDAY OF EASTER – SYMBOL: A DOVE

A member of the group places a representation of a dove in the middle of the three candles.

THE WORD OF GOD IN THE GOSPEL READING FOR THE SIXTH SUNDAY OF EASTER OF THE RELEVANT YEAR.

Year A: John 14.15-21

Year B: John 15.9-17

Year C: John 5.1-9

Think about the story together (see suggestions in Session 1).

Then follow the pattern of Session 1 above.

ON OR AFTER THE SEVENTH SUNDAY OF EASTER – SYMBOL: A PICTURE OF JESUS PRAYING

A member of the group places a representation of a picture of Jesus praying in the middle of the three candles.

THE WORD OF GOD IN THE GOSPEL READING FOR THE SEVENTH SUNDAY OF EASTER OF THE RELEVANT YEAR.

Year A: John 17.1-11

Year B: John 17.6-19

Year C: John 17.20-26

Think about the story together (see suggestions in Session 1).

ART, CRAFT AND OTHER ACTIVITIES

As for Session 1.

THE CONCLUSION

We all say this prayer together.
Come, O Spirit of God,
and make your home within us.
May our darkness be dispelled by your light,
and our troubles calmed by your peace.
Amen.

[DP 354 adapted]

The Lord's Prayer is said.

May the Holy Spirit of God bless and sanctify us so that we may be consecrated in the truth. Amen.

[DP 354]

On or after Pentecost

Symbol: Pentecost is a significant feast that can sometimes be rather overlooked. Ensure that this does not happen by making it special. Instead of placing a picture on the table, give everyone a sparkler to hold. In party shops you can get little sparklers that are usually used on cakes and are designed for use inside. If you can't get hold of them, or you judge there will be people who will be afraid to hold them, you could use balloons or windmills instead.

The Word of God in the story of Pentecost in Acts 2.1-21

Think about the story together (see suggestions in Session 1).

Then follow the pattern for the Seventh Sunday of Easter (above).

Adults

After Easter – Symbol: The stone

Scripture passage – Mark 16.1-8: The women visit the tomb of Jesus

Read the passage aloud, but try to make sure people can see it either in their own Bibles or on a specially printed sheet.

Allow a short silence for reflection on the reading

Comment

Allow anyone who wishes to offer a question they would like an answer to that emerges from the reading. If possible write them down and then use them in turn as discussion starters.

Symbol and reflection

A member of the group places a large stone in the middle of the three candles.

Each member of the group is invited to reflect on what the stone that was rolled away from the tomb means to them. Each person could ask questions such as:

- How do I respond when I know I need to do something that is going to be difficult for me?
- What happens when I am faced with something so astounding that I cannot comprehend it?
- How do I bear good news?

Those who feel able are invited to share their thoughts with the rest of the group. Be aware that this may stir up some very personal thoughts that people may not want to share, so this part of the exercise should not be forced.

Silence is kept for further reflection.

Comment on the stone

Matthew tells us that the chief priests and the Pharisees, recalling that Jesus had said 'After three days I will rise again', asked that the tomb should be guarded. The stone was sealed and a guard granted. In going to the tomb, therefore, the three women were likely to be kept at a distance and shut out of the tomb. Mark tells us that they were asking themselves how they would enter while Luke says that they had carefully noted the situation of the tomb so that after the Sabbath they could return with the spices. Only Matthew tells us of the earthquake, providing an explanation for the removal of the stone, but all the evangelists tell us that there had been a stone across the entrance to the tomb and that this had moved. Clearly those who went to the tomb (the details vary slightly in the four accounts) were shocked by what they found. The women had gone, in what they recognized was a somewhat vain attempt, to complete the burial ritual. They had been carrying the necessary equipment and, if it was at all possible, were prepared to do the job. They did not expect what had happened. Luke tells us that Peter went to the tomb simply to check that what the women had said was true. No one at all had expected to find the stone had moved. Curiously it was Jesus' enemies who were concerned about his talk of rising: it does not seem to have entered the heads of the various people who went to the tomb.

The stone, the closure of the tomb, marks a decisive end, as the does the closure of any grave, or indeed, the closure of the crematorium curtain. This end is marked by ritual. That is one of the characteristics of being human: even in the most adverse circumstances human beings seek to deal with their dead with dignity and respect. And yet it is not the end, for we continue to remember the dead. The stone marks one kind of end, but an end that is a transformation. The new beginning that is characterized by the resurrection of Jesus marks a radical transformation, perplexing and shocking for the disciples, unexpected and unsought, but initiating a new era in the relationship between God and humanity, assuring us that death is not the end and full of a hope that is eternal.

DISCUSSION

What are your experiences of endings?

Does anyone have the experience of undertaking apparently ridiculous and hopeless missions?

What does the resurrection mean to you? Do you know people whose views are different?

We return to the Office of Prayer …

RESPONSE

A song may be sung or a quiet piece of music played.

Blessed are the peacemakers,
for they will be called children of God.

Matthew 5.9

PRAYER

The leader puts a basket of rough stones onto the table.

Each person takes a stone and holds it in his or her hands.

Some music is played; all present look at the stone they have chosen. They are invited to reflect on what the obstacles to faith are for them at the present time, and what seals their belief.

When the music stops, a short silence is kept.

All say this prayer
Christ yesterday and today,
the beginning and the end,
Alpha and Omega,
all time belongs to you,
and all ages;
to you be glory and power
through every age and for ever.
Amen.

The Lord's Prayer is said.

THE CONCLUSION

May the risen Christ give us his peace.
Alleluia. Amen.

[DP 79]

After Easter 2 – Symbol: The wounds

SCRIPTURE PASSAGE – JOHN 20.34-31: JESUS APPEARS TO THOMAS

Read the following passage aloud, but try to make sure people can see it either in their own Bibles or on a specially printed sheet.

Allow a short silence for reflection on the reading.

COMMENT

Allow anyone who wishes to offer a question they would like an answer to that emerges from the reading. If possible write them down and then use them in turn as discussion starters.

SYMBOL AND REFLECTION

A member of the group places bandages and other medical items on the table.

Each member of the group is invited to reflect on how they regard this encounter between Thomas and the risen Jesus. Each person could ask questions such as:

- When do I need proof?
- Are there limits to my faith? Do I know what they are?
- What helps my faith?

Those who feel able are invited to share their thoughts with the rest of the group. Be aware that this may stir up some very personal thoughts that people may not want to share, so this part of the exercise should not be forced.

Silence is kept for further reflection.

COMMENT ON THE WOUNDS

Thomas does not share the meeting with Jesus that the other disciples experience, and he cannot believe their testimony. He may have felt excluded: the experience of being in a minority of one is not affirming and the testimony of everyone else to something you have missed can be irritating to say the least. Faith flourishes in community; without community it can falter. Thomas may well have reprimanded himself that he had missed such an important event. Yet when Jesus appears he does not pursue the need for the proof that he had so boldly stated that he required. In response to the risen Christ he makes a profound confession of faith in the divinity of his master: 'My Lord and my God!' Thomas may have been wounded by his exclusion, but his apparently macabre demand to see proof of Christ's journey through death by touching the wounds inflicted by his suffering all come to nothing when he actually encounters his risen master.

DISCUSSION

Today we are bombarded with images of violence, wounding and death. This happens not just to those who choose to watch horrendous films but to all who watch the TV news or read the paper. It is not something that we can opt out of. Nor do we have the luxury of being unaware, as was perhaps the case in earlier generations. Thomas thought that witnessing the wounds of Christ would be the proof he needed, but in the event it proved to be the encounter with the person he loved that provoked the act of faith. What does that have to say to us today?

We return to the Office of Prayer ...

RESPONSE

A song may be sung or a quiet piece of music played.

Blessed are the peacemakers,
for they will be called children of God.

Matthew 5.9

PRAYER

The leader puts a variety of pictures of Jesus on the table, and a basket of nails.

Each person chooses a picture and takes a nail and holds them in his or her hands.

Some music is played as each person looks at the picture he or she has chosen. They are invited to reflect on what helps their belief that Jesus is Lord and God and how that influences their response to the wounded in body, mind and spirit.

When the music stops a short silence is kept.

Conclude the session by following the pattern under 'Prayer' on p. 201.

After Easter 3 – Symbol: The journey

SCRIPTURE PASSAGE – LUKE 24.13-35: ON THE ROAD TO EMMAUS

Read the passage aloud, but try to make sure people can see it either in their own Bibles or on a specially printed sheet.

Allow a short silence for reflection on the reading

COMMENT

Allow anyone who wishes to offer a question they would like an answer to that emerges from the reading. If possible, write them down and then use them in turn as discussion starters.

SYMBOL AND REFLECTION

A member of the group places walking sticks or walking boots (or other items symbolizing a walk) and some bread on the table.

Each member of the group is invited to reflect on how they regard this encounter between the two travellers and the risen Jesus. Each person could ask questions such as:

- How do you respond when you are joined unexpectedly by a stranger?
- How do you find detailed explanations of things you are puzzling about?
- Have you ever invited a complete stranger into your home?

Those who feel able are invited to share their thoughts with the rest of the group. Be aware that this may stir up some very personal thoughts that people may not want to share, so this part of the exercise should not be forced.

Silence is kept for further reflection.

COMMENT ON THE EMMAUS JOURNEY

This is not a story just about Jesus. All the resurrection appearances describe encounters between the risen Jesus and those who recognize him and we see that an encounter with the risen Christ, on each occasion, requires an act of recognition. It is not immediately obvious who this person is. In the account of the walk to Emmaus, Jesus joins the two people on their journey, but it is they who extend the hospitality. First they share their anxieties with Jesus, then they listen to what he has to say. It seems to be an extended and demanding explanation: 'Then beginning with Moses and all the prophets, he interpreted to them the things about himself in all the scriptures.' Still they do not recognize the person who is with them. It is only when they reach their destination and sit down to eat that they recognize Jesus as he breaks the bread. It is not all the action of Jesus that brings this about: the travellers are vital in the process: if they had not invited Jesus in, presumably they would not then have had the opportunity to recognize him. Hospitality is a key Christian value as, indeed, it is a Jewish one. Again and again, throughout the Hebrew Scriptures, we read of revelation in response to hospitality. A feature of several of the resurrection appearances as Jesus appears to groups of gathered friends, it is clearly the key to this one. The two travellers welcome the stranger to walk with them, they attend to what he has to say and then they invite him to share their accommodation and their meal.

DISCUSSION

How do we practise hospitality?

How do we each respond to the stranger in our midst?

What opportunities does this offer to us?

What do you feel about the possibility of 'entertaining angels unawares'?

We return to the Office of Prayer …

RESPONSE

A song may be sung or a quiet piece of music played.

Blessed are the peacemakers,
for they will be called children of God.

Matthew 5.9

PRAYER

Some music is played and the bread is passed around the group, each person giving his or her neighbour a piece. No words are necessary. All are invited to reflect on encounters with others that have led them to a deeper understanding of their relationship with Jesus.

When the music stops a short silence is kept.

Conclude the session by following the pattern under 'Prayer' on p. 201.

After Easter 4 – Symbol: The Shepherd

SCRIPTURE PASSAGE – JOHN 10.1-18: THE GOOD SHEPHERD

Read the passage aloud, but try to make sure people can see it either in their own Bibles or on a specially printed sheet.

Allow a short silence for reflection on the reading

COMMENT

Allow anyone who wishes to offer a question they would like an answer to that emerges from the reading. If possible, write them down and then use them in turn as discussion starters.

SYMBOL AND REFLECTION

A member of the group places a shepherd's crook or a walking stick and some toy sheep or a cuddly lamb on the table. A picture of Jesus the Good Shepherd would also be appropriate.

Each member of the group is invited to reflect on this reading. Each person could ask questions such as:

- Have I watched a shepherd working with his sheep, and what have I noticed?
- Can I imagine the presence of the wolf among the flock?
- Which 'figures of speech' about Jesus are the most powerful for me?

Those who feel able are invited to share their thoughts with the rest of the group. Be aware that this may stir up some very personal thoughts that people may not want to share, so this part of the exercise should not be forced.

Silence is kept for further reflection.

COMMENT ON THE GOOD SHEPHERD

Although they do not describe resurrection appearances, it has become customary on the fourth Sunday of Easter to have readings from John 10 where Jesus talks of being the Good Shepherd. The image of God as a shepherd caring for his sheep is strong in the Old Testament: we find it in the Psalms (23 and 80), in Jeremiah 23 and in Ezekiel in chapters 34 and 36. In William Temple's translation and commentary on St John's Gospel he points out that the particular meaning of 'good' in this context is 'beautiful', so he writes verse 11 as 'I am the shepherd, the beautiful one.'[4] In the time of Jesus, shepherds would bring in their sheep to the fold for the night, and in the morning each shepherd would call out his own sheep by name and lead them to pasture. The good shepherd, the beautiful one, was the one who knew his sheep intimately, by name. He knows their particular needs, he knows their strengths and weaknesses. He knows when they are present and when they are missing. In following Jesus, we become like him. We need to know one another's needs, to rescue one another when we falter and fall. We will make God known by what we do rather than by what we say. In the resurrection, God takes us beyond words, to the experience of a new life, the manifestation of something very beautiful.

DISCUSSION

How do you recognize the call of the Good Shepherd?

Why do you follow him?

What do you feel about the idea of Jesus as 'the beautiful one'?

We return to the Office of Prayer …

RESPONSE

A song may be sung or a quiet piece of music played.

Blessed are the peacemakers,
for they will be called children of God.

Matthew 5.9

PRAYER

Some music is played and all stand in a circle, holding hands if this is appropriate. Be aware of the person on each side of you: what are their needs that you might meet and what can you accept from them?

When the music stops, a short silence is kept.

Conclude the session by following the pattern under 'Prayer' on p. 201.

After Easter 5 – Symbol: The net

SCRIPTURE PASSAGE – JOHN 21.1-14: THE MIRACULOUS CATCH OF FISH

Read the following passage aloud, but try to make sure people can see it either in their own Bibles or on a specially printed sheet.

Allow a short silence for reflection on the reading.

COMMENT

Allow anyone who wishes to offer a question they would like an answer to that emerges from the reading. If possible, write them down and then use them in turn as discussion starters.

SYMBOL AND REFLECTION

A member of the group places a fishing net, or something to symbolize a fishing net, on the table. If you can't get real fishing net, use some garden netting. If you are really pushed, a satsuma net bag would do.

Each member of the group is invited to reflect on this reading. Each person could ask questions such as:

- Have I been quick to recognize the work of God when others haven't?
- Have I been slow to recognize the work of God when others have readily seen it?
- Why did the disciples not mention that they knew it was Jesus?

Those who feel able are invited to share their thoughts with the rest of the group. Be aware that this may stir up some very personal thoughts that people may not want to share, so this part of the exercise should not be forced.

Silence is kept for further reflection.

COMMENT ON THE APPEARANCE ON THE SEA OF TIBERIAS

The disciples have returned to their own occupation, fishing. They are at work in the way that they had been accustomed, and on this occasion they had not had much luck. Has this three-year career break meant that their skills need honing again? It is Peter who recognizes Jesus first – as it was he who first believed the evidence of the resurrection on Easter morning. Impetuously he jumps into the water and sets off for the shore, leaving his colleagues to deal with burgeoning net. When they arrive with it, there is already fish to eat on the beach – the Lord will provide. And, although the net is full, it does not break: God is always generous, but he never gives us more than we can manage.

So often Jesus appears to us in what we know well; in what is routine. And sometimes it is difficult for us to recognize what is going on.

DISCUSSION

Are we like Peter, the first to recognize, but then forgetting the needs of those around us?

Or like the others, plodding on with whatever there is to be done and recognizing only slowly, but nevertheless open in the end?

And which is the better way? Or does it depend on who we are?

We return to the Office of Prayer …

RESPONSE

A song may be sung or a quiet piece of music played.

Blessed are the peacemakers,
for they will be called children of God.

Matthew 5.9

PRAYER

Some music is played. Pray that you will recognize the presence of the risen Christ and be ready to lead others to him.

When the music stops a short silence is kept.

Conclude the session by following the pattern under 'Prayer' on p. 201.

After Easter 6 – Symbol: The Paraclete

SCRIPTURE PASSAGE – JOHN 14.15-21 JESUS PROMISES THE HOLY SPIRIT

Read the following passage aloud, but try to make sure people can see it either in their own Bibles or on a specially printed sheet.

Allow a short silence for reflection on the reading.

COMMENT

Allow anyone who wishes to offer a question they would like an answer to that emerges from the reading. If possible write them down and then use them in turn as discussion starters.

SYMBOL AND REFLECTION

A member of the group puts onto the table a picture of the Ten Commandments and a dove.

Each member of the group is invited to reflect on this reading. Each person could ask questions such as:
* How do I keep the commandments?
* How do we know the Spirit of truth?
* How does the Holy Spirit act as an advocate (or defender) for us?

Those who feel able are invited to share their thoughts with the rest of the group. Be aware that this may stir up some very personal thoughts that people may not want to share, so this part of the exercise should not be forced.

Silence is kept for further reflection.

COMMENT ON THE APPEARANCE OF THE PARACLETE: THE HOLY SPIRIT, ADVOCATE AND GUIDE

Those familiar with the Eucharist in *The Book of Common Prayer* will remember the Comfortable Words: 'Hear what St John says: "If anyone does sin, we have an advocate (parakletos) with the Father, Jesus Christ the righteous" (1 John 2.1).

The sixth Sunday of Easter represents a marker in the season as we move towards the parting of Christ from the apostles and the coming of the Spirit. Although Pentecost itself is a great and dramatic occasion, it marks the fulfilment of a promise and the beginning of a new era. Jesus is no longer bodily present with the disciples but everyone knows now that this is a story that will run, and they are becoming aware of just how that will be possible.

Parakletos, a Greek word for 'Spirit', means literally 'one who is called or appealed to'. He is the defender, 'the advocate'. Another word sometimes used is 'counsellor'. This term enables us to see the relationship between Christ's action and that of the Holy Spirit. In the upper room, on the eve of his passion, Jesus announced the coming of the Holy Spirit: 'The Father will give you another advocate.' Jesus is the first Paraclete, the first advocate or defender. The Holy Spirit's action will be like his and will continue his work.

The advocate (defender) defends us from the penalty due for our sins, and saves us from the danger of losing eternal life. This was the work of Jesus and the Holy Spirit is called the Paraclete because he continues Christ's redemptive work that freed us from the consequences of sin.

But there is more than this. Jesus is assuring the apostles that the Holy Spirit will be their advocate-defender and so the advocate-defender of all those down through the centuries who will be the heirs of their witness. 'They will hand you over to councils … you will be dragged before governors and kings … When they hand you over, do not worry about how you are to speak or what you are to say … for it is not you who speak, but the Spirit of your Father speaking through you' (Matthew 10.17-20).

DISCUSSION

What challenges do we face in keeping Jesus' commandments?

How are we aware of the Spirit?

Do we think of the Spirit as our 'defender'?

We return to the Office of Prayer …

RESPONSE

A song may be sung or a quiet piece of music played.

Blessed are the peacemakers,
for they will be called children of God.

Matthew 5.9

PRAYER

Some music is played. Pray that you may know the comfort of the Holy Spirit and that you will be open to the Spirit's guidance.

When the music stops a short silence is kept.

Conclude the session by following the pattern under 'Prayer' on p. 201.

After Easter 7 – Symbol: Christ in majesty

SCRIPTURE PASSAGE – JOHN 17.1-11: JESUS PRAYS FOR HIMSELF AND HIS FOLLOWERS

Read the passage aloud, but try to make sure people can see it either in their own Bibles or on a specially printed sheet.

Allow a short silence for reflection on the reading.

COMMENT

Allow anyone who wishes to offer a question they would like an answer to that emerges from the reading. If possible, write them down and then use them in turn as discussion starters.

SYMBOL AND REFLECTION

A member of the group puts a picture of Christ in Majesty on the table. A good source of images is www.textweek.com.

- What is my experience of something that is glorious?
- How do I imagine Christ glorified?
- How do we give glory to God?

Those who feel able are invited to share their thoughts with the rest of the group. Be aware that this may stir up some very personal thoughts that people may not want to share, so this part of the exercise should not be forced.

Silence is kept for further reflection.

COMMENT ON CHRIST IN MAJESTY

In the time between Ascension and Pentecost things move quickly. Jesus leaves the apostles. It is a departure at once sad and exciting. The Master is no longer with them, yet he is in glory and the next stage of the adventure is about to begin. Adventures are both exciting and scary. In fact sometimes they are only exciting after they have been scary, and maybe there is something of this for the apostles at this time.

The word 'glory' runs through the Gospel accounts like a golden thread. Simeon, in Luke 2, declares that Jesus will be 'the glory of your people Israel'. William Temple[5] suggested that John 17 'is, perhaps, the most sacred passage in the four Gospels – the record of the Lord's prayer of self dedication as it is lived in the memory and imagination of His most intimate friend'.

Yet reading this chapter is not easy. There are beautiful words and a tenderness that is testimony not just to the intimacy between Jesus and the beloved disciple but between Jesus and the Father. In many translations it has been titled 'The Prayer of Jesus'. It is an outpouring of Jesus' heart to his Father in the last hours before his arrest. Yet what is he saying? Perhaps it is more rewarding to listen to this as poetry. And perhaps, too, it begins to be unpacked when we look at it alongside a picture of Christ in Majesty.

Long before pictures of Christ on the cross were regular features of Christian art, Christ in Majesty decorated churches. Christ in glory was the most common image carved over the west doors of churches until the diversity that emerged in the Gothic period. The oldest images of Christ as king are from the fourth century and mirror portrayals of the Emperor, with his court. Here the court is the saints, often represented primarily by the four evangelists. The head of Christ is surrounded by a halo and his hand is usually raised in blessing. Often he sits among the stars, for he is one with creation, glorious before the world began. So, in listening to these words, and hearing them read aloud is probably the best way to encounter them, we may do well to look too at a picture that will help to lift them off the page, and direct us, too, to heaven.

DISCUSSION

What do you like best about this prayer of Jesus?

How might we better glorify God?

We return to the Office of Prayer …

RESPONSE

A song may be sung or a quiet piece of music played.

Blessed are those who mourn,
for they will be comforted.

Matthew 5.4

PRAYER

Spend some time listening to some music while looking at the image of Christ in Majesty that you have chosen. Appropriate music would be a setting of the Gloria in excelsis or the Te Deum.

When the music stops a short silence is kept.

All say this prayer
O King enthroned on high,
Comforter and Spirit of truth,
you that are in all places and fill all things,
the treasury of blessings and giver of life,
come and dwell with us,
cleanse us from every stain
and save our souls, O gracious one.
Amen.

[DP 84]

The Lord's Prayer is said.

THE CONCLUSION

May the grace of the Holy Spirit enlighten our hearts and minds.
Alleluia. Amen.

The Lenten tree at home

As in Lent, create a special space in your home to become a prayer focus for the whole household. You could transform your Lenten cross into an Easter cross by the addition of flowers and Easter eggs. A candle could be placed there to be lit each day when the household gathers for Easter prayers. It might also be the centrepiece of the dining table if the household eats together. You could share pieces of Easter egg after the prayers on each occasion. You might keep this all fresh by looking out for the first newly emerged leaves and flowers from trees and bushes as they come into leaf and blossom as spring progresses. People might like to tell one another where they found their leaves and flowers. You could try to identify what they are: you might even keep a diary and compare it from year to year, if this way of praying becomes a custom in your household. 'The Eighth Day of Creation' is a phrase sometimes used to describe Easter – the day of resurrection, the day of fresh beginnings, the day of new creation. The New Zealand hymn writer Shirley Erena Murray, says in her hymn, 'Because you live, O Christ', that 'the garden of the world has' once more 'come to flower'.[6] At a time when we are so conscious of the fragility of the world and its resources, this may be a helpful way of tying in this awareness with the rejoicing of the Easter season.

Here is a very short order for prayer around the transformed Easter cross.

Short prayer around the Easter cross

When everyone is ready, a candle may be lit.

Blessed are the peacemakers
for they will be called children of God.

Matthew 5.9

The reading for the day is read

Signs of new life

Signs and pictures of new life may be placed around the cross. People may talk about where they found these; flowers and leaves can be identified; dates might be recorded.

Prayer

Someone asks
Who is in our thoughts today?
Names or situations are mentioned.

Silence is kept as we share our thoughts about them with God.

We say The Lord's Prayer
Our Father …

Someone says
May the risen Christ give us his peace.
Alleluia. Amen.

The Lenten tree in outreach

An interactive Easter garden

Make an outside Easter garden and make it as attractive and intriguing as possible. Imagine the significance of placing a resurrection garden in a graveyard! And even if you do not have a graveyard, the presence of a living, growing garden with which people are invited to interact will be very significant.

One of the advantages of a garden outside is that living plants (as opposed to cut flowers) do well in it (which they tend not to in a church because the lack of light eventually makes them wilt and go pale and 'leggy'). Invite people to bring plants in pots to plant in it and encourage them to undertake the planting themselves. (Remember that tender house plants might be affected by frost early in the season but, in an interactive garden, people can plant things for a while and then replace them with something else.) You might like to include a solar-powered fountain or waterfall: these are now available from DIY and garden centres at a relatively modest cost. You could grow some summer herbs and invite people to help themselves as they need them. Keep the garden constantly fresh and changing. If you prepare early, this could be done by using a sequence of bulbs in pots that flower at different times over the spring and early summer. Add them and take them away as they come into flower and fade. Perhaps you could invite different community groups to do

this. You might also like to add representations of various resurrection accounts. Sometimes churches have Easter garden figures that are put into a scene beside the tomb, but you could extend this idea so that, after the tomb, you create the walk to Emmaus; Thomas and Jesus; scenes on the beach and so on, moving towards the Ascension and then Pentecost. The constantly changing scenes again emphasize the growing, dynamic aspects of the resurrection and its location within a dynamic creation.

You might like to create an explanatory leaflet to accompany your garden, which can be left beside it, either for people to read in situ, or to take away. Even if it is outside, this is possible: simply laminate those to be left outside. You might also like to ask people to respond to it and leave behind their responses to share.

Easter:
The Head, hands and heart pathway

Head, hands and heart in groups

Children

The following materials are all based around post-resurrection encounters with Jesus. The overall aim is to provoke some thinking about what the encounters show us about Jesus and ourselves and to look at what the characters learned from their meeting with Jesus. These are all great stories of post-resurrection appearances. There is a wealth of detail in the accounts and the writers are keen to emphasize the bodily resurrection of Jesus – details such as his invitation to Thomas to touch his wounds; his request for food; the sharing of supper at Emmaus, all show that this is not a ghost but flesh and blood.

The telling of these stories is important. You will need to work carefully with the text and may wish to create dramatized versions of the texts for reading aloud. *The Storyteller Bible* by Bob Hartman and *The Book of Books* by Trevor Dennis both published by Lion are very good resources to help with the storytelling for these sessions. Both these books allow the stories to speak for themselves whilst presenting the text in an engaging and rich way. *The Miracle Maker* also gives powerful renditions of some of these passages of Scripture. There are valuable materials on the encounters between Jesus and Mary, and Jesus and Thomas in *The Life of Jesus Through the Eyes of an Artist* images and *The Life of Jesus Through the Eyes of an Artist Teacher's Guide* (see Resources, p. 240). The *Teacher's Guide* uses the images as a way in to reflection on the incidents in the Gospels and gives ideas for a session based around the image.

Each session outline contains suggested introductory materials, talking points and some suggestions for activity and/or prayer and worship.

Session 1

Character: **Mary**

Theme: **Surprise**

Senses: **Hearing and touch**

Bible: **John 20.1-18**

INTRODUCTORY MATERIALS

This meeting between Mary and Jesus is high in shock value! Mary goes to the garden in the early morning expecting to spend time crying at the tomb of Jesus, no doubt remembering all that has happened in the last few days. She is weeping and in grief. She finds that the stone across the tomb has been rolled away and, not only that, but two angels stand guard over an empty space. She must have been terrified – for a start it looked as if grave robbers had been at work and what's more – why these strange heavenly beings? Then she meets someone she thinks is the gardener who tells her that Jesus is not there. He calls her by name and suddenly she realizes who it is – Jesus himself.

Nothing is as it should be in this story. Mary believes she will never see Jesus again and then she meets him in the garden. The tomb should have been closed up but Mary finds that the stone has been rolled away from the entrance; crying turns into laughter; the gardener turns out to be Jesus; Jesus is back but can't be held on to; things are back to normal – but then everything is changed.

You might like to look at *The Miracle Maker* by Murray Watts which tells this story beautifully and with imagination (see Resources, p. 240).

TALKING POINTS

Talk about names
- How did you get your name – who chose it and why?
- Does your name have a special meaning?

Talk about baptism
- We are given a name in this service – why do you think this happens?
- How important is it that God knows us by name?

Talk about how people use names
- Proper names such as on a list or register;

- Nicknames
- The name your mum calls you when you are in trouble – Andrew rather than Andi;
- Pet names/family names – Boo; Buster; Toots, etc.
- The names boyfriends and girlfriends call each other – honeybun, etc.

In the garden Jesus just says 'Mary' – how did she know it was him from just this one word?

Here you might like to use 'A death rewound', from *Telling the Bible Stories and Readings for Sharing Aloud* (see Resources, p. 240).

The Bible talks a lot about how important we are to God – you might like to look at Psalm 139 or Isaiah 43.1: 'I have called you by name, you are mine.'

We also read that the hairs of our head are numbered.

The meetings Jesus has with individuals after the resurrection are all very personal moments where, if you like, he calls people by name and says something particular to each one.

WORSHIP

YOU WILL NEED

- An icon or picture of Christ displayed on a suitable stand with candles at either side of it.
- Non-toxic paints to make handprints.
- Wipes to remove spare paint from hands.
- Wallpaper lining paper on a roll.

WHAT TO DO

Place an icon of Christ or an image of the risen Christ centrally and lay out a long strip of lining paper in front of it.

Explain that we are loved by God and that God calls us by name to be a part of his life.

Our names are very personal to us and so are our handprints – so as a sign of us saying yes to God's love we are going to offer our handprints.

Everyone is invited to come and place a handprint on the paper. Position a helper at each side of the space to wipe the spare paint off hands when the prints have been made.

Read Isaiah 43.1-3

Invite the members of the group to place their handprints on the paper.

Sing a song together.

Say The Grace together.

Session 2

Character:	**Thomas**
Theme:	**Doubt**
Senses:	**Touch**
Bible:	**John 20.19-29**

INTRODUCTORY MATERIALS

Poor Thomas! He gets a bad name – we use the expression 'doubting Thomas' when we talk about people who never believe anything even when the evidence is right under their noses. Poor Thomas! He heard that Jesus was alive but he wanted to see Jesus with his own eyes. Second-hand experiences did not seem good enough for Thomas – perhaps it was that he loved Jesus so much that he did not want to believe that Jesus was alive if there was any possibility that it was not really true. Sometimes we understand things about God and then we forget them. Sometimes we feel that God is so close and then at other times we feel a long way away from God. Perhaps we have things in common with Thomas – other people's stories and other people's experiences of Jesus can't replace our own. Thomas also teaches us that asking questions and not knowing are an important part of relationship with Jesus – just as much as feeling certain about things is. Some people seem to be full of new experiences of God and seem to know what God wants them to do. And other people find it very difficult to be certain.

TALKING POINTS

- Have you ever had the experience of hearing about something and not quite believing that it was true? What was this experience and what happened?
- In church we speak as though things are obvious and true – is this our experience all the time?
- What about Thomas – can we feel sympathetic towards him?
- Jesus doesn't criticize Thomas for saying what he said – is it possible that doubt can help us to become stronger in our faith?
- Jesus doesn't give an easy answer to Thomas either, nor does he say stop doubting and get on with it! Instead he shows him his hands and invites him to reach out and touch.

- Jesus shows Thomas his wounded hands – how easy is it to imagine that these wounds are part of the God we know?

You might like to reflect on these ideas with the group – the theology is deep but important:
- Is it important to believe in a God who suffers – why?
- What difference do you think that this meeting made to Thomas?
- John's Gospel does not tell us that Thomas actually reached out and put his hand into the side of Jesus or felt the hands of Jesus – instead John tells us that Thomas expressed his belief. Maybe Thomas needed a personal encounter of his own with Jesus – he didn't just want to rely on what other people said. How easy is it to go along with other people's view of Jesus and how important is it to find our own meeting place with Jesus?
- Where is this place for each of us?

WORSHIP

YOU WILL NEED
- *The Creation of Adam* by Michelangelo as a focus for worship.
- A version of the image that gives a detail showing only the hand of God and the hand of Adam reaching out towards each other and with a small gap between the outstretched fingers. Place this image centrally as a focal point.

WHAT TO DO

Invite the group to look carefully at the picture and explore with them the fingers reaching and reaching and the longing to touch. Explore the presence of a gap between the fingers – no one is pulling the other; there is no force except the longing to reach the other.

Explore the idea that this is what friendship is like; that this is what love is like; and that this is what faith is like.

PRAYERS

Thank you God that you speak to us clearly
and thank you that sometimes we hear your voice in whispers and in silence.

Thank you that you come close to us
and thank you that you leave us the space to make

up our own minds to follow you.

Thank you that you are found when we have faith and thank you that you walk with us even when we feel alone and lose sight of you.

Thank you that you answer our questions and thank you that we never get to the end of all that there is to know about you.

Thank you for what we know of your love and thank you for all that we have yet to find out …
Amen.

Session 3

Characters:	**The disciples by the sea**
Theme:	**Recognition**
Sense:	**Sight and taste**
Bible:	**John 21.1-14**

INTRODUCTORY MATERIALS

This story starts as the disciples go fishing – a normal activity for them. However, they do not catch any fish. Jesus is standing on the beach but the disciples do not recognize him. He tells them to cast the net over the other side of the boat – and they catch so many fish that they can hardly pull the net in. On the shore Jesus has got a fire going and asks them for some of the fish and then he invites them to have breakfast. Then he gives them bread and fish to eat.

TALKING POINTS
- Clearly Jesus is not a ghost – he is eating breakfast. This is important because there would have been stories at the time that Jesus was not really alive – it was just a ghost dreamed up by desperate disciples.
- Can you think of another occasion when Jesus gives people bread and fish to eat?
- You might want to refer to this story in John 6 or another Gospel. Meals are very important to Jesus – he ate with his disciples, he ate with his enemies; he ate with people as a sign of inclusion and forgiveness. Jesus told stories about meals such as the Great Banquet and the Prodigal Son.
- Here Jesus meets with the disciples as they are going about their daily work – and he makes the experience something unusual. Have we had experiences when Jesus has changed our experience of daily life?

- What does it mean when we say that Jesus feeds us today – how and where?
- How are we fed in our faith by friends and by the church?
- Talk about the fish as a symbol for Christ himself and how we can see this story as a way of Jesus telling his disciples that all would be well and that he would feed them with himself.

WORSHIP

YOU WILL NEED

- A holding cross for each member of the group (see Resources, p. 241).
- A central cross as a focus for worship, displayed on red fabric.
- A recording of 'The King of love my shepherd is' or copies of Psalm 23 to read together.

WHAT TO DO

Play a recording of 'The King of love my shepherd is' or read Psalm 23 together.

What does it mean to you/me that God 'spreads a table for us'? (You might like to think about this in the context of special meals and there are also links to be made with the Eucharist.)

If you are familiar with working with Godly Play, you might like to work with the Good Shepherd. This is particularly pertinent if you are using this session where the lectionary reading provides a focus on 'I am the Good Shepherd'.

Invite the members of the group to take the cross in their hands and to feel the shape and the texture of the wood.

PRAYERS

Lord Jesus,
we thank you that you died for us;
we thank you that you were raised from the dead
*   and that you are with us always.*

Hold on to us when we are feeling lost and alone;
speak to us when we need to know where to go;
touch our lives with your presence
and help us to look for you and to find you every day
*   of our lives.*

Sing a suitable song together.

End by saying The Grace.

Session 4

Character:	**Peter**
Theme:	**Forgiveness**
Sense:	**Heart and mind**
Bible:	**John 21.15-19**

INTRODUCTORY MATERIALS

This meeting is quiet and almost private. Earlier, Peter let Jesus down badly. He was in a yard in the evening after following events as Jesus was arrested and tried. He was following but maybe he was also keeping his distance. Maybe he was just plain scared! When a serving girl asks him if he was a follower of Jesus he says no. He says 'no!' three times. After all his promises to follow Jesus, after everything he had said about being there for Jesus – events proved that he was all talk! In this meeting after the resurrection, Jesus comes up to Peter and says 'Do you love me?' and Peter says 'Yes' – three times! So each time he says yes it makes up for the time he said no earlier. Peter goes on to be vital to the Church as it grows and spreads. So important that he lives up to his name – Peter, the rock.

This meeting then transforms Peter's life. He was no doubt feeling depressed and guilty – after all, he did love Jesus. Jesus though knows how to forgive and how to set Peter free to go on to do what he was made for. Peter probably always remembered this moment and I wonder if it changed his relationships with other people who made the same mistakes …

TALKING POINTS

- Have you ever let someone down?
- Have you ever been let down by someone?
- What do these experiences feel like?
- How do people respond when someone lets them down? (You might like to explore a range of possibilities here – getting angry; punching people – or other violence; never speaking to the person again, etc.).
- Talk about how surprising and odd the reactions and responses of Jesus are to Peter. Jesus doesn't go over old ground or go on and on about how hurt or let down he felt – he simply gives Peter the chance to replace the no with a yes and then Peter goes on from this point to help build the Church.
- How important are second chances?
- Should we give other people second chances or not? Why?

- What is challenging for us about this meeting between Peter and Jesus?

WORSHIP

YOU WILL NEED

- Some stones – enough for each person in the group to have one.
- A small table on which will be placed a piece of cloth and a bowl (see below).
- A large bowl of water. This needs to be large and deep enough so that when all the stones are dropped into the water, the water does not spill over the top. You will need to experiment with this at home before doing it in worship!
- Some blue cloth on which to place the bowl. A clear bowl is good for this as the stones can be seen clearly on the bottom after they have been dropped into the water.

WHAT TO DO

Invite all present to choose a stone.

Invite them to hold the stone in their hand.

Talk about the stone and invite the holders to think about the shape, texture and the weight of it in their hands.

Invite the members of the group to remember the conversation between Peter the rock and Jesus … all that Peter needed to let go of …

Invite the members of the group to think about a situation that needs to be put right and their feelings about it.

Use suitable prayers of confession and absolution for the group context.

Use a verse from Scripture such as 'Behold, I am making all things new!'

Invite the members of the group to place their stones in the water.

Invite them to gather round the bowl and to see how the stones are transformed by the water. (You might like to remind them of baptism and how the water is a sign of change and transformation in us.)

Include a time for personal prayers if appropriate.

End by holding hands and saying The Grace together.

Session 5

Characters:	**The disciples on the road to Emmaus**
Theme:	**Believing**
Sense:	**Sight, taste and sound**
Bible:	**Luke 24.13-31**

INTRODUCTORY MATERIALS

This is a long passage and you will need to think carefully about how you tell the story in ways that are appropriate for the context. It is also a powerful story and there is a great deal in the passage about the importance of Scripture and the importance of sacraments in remembering Jesus. You might like to look at *The Miracle Maker* by Murray Watts (pages 284–9, see Resources, p. 240, for more details) which gives a very powerful account of the Emmaus road experience.

TALKING POINTS

- Jesus meets the disciples as they travel along puzzling over the events of the previous days and wondering why things did not seem to have turned out as they expected.
- Look at the questions the disciples ask.
- Look at how Jesus responds to them.
- Why do you think they did not know it was Jesus?
- Talk about meals
- What kinds of meal can you think of that you have been a part of? What sorts of meal do people share together?
  - Family meals/meals in the home.
  - Meals when guests are invited.
  - Special meals.
  - Parties and feasts.
- What experiences have we had of these?

Look at what happens in the story. Jesus and the disciples are deep in conversation and it is getting dark as they approach Emmaus. The disciples invite Jesus in (though they do not yet know who he is). (Explain traditions of hospitality in the region at the time).

Reread the account of Jesus taking, blessing and breaking the bread and how the disciples finally realized who he was.

You might like to share other stories Jesus told about meals – for example, the Great Banquet, the Prodigal Son or imagery in Isaiah about feasts at the end of time.

Why do you think Jesus was so keen on telling stories about food and sharing and hospitality – what do you think these images tell us about God?

Think about the Eucharist – what does this show us about the love and generosity of God?

You will need to be alert here to feelings around the subject of children and communion. Children's experiences of inclusion in the meal at the heart of the Church may depend on the view held in the congregation of children and communion before confirmation and whether children have had a long experience of being welcomed to participate at the table of the Lord or not.

How do we remember Jesus? Talk about places, times and people that are important in this.

WORSHIP

YOU WILL NEED

- An image of the Last Supper as a focal point for the gathering.

WHAT TO DO

Light a candle and say:

Jesus said,
Where two or three are gathered together, there am I
*   in the midst of them.*

PRAYER

Lord Jesus, we thank you that you meet us
in the people we know and love – our friends and
*   those who care for us;*
in the church when we meet for prayer and worship;
in our daily lives as we struggle to make sense of
*   events;*
in the Bible and the stories of our faith;
in bread and wine – the signs of your presence with
*   us for all time.*

Offer the opportunity to say thank you prayers for the times and places where we meet Jesus and for the people who are the presence of Jesus for us.

Say the Lord's Prayer together.

Adults

There are two schemes for group reflection and study provided here. The first looks at encounters with the resurrected Christ and invites reflection on particular aspects of the Eucharist.

The second explores the Church as the body of Christ and uses the letters of Paul to the Romans and to the Ephesians as its basis.

Encounters with Jesus

These sessions encourage groups to reflect on some of the meetings with Jesus described in the Gospels and then to consider how we might meet Christ at various points in the Eucharist. The links have been made with the Eucharist for several reasons:

- The Eucharist is the primary place where we encounter Christ in symbols and through our senses as much as through the words – the bodily and tactile dimensions are fundamental to the whole experience.
- This encounter is not dependent on how much we understand.
- We are reminded of God's generosity and grace.
- We remember not just the death but also the resurrection of Christ.
- We appreciate and take hold of the grace of God in receiving bread and wine.
- We receive Christ through the bread we hold in our hands.
- It is an experience many members of the body of Christ share in together – irrespective of age or stage. This is particularly true where children are welcomed to receive bread and wine alongside the adults.
- Through the offering of ourselves, we become the Eucharist for others – pouring out ourselves for the sake of the world.

Session 1 Remember who you are: Jesus meets Mary (John 20.1-18)

Link to the Eucharist: The Greeting, the Peace,
**   the Intercessions**

Symbolic objects: Bowl of water and candle

INTRODUCTORY NOTES

There is much in this passage about being called by name. In the half-light, Mary goes to the tomb of Jesus early in the morning. You might like to invite the group to listen carefully as you read this atmospheric passage out loud, asking them to concentrate on the atmosphere in the garden, the darkness just before dawn, Mary's emotional state, the events of the previous days, the raw grief of someone who loved Jesus and who is now facing the loss of him. Invite the group to consider the journey that Mary had made to the garden and her shock at finding the stone rolled away from the entrance to the tomb and the tomb empty.

YOU WILL NEED

- Large bowl for water;
- Large jug of water (to be poured into the bowl during the worship);
- Night lights – enough for each person in the group to have one;
- Large candle and a stand on which to place it.

PREPARATION

Position the bowl on a small table or stand and set the candle alongside. Place the jug of water on the floor to the side of the table. If you have a floor-standing candlestick, this could be used instead. Place a basket or bowl containing the individual candles alongside the table.

FOR REFLECTION

- Why is naming so bound up with identity? You might like to refer here to the importance of names and naming generally.
- Talk about the meanings of the names of the group members and what they know about the reasons why they were given their own names.
- Reflect on the importance of Jesus calling Mary by her name in the passage.
- You might like to consider another garden where naming is important – the Garden of Eden. How do these two gardens tell the story of paradise lost and paradise restored?
- Who are the people we need to recognize and name in our church today?
- Why is it important in this passage that Jesus tells Mary not to touch or to hold on to him?
- Can you think of ways in which we as individuals or as the church fail to let go and move on? Are there ways in which we as individuals and as the church want to 'hold on' to a particular way of knowing Jesus?
- Think together about the places in the liturgy where welcome is extended and where people may be named.

CLOSING WORSHIP

- Use the 'Thanksgiving for Holy Baptism' from *Common Worship* (pp. 48–9) as a basis of an act of worship together. Or
- Read Isaiah 43.1-3a.
- Keep silence together.
- Pour water from the jug into the large bowl. You might like to use the following prayer from *Common Worship*:

Blessed are you, sovereign God of all,
to you be glory and praise for ever.
You are our light and our salvation.
From the deep waters of death
you have raised your Son to life in triumph.
Grant that all who have been born anew by
*   water and the Spirit,*
may daily be renewed in your image,
walk by the light of faith,
and serve you in newness of life;
through your anointed Son, Jesus Christ,
to whom with you and the Holy Spirit
we lift our voices of praise.
Blessed be God, Father, Son and Holy Spirit:
Blessed be God for ever.

[CW 48]

- Invite the members of the group to dip their fingers into the water and to use the water to sign themselves with the sign of the cross.

PRAYERS

God has brought us through the waters of death and God will open the path before us.

God will bring us through the waters that threaten to overwhelm us today

and in the fullness of time will lead us home.

Invite members of the group to light a candle and to place it around the bowl of water as a sign of commitment to live out their baptism in the world.

Keep silence together.

O God
You love us with a love that is stronger than death.
You know us with understanding too deep for words.
Call us again by our own name
and summon us into new life.
Speak to us in gentleness
and awaken us to new adventures of faith.
Give us grace to listen for your voice

*and to respond with open hearts to your call
that we might walk with you into the world
to speak your word of love to the lost and broken-
hearted.*
Amen.

*Session 2   Remember what you believe: Jesus
meets Thomas (John 20.19-30)*

Link to the Eucharist: Creed

**Symbolic objects: Celtic cross – the kind that
has carvings of the Christian
story etched into it
or cross with images on
it of the life of Christ (see
CD-ROM for an example
of this).**

INTRODUCTORY NOTES

We use the term 'doubting Thomas' in a derogatory
way – but what might this passage have to teach us
abut the relationship between faith and doubt? This
passage is very physical – Jesus invites Thomas to
put his finger on the wounds in his hands and to
place his hand in his side. What is important here
is the emphasis on bodily resurrection – a real body
not a ghost; a body that eats and drinks; that walks
about and that can be touched. Another aspect of
this encounter is the presence of the wounds on the
resurrected body – we are not to forget the sufferings
that Christ endured now that he has been raised.

YOU WILL NEED

- Celtic cross as described above or similar –
  many crosses from South America are decorated
  with images telling the salvation story.

PREPARATION

Display the cross on a background cloth placed on a
table.

FOR REFLECTION

You might need to have copies of the creeds and credal
statements available here and invite the group to look at
these in their reflection on the following questions:
- In what ways does this encounter inform or
  challenge our credal statements?
- What balance do we need to find between the
  divine and the earthly and bodily?

- If we emphasize one aspect over the other, how
  might this distort our worship or our gospel
  message?
- Where do we express both these aspects of
  Christ in worship and in the creeds?
- Do you think we are tempted to forget that the
  resurrected Lord is still a wounded saviour?
- What place could or should be given to the
  expression of doubt in worship or prayer?
- In a culture obsessed with youth and beauty,
  what particular challenges does the Church face
  in communicating the gospel of the wounded
  saviour?

ACTIVITY

Invite members of the group to consider which
stories and which incidents they think are crucial in
the communication of the gospel in the world.

CLOSING WORSHIP – AN ORDER FOR NIGHT PRAYER (COMPLINE)

Say Compline together.

PREPARATION

*The Lord almighty grant us a quiet night and a
perfect end.*
Amen.

Our help is in the name of the Lord
who made heaven and earth.

A period of silence for reflection on the past day may
follow.

The following or other suitable words of penitence
may be used
**Most merciful God,
we confess to you,
before the whole company of heaven and one
    another,
that we have sinned in thought, word and deed
and in what we have failed to do.
Forgive us our sins,
heal us by your Spirit
and raise us to new life in Christ. Amen.**

O God, make speed to save us.
O Lord, make haste to help us.

**Glory to the Father and to the Son
and to the Holy Spirit;
as it was in the beginning is now
and shall be for ever. Amen.
Alleluia.**

The following or another suitable hymn may be sung

Before the ending of the day,
Creator of the world, we pray
That you, with steadfast love, would keep
Your watch around us while we sleep.

From evil dreams defend our sight,
From fears and terrors of the night;
Tread underfoot our deadly foe
That we no sinful thought may know.

O Father, that we ask be done
Through Jesus Christ, your only Son;
And Holy Spirit, by whose breath
Our souls are raised to life from death.

[CW 81-2]

The Word of God

Psalm 104.1,21-33

Bless the Lord, O my soul.
O Lord my God, how excellent is your greatness!

You appointed the moon to mark the seasons,
and the sun knows the time for its setting.

You make darkness that it may be night,
in which all the beasts of the forest creep forth.

The lions roar for their prey
and seek their food from God.

The sun rises and they are gone
to lay themselves down in their dens.

People go forth to their work
and to their labour until the evening.

O Lord, how manifold are your works!
In wisdom you have made them all;
*   the earth is full of your creatures.*

There is the sea, spread far and wide,
and there move creatures beyond number, both
**   small and great.**

There go the ships, and there is that Leviathan
which you have made to play in the deep.

All of these look to you
to give them their food in due season.

When you give it them, they gather it;
you open your hand and they are filled with good.

When you hide your face they are troubled;
when you take away their breath,
they die and return again to the dust.

When you send forth your spirit, they are created,
and you renew the face of the earth.

May the glory of the Lord endure for ever;
may the Lord rejoice in his works;

Glory to the Father and to the Son
and to the Holy Spirit;
as it was in the beginning is now
and shall be for ever. Amen.

[CW 715–17]

Short reading

The servants of the Lamb shall see the face of God, whose name will be on their foreheads. There will be no more night: they will not need the light of a lamp or the light of the sun, for God will be their light, and they will reign for ever and ever.

Revelation 22.4,5

The following responsory may be said

Into your hands, O Lord, I commend my spirit.
*   Alleluia, alleluia.*
For you have redeemed me, Lord God of truth.
Alleluia, alleluia.
Glory to the Father and to the Son
*   and to the Holy Spirit.*
Into your hands, O Lord, I commend my spirit.
**   Alleluia, alleluia.**
Keep me as the apple of your eye.
Hide me under the shadow of your wings.

[CW 85 adapted]

Gospel Canticle

The Nunc dimittis (*The Song of Simeon*) is said or sung

Alleluia. The Lord is risen, alleluia,
as he promised to you. Alleluia, alleluia.

Now, Lord, you let your servant go in peace:
your word has been fulfilled.

My own eyes have seen the salvation
which you have prepared in the sight of every
*   people;*

*A light to reveal you to the nations
and the glory of your people Israel.*

Luke 2.29-32

**Glory to the Father and to the Son
and to the Holy Spirit;
as it was in the beginning is now
and shall be for ever. Amen.**

**Alleluia. The Lord is risen, alleluia,
as he promised to you. Alleluia, alleluia.**

[CW 86 adapted]

PRAYERS

Intercessions and thanksgivings may be offered here.

The Collect

Silence may be kept.

Almighty God,
*by triumphing over the powers of darkness
Christ has prepared a place for us in the new
   Jerusalem:
may we, who have this day given thanks for his
   resurrection,
praise him in the eternal city
of which he is the light;
through Jesus Christ our Lord.*
Amen.

[DP 344]

The Lord's Prayer may be said.

THE CONCLUSION

In peace we will lie down and sleep;
for you alone, Lord, make us dwell in safety.

Abide with us, Lord Jesus,
for the night is at hand and the day is now past.

As the night watch looks for the morning,
so do we look for you, O Christ.

[CW 87]

BLESSING

*May the risen Lord Jesus bless us.
May he watch over us and renew us
as he renews the whole of creation.
May our hearts and lives echo his love.*

[DP 353]

Session 3 Remember grace received: Jesus meets Peter (John 21.9-19)

Link to the Eucharist: Forgiveness and absolution

Symbolic objects: Stones and a cross

INTRODUCTORY NOTES

This passage needs to be read in conjunction with the passage that deals with Peter's denial of Jesus – John 18.15-27. The threefold affirmation of Peter's love wipes out his earlier threefold denial and Peter becomes a crucial part in the building of the Church. It is worth reflecting on the ways in which Peter's experience later affected his leadership. (In passing it is also worth noting that this is another instance of names being significant – Peter the rock of the Church.)

YOU WILL NEED

- Bibles.
- A small table on which should be placed a white cloth and a simple cross, lying down on the cloth. Members of the group will later be invited to place their stones on or around this cross so it will need to be quite large. Simple pieces of wood arranged in a cross shape and bound together will work.
- Several pebbles or stones – enough for members of the group to have one each.

PREPARATION

- Set the table in the centre of the room with the cross arranged on it.
- Place the stones in a bowl or basket and position the bowl or basket near the table with the cross on it.

FOR REFLECTION

Set out this conversation between Peter and Jesus alongside Peter's denials described in John 18. Do you think the two are related?

Reflect together on your feelings about the poem that is verse 18.

Is absolution a comfort or challenge?

CLOSING WORSHIP

Use penitential materials from *Common Worship*, e.g. the Kyrie Confessions (p. 133).

Invite the members of the group to come forward, to take a stone and to place it on the cross.

Allow time for this.

Say words of absolution in the appropriate form.

Give space for intercession as appropriate.

End by saying The Grace together.

Session 4 Remember the gospel: Jesus meets his disciples on the road to Emmaus (Luke 24.1-27)

Link to the Eucharist: Liturgy of the Word (reading and preaching)

Symbolic objects: Open Bible placed on a lectern or velvet cushion; candle

INTRODUCTORY NOTES

Sessions 4 and 5 form a pair, just as the Liturgy of the Word and the Liturgy of the Sacrament are inextricably linked in our eucharistic practice. Jesus opens up the Scriptures to the downcast disciples who are struggling to interpret the events of the past days and to make sense of Christ's death in the light of what they had believed – that he was the one to save Israel. Later (in the passage set for the next session) the disciples welcome the traveller into their home and the visitor takes bread, blesses and breaks it and gives it to them and 'then their eyes were opened and they recognized him' (Luke 24.31).

YOU WILL NEED

- Bibles;
- A large Bible to be used as a focal point;
- A lectern or cushion on which to place the large Bible;
- A candle,

PREPARATION

- Place the lectern or cushion on a piece of white fabric over a small table.
- Put the Bible on the lectern or cushion and set the candle alongside it.

FOR REFLECTION

- Jesus meets the disciples as they are travelling and as they are struggling to make sense of events in the light of what they had seen and heard of Jesus. What can we learn from this about mission?
- If we want to speak of the things of God, how important is it to travel alongside others first and do what they are doing in order to hear their story?
- What can we learn about when to speak and when to keep silent as we accompany people on their journey of faith?
- How can we tell the story in ways that make people's hearts burn within them?
- How important is hospitality to mission? Why might it be important?
- How can we let the word and the culture speak to and be informed by each other in our worship and our learning in the Church?

CLOSING WORSHIP: ACT OF WORSHIP BASED ON THANKSGIVING FOR THE WORD

PREPARATION

Your word is a lantern to our feet
and a light upon our path.
The light and peace of Jesus Christ be with you.
and also with you.

PRAYER OF THANKSGIVING

Blessed are you, Lord our God.
How sweet are your words to the taste,
sweeter than honey to the mouth.
How precious are your commands for our life,
more than the finest gold in our hands.
How marvellous is your will for the world,
unending is your love for the nations.
Our voices shall sing of your promises
and our lips declare your praise
for ever and ever.
Amen.

FIRST READING

You might like to use some verses here from the passage you have been looking at.

PRAYERS OF PENITENCE

Your word is life to the lost and drink to the thirsty soul.
For our failure to tell the stories of faith, keeping the rumours of glory alive,
and singing the song of your unending love,
Lord, have mercy.
Lord, have mercy.

Your word is a lantern to our feet showing us the way to go.
For our failure to respond to your call of love, insistent in its longing
and revealing to us your mercy and truth,
Christ, have mercy.
Christ, have mercy.

Your law is my delight and I will tell of your works for ever.
For our inability to tell the story afresh from generation to generation,
inspiring others to follow in the way,
Lord, have mercy.
Lord, have mercy.

May the God of all healing and forgiveness draw us to himself,
and cleanse us from all our sins
that we may behold the glory of his Son,
the Word made flesh,
Jesus Christ our Lord.
Amen.

Song (as appropriate)

SECOND READING

INTERCESSIONS ARE OFFERED

Almighty God,
we thank you for the gift of your holy word.
May it be a lantern to our feet,
a light upon our paths,
and a strength to our lives.
Take us and use us
to love and serve all people
in the power of the Holy Spirit
and in the name of your Son,
Jesus Christ our Lord.
Amen.

[CW 47]

The Lord's Prayer is said.

THE ENDING

The Word of life which was from the beginning
we proclaim to you.
The darkness is passing away
and the true light is already shining;
the Word of life which was from the beginning.
That which we heard, which we saw with our eyes,
and touched with our hands,
we proclaim to you.
For our fellowship is with the Father,
and with his Son, Jesus Christ our Lord.
The Word of life, which was from the beginning,
we proclaim to you.

[CW 47]

Song

SENDING OUT

Let us bless the Lord.
Thanks be to God.

Session 5 Remember Christ: Jesus meets his disciples in the breaking of bread
(Luke 24.28-35)

Link to the Eucharist: Liturgy of the Sacrament (moment of fraction)
What does it mean to be a community shaped by the Eucharist? What might be the markers of this?
Symbolic objects: Bread and wine

INTRODUCTORY NOTES

This session links back to the material covered in the previous session. You will need to begin by giving a recap of the key points raised in discussion of the passage set for the previous session and perhaps by rereading the first part of the biblical narrative of the journey to Emmaus. The Supper at Emmaus by Caravaggio is an interesting way in to reflecting on this encounter between Jesus and the disciples present. The food in this picture is very vivid and the action seems almost to move out of the frame. It manages to capture the sense of the drama of the moment as, for the disciples, past experience and memory; previous meals shared with Jesus; the habitual actions over food at shared meals and the remembrance of both the Last Supper and the death of Christ all collide in the moment when Christ takes, blesses, breaks and shares the bread at table.

- Cup and paten;
- Red cloth on which to place these items.

Preparation

Arrange the red cloth over a table and place the cup and paten on it as a focal point in the room.

For reflection

- What links can you see between word and sacrament in these two parts of the journey to Emmaus? Could you have one without the other?
- How important is this balance in our eucharistic celebration?
- Think about the moment when the bread is broken. What can we learn here about the nature of the eucharistic community?
- How important is this moment in the Eucharist for you?
- How important is it that we can see and hear what is happening here?
- How much time is there for reflection during the Liturgy of the Sacrament?
- How can eating together and hospitality help people into a fuller experience of the Eucharist?

Closing worship

If appropriate, you might like to hold a meditative Eucharist together that helps to focus attention on the sensory aspects of this act of worship.

Intercessions

Faithful God,
we call to mind and give thanks for all that reveals to us your loving purposes
for the world which you have made.
For your continual renewing of the face of the earth
and for the work you continue to do in our lives,
we praise your name.

Ever-present God,
we call to mind and give thanks for all that reveals you to us in the midst of life;
for your presence along the way,
for times when we encounter you in other people
and signs of your grace in the joy and pain of daily life,
we praise your name.

Living God,
we call to mind and give thanks for your gift of new life in Christ,
for your work of salvation through time and in our lives,
for your word which speaks and challenges
and for the life we share in the fellowship of your people and all the saints,
we praise your name.

God of creation,
renew your image in us
that in all our ways and works we may witness to your unfailing goodness.

Merciful God,
we bring before you our cry for your healing and grace:
from all that limits our service and witness,
from all that keeps us from showing hospitality to others,
from conflict in our communities and our world,
Lord, deliver us.

Ever-loving God,
we bring before you our need of your mercy:
from thinking too well of ourselves,
from casual words which fail to heal,
from failure to speak of you in our communities and neighbourhoods,
Lord, deliver us.

Almighty God,
we bring before you all we are and all we have
in loving fellowship with others,
in ways peaceful and true,
in open and tender-hearted service,
keep us by your grace.

God of all,
may we be joyful in hope and faithful in prayer,
living and working to your praise and glory
until we come at last to your eternal kingdom.
Amen.

'Now you are the body of Christ and individually members of it.' (1 Corinthians 12.27)

In the Church, the outworking of our Lenten discipline and our Easter hope can be seen in the work to become the body of Christ, respecting one another, honouring the weakest members for the sake of the whole, learning to make best use of our different gifts to build up the body and suffering and rejoicing together.

In the group materials on Paul's letters provided here, you will find two suggested passages of Scripture for each session, one from Paul's letter to the Romans and a comparable passage from Paul's letter to the Ephesians. You can choose to look at one of the letters on its own or to look at the parallel passages and explore the similarities and the different contexts for each book.

WHY THESE TWO BOOKS?

Romans has often been viewed as a complex book – densely expressed and packed with theological argument. It has a different 'feel' from the other letters and some scholars believe that it more resembles a testament than a letter. Written for a church Paul had no hand in founding, the letter to the Romans does not contain the responses to practical situations and the pressing theological questions within a particular context that make the other letters distinctive. It is rather that Paul is setting out his understanding of God and of the work of Christ and making clear what lies at the heart of his own faith.

Ephesians, on the other hand, is a letter to the church in Ephesus, possibly a circular letter that did the rounds of the churches in the Lycus valley area. It is written to a congregation in a particular context as well as being written to communicate issues of more general concern to the wider community of the faithful. There is some debate amongst scholars as to the authorship of the letter to the Ephesians but there are nevertheless themes and images that are central to Paul's other writings so for the purpose of this discussion we will view Paul as the author.

Paul wrote the letter to the Romans in AD 58, just before he embarked on a journey to Jerusalem to take gifts from the church in Corinth. He longed then to visit Rome, arguably the greatest city of the greatest empire in the world – and a gateway to the spreading of the Christian message to the West. It is possible that in this letter Paul was setting out his standpoint on matters of faith to pave the way for a later visit. The hope was that, when he arrived in Rome, he would be treated sympathetically and welcomed. It was, however, a journey that he was never to make. Whilst in Jerusalem, he was arrested and was never freed again. The letter to the Ephesians was written from prison, when Paul was in a situation of great hardship and suffering.

There is, then, an interesting way in which these letters can speak to us in this part of our journey through the church year. On the one hand, the letter to the Romans sets out the core of belief in the Christ who died and who was raised from the dead and grapples with ways of expressing this belief – with doctrine, if you like. The letter to the Ephesians gives us a window into the working out of belief in daily life, in relationships and in community – and in Paul's own case in the midst of suffering. Both letters, then, show us something of the working out of discipleship and tell us that faith needs to be worked at constantly and thought through in response to very real situations that pull and push against the theological statements we make. Both letters together call us to live a life worthy of the gospel – and to hold a faith that touches our minds, our bodies and our hearts.

WHAT YOU WILL FIND FOR EACH SESSION

In the following materials you will find the passages for suggested study and reflection for each session. You will also find suggestions for images and for music and poetry. These are suggestions and you may well have other ideas of your own, suggested to you from the passages and the ideas contained in them. The images can be used as focal points within the space where the gathering takes place. They can then become a focus for prayer and reflection if the group has a time for prayer and worship at the end of the session.

Similarly, you might like to use the suggested music as the group gathers or, where suitable, in the time of prayer or worship. You will need to listen to the suggested items beforehand and decide how best to use them within your context, or find replacements.

VERSIONS OF SCRIPTURE AND COMMENTARIES

Nothing can replace reading and rereading the texts for yourself. You might like to read the texts in a couple of different versions. Alongside the NRSV, you might like to look at Rob Lacey's *Street Bible* and Tom Wright gives his own translations in his commentaries. You might like to look at Tom Wright's books: *Paul for Everyone: Romans* and *Paul for Everyone: The Prison Letters*, published by SPCK. *The New Daily Study Bible: The Letter to the Romans* by William Barclay, published by Saint Andrew Press, is also a good support for leaders of Bible study and reflection on these letters.

Christ makes all things new: Reflections on Paul's letter to the Romans and Paul's letter to the Ephesians

SESSION 1 A NEW HOPE

SCRIPTURES: ROMANS 5.1-11; EPHESIANS 1.1-12 IN HIM WE HAVE REDEMPTION

(John 20.1-18 tells of the encounter between Jesus and Mary and makes an interesting link in terms of the post-resurrection appearance, calling Mary by name and sending her to bear witness to the resurrection and to tell the disciples what she has seen and heard.)

Image: *Michelangelo,* The Creation of Adam *(detail: God's hand and the hand of Adam).*

Music: *Vaughan Williams,* The Lark Ascending *or Nina Simone 'It's a new dawn' ('Feeling good').*

Poetry: *e. e. cummings, 'I thank you God for most this amazing' or Laurie Lee, 'April Rise'.*

INTRODUCTORY NOTES

The passage from Romans emphasizes the blessing that is ours because of the work of Christ 'through whom we have obtained access to this grace in which we stand' (v. 2). Grace is a keynote of this part of the letter to the Romans and indeed of the whole book. Paul speaks of reconciliation with God through the death of Christ and states that 'while we were still sinners Christ died for us' (v. 8). The word 'access' is important. In the Greek it is *prosagoge* which conjures up two images – that of being ushered into the presence of royalty and that of a harbour or haven. Jesus opens the way into God's presence and the safety of his grace.

FOR REFLECTION

- Where is the emphasis in this passage – on God's work or ours?
- What difference does this emphasis make to the way we live out our faith day to day?
- What difference might it make to our worship?
- Look carefully at the image of the hands of God and of Adam in the painting by Michelangelo – who is reaching out to whom and who is the initiator in this moment?

CLOSING WORSHIP – SEEDS OF FAITH

You will need a large tray of soil and some seeds.

Give each member of the group one of the seeds. Reflect with them on the growth of the Church from small beginnings and on God's generous response to our faith – however feeble and frail it might be. Say something like:

Generous God,
we plant these seeds as a sign of your promise to
    make all things new.
Nurture in us the hope of resurrection life
and bring your word to birth in our lives.

Keep silence and invite members of the group to come forward and to plant their seeds in the soil.

Pray for individuals and communities where resurrection life is crushed or denied.

Play a recording of 'The lark ascending' and read one of the poems over the music (you will need to practise this carefully!) or play the music and then read one of the poems afterwards in an attitude of meditation.

SESSION 2 A NEW CREATION

SCRIPTURES: ROMANS 8.18-39; EPHESIANS 2 A DWELLING PLACE FOR GOD

Image: *You will need a collection of images that speak of a new creation or of creation's need for renewal. Invite the members of the group to choose one that speaks to them and place these around the candle during the worship time.*

Poetry: *Gerard Manley Hopkins 'God's Grandeur'.*

Music: *'St Patrick's Breastplate'.*

INTRODUCTORY NOTES

Romans 8.18-39 is a great and poetic vision of the renewal of the face of the earth. Paul describes the bondage that creation is in and the suffering that mars not only human existence but the life of the world. He then goes on to describe a future liberation and coming glory. This dream of a renewed earth was dear to the heart of Jews and it is a feature of the Old Testament Scriptures (for example, see Isaiah 65.17); between the testaments, when the Jews were enslaved and oppressed, the dream of a new heaven and a new earth were a part of their sustaining vision. The idea of the renewal of the whole earth is part of the 'now and not yet' of the Easter hope expressed in the Exsultet 'this is the night' – now and yet to come. There is another reminder of the Garden of Eden here too. Human sin brought all creation into bondage 'cursed is the ground because of you' (Genesis 3.17). And in another garden just recently in our Easter story, life springs out of death and hope is reborn.

The passage from Ephesians places its emphasis on renewed relationships – with God and with one another. Grace is again a keynote here – this time in terms of membership of the household of God. Grace is apparently without boundaries or restrictions too – it is peace for those who are far off and those who are near. The passage highlights the dramatic change that Christ's death brings to individuals but reminds us that this is worked out in renewed relationships.

FOR REFLECTION

- In what ways do you see salvation as individual and in what ways is it corporate?
- How might this affect the way we approach mission and evangelism?
- What does the passage from Romans have to teach us about the effects of our actions and choices on the natural world?
- Do you think sin has consequences for the world and for the created order?
- In what ways do we see this being worked out in the world today?
- What kinds of 'footprint' do we leave on the earth today – what are the effects of our attitudes to the earth?
- What does our Celtic heritage have to teach us about our relationship with the created order?
- Peace to those who are far off and peace to those who are near – how does the Church communicate this gospel in the world? How might this affect our understanding of worship and of mission?

CLOSING WORSHIP

Light a candle and place it centrally in the group.
Keep silence for a few moments.
Invite members of the group to place their images around the candle.

Say something like:

We offer our penitence to you this night, O Lord,
for our failure to use the earth's resources wisely.
For our failure to see your hand in the beauty of
*   creation;*
for our neglect of the gift of the earth that you have
*   made*

and our greed and selfishness with your generous gifts.

Keep silence or invite spoken prayer.

We give thanks this night for the signs of your
*   continued presence in the world.*
For love where there has been hatred;
for truth in the place of deceit and joy where all
*   seemed lost.*

Keep silence or invite spoken prayer.

We pray this night for places and people who need
*   to hear again your invitation of grace.*
For all who are lost or alone; for suffering peoples of
*   the earth*
and those in situations of bloodshed and conflict;
and for all who need to know again that they are
*   loved by you.*

Keep silence or invite spoken prayer.

Read the poem 'God's Grandeur'.

Say the Lord's Prayer together.

SESSION 3 A NEW COMMUNITY

SCRIPTURES: ROMANS 12.1-21; EPHESIANS 4.1-16
GROW UP IN EVERY WAY INTO CHRIST

> **Image:** *Rublev*, The Holy Trinity.
>
> **Music:** *'Ubi caritas et amor' (Taizé chant or version by Fauré, which you can play from a CD).*

INTRODUCTORY NOTES

Romans 12.1-21 presents us with the image of the body of Christ and sets out ethical teaching for right relationships or community. Again it is the corporate dimension of salvation that we are being urged to attend to here. The passage from Ephesians urges the believer to live 'a life worthy of the calling to which you have been called' (Ephesians 4.1). The markers of a renewed community are unity and peace and the exercising of gifts for the sake of the whole body 'to equip the saints for the work of ministry, for building up the body of Christ' (Ephesians 4.12).

Salvation, we are reminded again, is not a private affair. It challenges the way we live and is tested out in the demands of human relationships.

FOR REFLECTION

- How well do we understand, recognize, and use the gifts of those in our church community?
- Are some gifts easier to deal with than others?

- Are some gifts more in evidence than others? Does this matter?
- Where is the gift of prophecy in your congregation?
- If we are to take seriously the idea that the salvation Christ offers is to renew relationships and the whole of creation, why might we need to find spaces for the prophetic voice to be heard in our congregations?
- In a situation where we live with the frustrations of the 'not yet', how important are imagination and story in keeping the rumours of glory alive?
- How successful are we as church at nurturing the kind of love-in-relationship that Rublev's icon shows us?

CLOSING WORSHIP

You might like to say Compline together (see Encounters with Jesus, session 2).

SESSION 4 A NEW CALLING

SCRIPTURES: ROMANS 13.8-14; EPHESIANS 6.10-18 PUT ON THE WHOLE ARMOUR OF GOD

Music: *'Amazing grace'.*

INTRODUCTORY NOTES

What armour is the Christian expected to be wearing? Truth; righteousness; the gospel of peace; the shield of faith and the helmet of salvation. The only attacking weapon is the sword of the Spirit, which is the word of God. Clearly the resurrection posed problems for the ruling authorities of the time and, in view of the spread of Christianity and the growth of the Church, Christians themselves were coming under more and more scrutiny. Increasingly efforts were made to lure Christians away from the central truths of the faith and this reminder from Paul was designed to help the young Church to stay true to its message of Christ's death and resurrection. In a situation where attacks on the Christian faith are not necessarily overt (persecution), it is interesting to ask whether Christians today are often caught out because they are not watchful enough against what runs contrary to the gospel.

FOR REFLECTION

- How do you respond to the military imagery in the passage from Ephesians? Do you find it helpful to be reminded of a battle?
- What do you think is being referred to in each of these items of armour?

- The passage from Romans talks about the 'armour of light'. What do you think this means?
- In what ways do Christians today need to wake up as this passage from the letter to the Romans suggests?
- The passage from Romans also speaks of the commandment to 'love your neighbour as yourself' as being the fulfilment of the law. Why do you think there is such an emphasis on loving others as the outworking of salvation?
- In church, do you think we place the emphasis on the individual or the corporate dimension of salvation?
- How do you understand the idea of the Christian life being a battle?
- In what ways do you think Christianity is itself under threat today?

CLOSING WORSHIP

An Order for Night Prayer (Compline) (See Encounters with Jesus, Session 2).

Head, hands and heart at home

This Head, hands and heart pathway encourages us above all to make the best use of our senses to help us explore the Lent, Passiontide and Easter seasons and so, as the period reaches its climax and conclusion, we can make the best of this.

Make an 'Easter place' in your home. If you have Easter eggs – and they are not all eaten at once – keep them there. Share them around at some time during the day when people can gather. Keep the place decorated with flowers. Don't use chrysanthemums from the supermarket, really try to make sure that your flowers are representative of the season and change as the early spring transforms over the six weeks into early summer. Watch the opening up of the buds and the warming of the ground. The flowers pass from daffodils to jonquils to grape hyacinth and tulip, then to bluebells and all the early tree and shrub blossoms. If you want a book to read together as a family (or indeed, if you are a household without children you can still read it) try *The Secret Garden* by Frances Hodgson Burnett. Another helpful book (for adults) that uses the garden allegory to explore Easter and includes reflections on Frances Hodgson Burnett's book is *Easter Garden* by Nicola Slee.

Watch for other signs of new life. Are there birds nesting anywhere near where you live or pass time? If you have small children, go and find some frogspawn, bring some home in a tub with some weed and watch the eggs develop for a while. Take them back to where you found them at some stage before they turn into frogs and need to breathe out of the water. On Good Shepherd Sunday (Easter 4), go out and watch lambs (if there is anywhere within easy travelling distance to make this possible). When the resurrection appearance beside Lake Tiberias is the Sunday Gospel reading, prepare a meal of bread and fish, then read the story together before you eat it.

On Rogation Sunday (Easter 6) **go out for a walk in the countryside** if at all possible: look at the crops in the fields and see what you can identify. Pray that there will be a good growing season and a prolific harvest. Give thanks for all who grow our food. You might take the opportunity to take part in one of the present aid schemes that supply animals to families farming in poor communities across the world.

The horse chestnut has sometimes been called the ascension tree because its flowers are often in blossom at Ascensiontide. If this is so, **pick some flowers to decorate your Easter place**. (Get permission from the tree's owner if necessary, of course, but you don't need to worry about damaging the tree, as they flower prolifically. At Pentecost celebrate with kites and sparklers.

As a Bible study throughout the season **read the Acts of the Apostles** with its stories of the newly emerging Church. You could use a commentary to help if you wish but you could just enjoy the stories and accounts as the season moves on. There are 28 chapters and 50 days between Easter and Pentecost, so this works out at about half a chapter a day, and a chance to read on when it's too exciting to stop!

Head, hands and heart in outreach

The Easter Vigil

This can be an evangelistic opportunity. Many people who would not normally attend church are drawn to the sense of mystery that this liturgy can offer them when it is done well. Thought needs to be given to how invitations can be issued in the community. It is a service full of ritual and poetry; of storytelling and symbolic action. Simple things can help people's experience of the service. For example: have a decent sized fire – whilst respecting health and safety regulations of course! Play up the other visual symbolism and the storytelling in this

service. Make sure that the church building really is dark so that the contrast of the light against the darkness is made effectively; ensure that the Exsultet is sung confidently; give careful consideration to the arrangement of ministers within the space; to the positioning of the Paschal Candle and to sight lines.

Flowers

The Head, hands and heart pathway commends itself particularly to flower arrangers. While big flower festivals might only be for the experienced and semi-professional, a smaller festival of Easter flowers might provide a specific occasion to invite people who enjoy working with flowers and plants to convey ideas and feelings, and any such occasion provides the opportunity to invite people to see the flowers and for some carefully targeted invitations.

Use the encounters described in the study material and suggest people work in these incidents in creating flower arrangements or planted gardens. Remember that a carefully planted garden could last for quite some time, and that those passing it on a regular basis will look at it and remember.

Here are the incidents on which you might like to base creative ideas:

Character: Christ meets Mary in the garden
   Theme: Surprise
   Senses: Hearing and touch
   Bible: John 20.1-18

Character: Thomas meets the risen Christ
   Theme: Doubt
   Sense: Touch
   Bible: John 20.19-29

Characters: The disciples meet Jesus on the beach
   Theme: Recognition
   Senses: Sight and taste
   Bible: John 21.1-14

Character: Peter
   Theme: Forgiveness
   Senses: Heart and mind
   Bible: John 21.15-19

Characters: The disciples on the road to Emmaus

Theme: Believing

Senses: Sight, taste and sound

Bible: Luke 24.13-31

Art

You might like to invite people to contribute or to suggest an image that they consider speaks about the themes of death and resurrection and display these in the gathering area of the church.

Outreach at Pentecost

- Make a **Wind Garden** – this could be sited in the church garden or discreet part of the churchyard. If your building always seems to be prone to stiff breezes, here is one occasion on which it will work to your advantage! Some decorations can be bought: children's handheld windmills, spinning Perspex strips, and wind chimes would make an interesting display. You could add to these some homemade decorations – tissue paper windsocks, streamers, foil shapes, paper doves, etc. All these items could be attached with strings to bamboo canes painted red or covered with a twisting red ribbon; or they could be hung from a convenient tree.

- Hold a **Pentecost Workshop** – this could be the perfect opportunity for creating some of the decorations that will liven up the church building for Pentecost, as well as being creative fun for people of all ages. At its simplest, three banners, one with a dove, one with fire and one with water could be made. Consider also making collages (individual or collective), and mobiles with symbols of the Holy Spirit, or kites (see note below). Now could also be the time to make some of the items for the Wind Garden (described above). Jam jars can be painted with glass paints to make holders for night lights (pre-test your jars to make sure that they will withstand the heat of the night light). A grouping of these painted jars produces a beautiful, shimmering light. You could make candles, or simply paint designs onto them using acrylic paints. You could make candles by pouring blue wax into scallop shells and adding wicks. They make a beautiful addition to the display on the theme of water.

- Make **kites** – for display and/or flying. Simple diamond-shaped kites can be made from two garden sticks, a large sheet of stiff paper, sticky tape, some string and some thin nylon thread (needed if you intend to fly them). Bind the two sticks into a cross shape with sticky tape. Run string around the perimeter of the shape and secure with tape. Now cover the front with the stiff paper (try coloured tracing paper, which is both stiff and light), folding a small tab over each of the four sections of string that make up the diamond shape and securing them with tape or strong glue. You can add a tail of string with bows of crêpe paper tied into it at intervals. If you are going to fly the kites after the service, take a prototype for a test flight and make any necessary adjustments. Choose Pentecost colours for your kites. The front of the kite can be used for Pentecost symbols, e.g. a dove, fire, water, wind, or oil. Older children will enjoy creating these kites from scratch and working on some variations of their own. Younger children could be given the basic kite model to decorate. If your church has pillars, why not attach these kites to them to prepare people for Pentecost worship?

  Alternatively, small kites and crayons (safe for clothes!) could be made available to those who would like them with their service sheet. They could create Pentecost designs on them while the liturgy unfolds and attach them to a display in the last hymn or carry them in the procession. Do not make the creation of kites into a competition – you want the artists (child or adult) to be thinking about the Holy Spirit, not about winning or losing.

- Hold a **Picnic or Street Party or Barbecue**. Pentecost is the perfect occasion for 'outward-looking' festivities that appeal to those on the fringe and those with no church connections at all. Go out of your way to welcome all-comers and to give things away openhandedly. Have plenty of bright decorations and theme some of the food to the occasion. You could decorate a cake with Pentecost symbols and arrange for people to ice their own biscuits in Pentecost colours. You could use helium-filled balloons to create a display, and organize Pentecost face-painting and hair-braiding, or invent some nonalcoholic cocktails with Pentecost names and colours. You could conclude the event with a brief act of open-air worship.

Easter:
The Stations pathway

The Stations in groups

Children

Stations of the Resurrection

The idea of Stations of the Resurrection is relatively new and probably developed in Spain. As with the Stations of the Cross, in the Stations of the Resurrection liturgy in *Times and Seasons* each station represents an incident described in the New Testament, some in the Gospels and some in the Acts of the Apostles. Few church communities will possess pictures of these stations, so what is made by the children may be the first set of artistic representations of these readings. It will be important as you prepare for this that you remember that 'The resurrection appearances are more than just stories or history, they are a record of personal encounters with our risen Lord' (*Times and Seasons* p. 443)

THE STATIONS

Below is a table of the nineteen incidents chosen to be Stations of the Resurrection in the *Times and Seasons* liturgy. This is a good many and you may not wish to use all of them. It is perfectly legitimate to make a choice.

1	The earthquake	Matthew 28.2-4
2	Mary Magdalene finds the empty tomb	John 20.1,2
3	The disciples run to the empty tomb	John 20.3-8
4	The angel appears to the women	Matthew 28.5-8 or Mark 16.3-8 or Luke 24.2-9
5	Jesus meets the women	Matthew 28.9-10
6	The road to Emmaus	Luke 24.28-35
7	Jesus appears to the disciples	Luke 24.36-43 or John 20.19,20
8	Jesus promises the Spirit	Luke 24.44-49
9	Jesus commissions the disciples	John 20.21-23

10	Jesus breathes the Spirit in the upper room	John 20.22,23
11	Jesus reveals himself to Thomas	John 20.24-29
12	Jesus appears at the lakeside	John 21.9-13
13	Jesus confronts Peter	John 21.15-19
14	Jesus and the beloved disciple	John 21.20-23
15	Jesus appears to five hundred at once	1 Corinthians 15.3-6
16	Jesus commissions the disciples on the mountain	Matthew 28.16-20
17	The ascension	Acts 1.3-11
18	Pentecost	Acts 2.1-11
19	Jesus appears to Saul (Paul)	Acts 9.1-18 or 1Corinthians 15.8

[T&S 445]

HOW TO USE THE IDEAS

As with the Stations of the Cross, this material is designed to be used at any time. It could be used on a Sunday morning or it might be used in a midweek group. It could even be used all together in one long session. There are seven Sundays of Easter and the season finally ends on Pentecost. One of the problems of this long season is that it is sometimes difficult to keep up the impetus. One valuable asset of this project might be that it works *towards* the end of the Easter season when you might wish to 'unveil' the set of pictures on say, the seventh Sunday of Easter, which follows Ascension and anticipates Pentecost. This material is not divided into weekly blocks. The activity of making the stations is completely flexible and will depend on the number of participants you have and how long you meet for. It will also depend in part on the age and competence of the children involved, and how far you want the material to look 'finished' or are happy to display it as work in progress. You may need to have a team of adults and older children who are prepared to meet to finish things off and tidy up each panel ready for it to be hung.

Again, as with the Stations of the Cross, hanging the panels will depend on their location. You could use a cane through a channel in the top of each and then attach a cord to each end of the cane to hang them by. If they are to be hung against a soft surface, they could be mounted onto it with pins. Or they could be mounted onto board or really stiff card and propped up, say in a window alcove

PREPARATION

The Easter panels should be in marked contrast to those made in Lent. They must be bright, sparkling and flamboyant, reflecting the glory of Easter and the celebration of this season. Nevertheless, the opening of the series is shrouded in mystery: while the earthquake is awe-inspiring, the first encounters with the risen Christ are puzzling and not really understood. Easter is marked by dawning realization, and it may be possible to allude to this through the use of colour.

YOU WILL NEED

- Bright, shimmering material to use as the background for the scenes, in colours of white, cream and yellow through to gold. You will need to decide on a size and then cut 15 pieces the same size. Secure the sides first. You could sew them, but if time is an issue then simply use iron-heat activated bonding ribbon (sometimes called hemming tape), which can be bought very easily now from sewing shops and even from supermarkets.
- Smoother, gentler fabrics will be required – felt is good as it sticks easily, doesn't fray and can be drawn on. You could use silk or something similar for faces, hands and feet. You might like to cut out lots of these so people can help themselves to what they need. Another possibility is to use the flesh-coloured paper people shapes that are now available in stationers and in educational catalogues. They come in different skin tones, which adds diversity.
- When you have chosen the particular stations you wish to explore and illustrate, you will have some idea of the other materials you will need to make them. There are several garden scenes,

several mountain scenes and several lakeside scenes, for example, and you might like to use the same fabric for each mountain, garden or lakeside scene to give some coherence to the set of pictures.
- Shapes of figures to copy: the pictures in *The Good News Bible* are really helpful from this point of view as they are simple and easy to emulate, yet very communicative. You might enlarge some on a photocopier to use as an inspiration.
- Adhesives: bonding fabric may be good to use with older children (in which case you will also need an iron); PVA glue sticks just about anything and can be bought in a washable variety; sewing cotton and needles might be helpful and staplers can also be used; scissors and pencils.

Have all these materials laid out on flat surfaces around the meeting room in preparation for each session.

THE WORSHIP TIME *(A STANDARD PATTERN FOR EACH WEEK)*

THE FOCAL TABLE

Cover the table with white or gold fabric each week. Use lots of flowers or plants. Perhaps you could have a basket of tiny Easter eggs throughout the season. Add something to represent each of the incidents you will be considering and responding to on that particular occasion.

Open with a greeting:
Alleluia. Christ is risen.
He is risen indeed. Alleluia.

This acclamation may be used:
Praise to you, Lord Jesus:
Dying you destroyed our death,
rising you restored our life:
Lord Jesus, come in glory.

God of glory,
by the raising of your Son
you have broken the chains of death and hell:
fill your Church with faith and hope;
for a new day has dawned
and the way to life stands open
in our Saviour Jesus Christ.
Amen.

[T&S 447]

Praise the God and Father of our Lord Jesus Christ.
**He has given us new life and hope
by raising Jesus from the dead.**

God has claimed us as his own.
**He has brought us out of darkness.
He has made us light to the world.**

Alleluia. Christ is risen.
He is risen indeed. Alleluia.

[T&S 407]

*The different stations in sequence allocated by
week*

A simple version of the reading has not been
provided as the texts themselves are short and very
dramatic. If you prefer a translation with a more
direct and contemporary style of language, use
Eugene Peterson's *The Message* or *The Good News
Bible*. If the teller of the story can possibly learn
the text of each passage and tell the story without
reading it from a book, that would be fantastic.

Pondering questions are provided after each reading.

STATION 1: THE EARTHQUAKE

READING

*Suddenly there was a great earthquake; for an angel
of the Lord, descending from heaven, came and
rolled back the stone and sat on it. His appearance
was like lightning, and his clothing white as snow.
For fear of him the guards shook and became like
dead men.*

Matthew 28.2-4

QUESTIONS

Have you ever seen anything scary and wonderful?
What if you had been a guard?

PRAYER

We praise you and we bless you, our risen Lord
    Jesus, King of glory,
for in your resurrection the power of love breaks
    open the earth
and frees life from death.
As the angel rolled away the stone from the prison of
    the tomb,
so release those imprisoned by life's misfortunes.
To you, Lord Jesus,

*whose life brings surprises beyond our wildest
    expectations,*
be honour and glory, now and for ever.
Amen.

[T&S 448]

STATION 2: MARY MAGDALENE FINDS THE EMPTY TOMB

READING

*Early on the first day of the week, while it was still
dark, Mary Magdalene came to the tomb and saw
that the stone had been removed from the tomb.
So she ran and went to Simon Peter and the other
disciple, the one whom Jesus loved, and said to
them, 'They have taken the Lord out of the tomb, and
we do not know where they have laid him.'*

John 20.1,2

QUESTIONS

What if you had arrived and found the stone gone?
What would you have said?

PRAYER

We praise you and we bless you, our risen Lord
    Jesus, King of glory,
for the love which drew Mary Magdalene to your
    tomb
to weep over your death.
As you broke into her grief with your death-shattering
    life,
so reach into our broken hearts with your promise of
    hope.
To you, Lord Jesus,
reaching into the deepest tombs of our despair,
be honour and glory, now and for ever.
Amen.

[T&S 449]

STATION 3: THE DISCIPLES RUN TO THE EMPTY TOMB

READING

*Peter and the other disciple set out and went towards
the tomb. The two were running together, but the
other disciple outran Peter and reached the tomb
first. He bent down to look in and saw the linen
wrappings lying there, but he did not go in. Then
Simon Peter came, following him, and went into the
tomb. He saw the linen wrappings lying there, and*

the cloth that had been on Jesus' head, not lying with the linen wrappings but rolled up in a place by itself. Then the other disciple, who reached the tomb first, also went in, and he saw and believed.

John 20.3-8

QUESTIONS

What if you had got there first?

How do you believe?

PRAYER

We praise you and we bless you, our risen Lord
*   Jesus, King of glory,*
for in you our God reveals the awesome power of
*   love that is stronger even than death.*
As in your dying you destroyed death,
so in your rising may we be raised above the trials
*   and torments of this world's woe.*
To you, Lord Jesus,
the fullness of your life revealed in an empty tomb,
be honour and glory, now and for ever.
Amen.

[T&S 450]

STATION 4: THE ANGEL APPEARS TO THE WOMEN

READING

The angel said to the women, 'Do not be afraid;
I know that you are looking for Jesus who was
crucified. He is not here; for he has been raised, as
he said. Come, see the place where he lay. Then go
quickly and tell his disciples, "He has been raised
from the dead, and indeed he is going ahead of
you to Galilee; there you will see him." This is my
message for you.'

So they left the tomb quickly with fear and great joy,
and ran to tell his disciples.

Matthew 28.5-8

QUESTION

What would you have told the disciples?

PRAYER

We praise you and we bless you, our risen Lord
*   Jesus, King of glory,*
for your resurrection overturns our expectations of
*   life*

and even your closest friends could not see truth
   before them.
As the angel helped them to grasp your triumph
and overcome their fear,
so help us to see your hand at work
   through the events that overtake us.
To you Lord, Jesus,
whose ways astonish beyond our imagining,
be honour and glory, now and for ever.
Amen.

[T&S 451]

STATION 5: JESUS MEETS THE WOMEN

READING

Suddenly Jesus met them and said, 'Greetings!'
And they came to him, took hold of his feet, and
worshipped him. Then Jesus said to them, 'Do not be
afraid; go and tell my brothers to go to Galilee; there
they will see me.'

Matthew 28.9-10

QUESTIONS

What would you have done?

Could you not have been afraid?

PRAYER

We praise you and we bless you, our risen Lord
*   Jesus, King of glory,*
for your simple word of greeting made the hearts of
*   the women leap with joy.*
Speak your word of love to those whose hearts are
*   broken,*
that they too may hear you, loving, beckoning call.
To you, Lord Jesus,
whose call summons us to life in all its fullness,
be honour and glory, now and for ever.
Amen.

[T&S 452]

STATION 6: THE ROAD TO EMMAUS

READING

As they came near the village to which they were
going, Jesus walked ahead as if he were going on. But
they [the two people he had met] urged him strongly,
saying, 'Stay with us, because it is almost evening and
the day is now nearly over.' So he went in to stay with
them. When he was at the table with them, he took

bread, blessed and broke it, and gave it to them. Then their eyes were opened, and they recognized him; and he vanished from their sight. They said to each other, 'Were not our hearts burning within us while he was talking to us on the road, while he was opening the scriptures to us?' That same hour they got up and returned to Jerusalem; and they found the eleven and their companions gathered together. They were saying, 'The Lord has risen indeed, and he has appeared to Simon!' Then they told what had happened on the road, and how he had been made known to them in the breaking of the bread.

Luke 24.28-35

QUESTIONS

Why did they invite Jesus in?

Would you have gone straight back to where you had just come from?

PRAYER

*We praise you and we bless you, our risen Lord
    Jesus, King of glory,
for you are with us,
even when our eyes are closed to your
    companionship.
Walk this day alongside the disconsolate and the
    despairing,
open their eyes to your gentle illumination,
and let their hearts burn within them at your invisible
    presence.
To you, Lord Jesus,
walking by our side,
be honour and glory, now and for ever.*
Amen.

[T&S 453]

STATION 7: JESUS APPEARS TO THE DISCIPLES

READING

While they were talking about this, Jesus himself stood among them and said to them, 'Peace be with you.' They were startled and terrified, and thought that they were seeing a ghost. He said to them, 'Why are you frightened, and why do doubts arise in your hearts? Look at my hands and my feet; see that it is I myself. Touch me and see; for a ghost does not have flesh and bones as you see that I have.' And when he had said this, he showed them his hands and his feet. While in their joy they were disbelieving and still wondering, he said to them, 'Have you anything here

to eat?' They gave him a piece of broiled fish, and he took it and ate in their presence.

Luke 24.36-43

QUESTION

What would you have said to Jesus?

PRAYER

*We praise you and we bless you, our risen Lord
    Jesus, King of glory,
for in your birth you were proclaimed the Prince of
    Peace,
and in your resurrection you breathe into your
    people peace beyond this world's understanding.
Be present, Lord, this day
with those whose lives are disfigured by conflict
and those whose hearts know no peace.
To you, Lord Jesus,
true bringer of the peace of heaven,
be honour and glory, now and for ever.*
Amen.

[T&S 454]

STATION 8: JESUS PROMISES THE SPIRIT

READING

Then he said to them, 'These are my words that I spoke to you while I was still with you – that everything written about me in the law of Moses, the prophets, and the psalms must be fulfilled.' Then he opened their minds to understand the scriptures, and he said to them, 'Thus it is written, that the Messiah is to suffer and to rise from the dead on the third day, and that repentance and forgiveness of sins is to be proclaimed in his name to all nations, beginning from Jerusalem. You are witnesses of these things. And see, I am sending upon you what my Father promised; so stay here in the city until you have been clothed with power from on high.'

Luke 24.44-49

QUESTION

What does a witness do?

PRAYER

*We praise you and we bless you, our risen Lord
    Jesus, King of glory,
for you promised that the same power*

that was at work when you were raised from the dead
would also be alive in us.
Show your power to those who are powerless;
reveal your love to those who feel unlovely
and through your Spirit enable all your people
 to be witnesses of your amazing grace.
To you, Lord Jesus,
daily renewing your people and your creation,
be honour and glory, now and for ever.
Amen.

[T&S 455]

STATION 9: JESUS COMMISSIONS THE DISCIPLES

READING

Jesus said to them again, 'Peace be with you. As the
Father has sent me, so I send you.' When he had said
this, he breathed on them and said to them, 'Receive
the Holy Spirit. If you forgive the sins of any, they are
forgiven them; if you retain the sins of any, they are
retained.'

John 20.21-23

QUESTION

What was Jesus sending the people for?

PRAYER

We praise you and we bless you, our risen Lord
 Jesus, King of glory,
for as you were sent by the Father, so you send us.
Equip your Church with the gifts to fulfil our calling
that we may love as you loved,
serve as you served,
and willingly follow wherever you lead.
To you, Lord Jesus,
gifting your people,
be honour and glory, now and for ever.
Amen.

[T&S 456]

STATION 10: JESUS BREATHES THE SPIRIT IN THE UPPER ROOM

READING

When Jesus had said this, he breathed on them and
said to them, 'Receive the Holy Spirit. If you forgive
the sins of any, they are forgiven them; if you retain
the sins of any, they are retained.'

John 20.22-23

QUESTION

What does it mean for sins to be forgiven?

PRAYER

We praise you and we bless you, our risen Lord
 Jesus, King of glory,
for you breathed new life into your astonished
 disciples.
As you turned unutterable grief into unshakeable joy,
so renew and refresh your turbulent world
and establish now your reign of peace.
To you, Lord Jesus,
transforming the pain of death into the fullness of life,
be honour and glory, now and for ever.
Amen.

[T&S 457]

STATION 11: JESUS REVEALS HIMSELF TO THOMAS

READING

Thomas (who was called the Twin), one of the
twelve, was not with them when Jesus came. So the
other disciples told him, 'We have seen the Lord.'
But he said to them, 'Unless I see the mark of the
nails in his hands, and put my finger in the mark of
the nails and my hand in his side, I will not believe.'
A week later his disciples were again in the house,
and Thomas was with them. Although the doors
were shut, Jesus came and stood among them and
said, 'Peace be with you.' Then he said to Thomas,
'Put your finger here and see my hands. Reach out
your hand and put it in my side. Do not doubt but
believe.' Thomas answered him, 'My Lord and my
God!' Jesus said to him, 'Have you believed because
you have seen me? Blessed are those who have not
seen and yet have come to believe.'

John 20.24-29

QUESTIONS

I wonder what Thomas felt when all the others
said 'We have seen the Lord?'
Why did Thomas say 'My Lord and my God!'

PRAYER

We praise you and we bless you, our risen Lord
 Jesus, King of glory,
for you come to us even in our doubting.
Through the sovereign work of your Spirit,

and the loving hands of your people,
continue to reveal yourself where doubt is stronger
    than faith.
To you, Lord Jesus,
whose resurrection body bears the murderous marks
    of the cross,
be honour and glory, now and for ever.
Amen.

[T&S 458]

STATION 12: JESUS APPEARS AT THE LAKESIDE

READING

*When they had gone ashore, they saw a charcoal fire
there, with fish on it, and bread. Jesus said to them,
'Bring some of the fish that you have just caught.' So
Simon Peter went aboard and hauled the net ashore,
full of large fish, a hundred and fifty-three of them;
and though there were so many, the net was not torn.
Jesus said to them, 'Come and have breakfast.' Now
none of the disciples dared to ask him, 'Who are
you?' because they knew it was the Lord. Jesus came
and took the bread and gave it to them, and did the
same with the fish.*

John 21.9-14

QUESTIONS

Why didn't the disciples dare to ask Jesus who he
was?

Why, do you think, they knew it was the Lord?

PRAYER

We praise you and we bless you, our risen Lord
    Jesus, King of glory,
for at the lakeside you showed concern for the daily
    needs of your disciples.
As you guided them to fill their nets with fish,
so guide all who are hungry
till their hunger is satisfied in you.
To you, Lord Jesus,
sharing with us the food of faith,
be honour and glory, now and for ever.
Amen.

[T&S 459]

STATION 13: JESUS CONFRONTS PETER

READING

When they had finished breakfast, Jesus said to

Simon Peter, 'Simon, son of John, do you love me
more than these?' He said to him, 'Yes, Lord; you
know that I love you.' Jesus said to him, 'Feed my
lambs.' A second time he said to him, 'Simon, son of
John, do you love me?' He said to him, 'Yes, Lord;
you know that I love you.' Jesus said to him, 'Tend
my sheep.' He said to him the third time, 'Simon, son
of John, do you love me?' Peter felt hurt because he
said to him the third time, 'Do you love me?' And he
said to him, 'Lord, you know everything; you know
that I love you.' Jesus said to him, 'Feed my sheep.
Very truly, I tell you, when you were younger, you
used to fasten your own belt and to go wherever you
wished. But when you grow old, you will stretch
out your hands, and someone else will fasten a belt
around you and take you where you do not wish
to go.' (He said this to indicate the kind of death by
which he would glorify God.) After this he said to
him, 'Follow me.'*

John 21.15-19

QUESTIONS

Why was Peter hurt?

How do you think Peter felt about going where he
did not wish to go?

PRAYER

We praise you and we bless you, our risen Lord
    Jesus, King of glory,
for even in the glorious victory of the resurrection
you understood the failure of Peter who denied you.
As you restored him to relationship with you,
remember all who feel downcast and worthless in
    this world's eyes
and give them a sense of purpose and value.
To you, Lord Jesus,
loving us despite our denial,
be honour and glory, now and for ever.
Amen.

[T&S 460]

STATION 14: JESUS AND THE BELOVED DISCIPLE

READING

*Peter turned and saw the disciple whom Jesus loved
following them; he was the one who had reclined
next to Jesus at the supper and had said, 'Lord, who
is it that is going to betray you?' When Peter saw
him, he said to Jesus, 'Lord, what about him?' Jesus
said to him, 'If it is my will that he remain until*

I come, what is that to you? Follow me!' So the rumour spread in the community that this disciple would not die. Yet Jesus did not say to him that he would not die, but, 'If it is my will that he remain until I come, what is that to you?'

John 21.20-23

QUESTION

Why do people spread rumours?

PRAYER

We praise you and we bless you, our risen Lord
    Jesus, King of glory,
for your single-minded commitment to your Father's
    will.
May we be free from distractions of envy or self,
that we might walk the way of the cross
and know the power of your risen life.
To you, Lord Jesus,
treading boldly on the path of suffering,
be honour and glory, now and for ever.
Amen.

[T&S 461]

STATION 15: JESUS APPEARS TO OVER FIVE HUNDRED AT ONCE

READING

For I handed on to you as of first importance what I in turn had received: that Christ died for our sins in accordance with the scriptures, and that he was buried, and that he was raised on the third day in accordance with the scriptures, and that he appeared to Cephas, then to the twelve. Then he appeared to more than five hundred brothers and sisters at one time, most of whom are still alive, though some have died.

1 Corinthians 15.3-6

QUESTION

Why is this important information?

PRAYER

We praise you and we bless you, our risen Lord
    Jesus, King of glory,
for your resurrection is a revelation to the whole
    world.
As you revealed yourself powerfully to so many,
reveal yourself now as the hope for our world.
To you, Lord Jesus,

going beyond the limits of our understanding,
be honour and glory, now and for ever.
Amen.

[T&S 462]

STATION 16: JESUS COMMISSIONS THE DISCIPLES ON THE MOUNTAIN

READING

Now the eleven disciples went to Galilee, to the mountain to which Jesus had directed them. When they saw him, they worshipped him; but some doubted. And Jesus came and said to them, 'All authority in heaven and on earth has been given to me. Go therefore and make disciples of all nations, baptizing them in the name of the Father and of the Son and of the Holy Spirit, and teaching them to obey everything that I have commanded you. And remember, I am with you always, to the end of the age.'

Matthew 28.16-20

QUESTIONS

What is authority?

How do you 'make disciples'?

PRAYER

We praise you and we bless you, our risen Lord
    Jesus, King of glory,
for you took the risk of passing your mission to frail
    disciples.
As you commissioned them to go into all the world,
so may all the world come to you, the King of
    nations.
To you, Lord Jesus,
with us to the end of the age,
be honour and glory, now and for ever.
Amen.

[T&S 463]

STATION 17: THE ASCENSION

READING

After his suffering he presented himself alive to them by many convincing proofs, appearing to them over the course of forty days and speaking about the kingdom of God. While staying with them, he ordered them not to leave Jerusalem, but to wait there for the promise of the Father. 'This', he said, 'is what you have heard from me; for John baptized with water, but you will be baptized with the Holy Spirit not many days from now.' So when they had come together, they asked him, 'Lord, is this the time when you will restore the kingdom to Israel?' He replied, 'It is not for you to know the times or periods that the Father has set by his own authority. But you will receive power when the Holy Spirit has come upon you; and you will be my witnesses in Jerusalem, in all Judea and Samaria, and to the ends of the earth.' When he had said this, as they were watching, he was lifted up, and a cloud took him out of their sight. While he was going and they were gazing up towards heaven, suddenly two men in white robes stood by them. They said, 'Men of Galilee, why do you stand looking up towards heaven? This Jesus, who has been taken up from you into heaven, will come in the same way as you saw him go into heaven.'

Acts 1.3-11

QUESTIONS

I wonder how they felt waiting in Jerusalem for forty days?

I wonder how they felt when Jesus vanished?

PRAYER

We praise you and we bless you, our risen Lord Jesus, King of glory,
for in your ascension you are crowned King of kings and Lord of lords.
As we worship you on your heavenly throne,
prepare our hearts for the coming of your Spirit.
To you, Lord Jesus,
who will come back in the same way you went up into heaven,
be honour and glory, now and for ever.
Amen.

[T&S 464]

STATION 18: PENTECOST

READING

When the day of Pentecost had come, they were all together in one place. And suddenly from heaven there came a sound like the rush of a violent wind, and it filled the entire house where they were sitting. Divided tongues, as of fire, appeared among them, and a tongue rested on each of them. All of them were filled with the Holy Spirit and began to speak

in other languages, as the Spirit gave them ability. Now there were devout Jews from every nation under heaven living in Jerusalem. And at this sound the crowd gathered and was bewildered, because each one heard them speaking in the native language of each. Amazed and astonished, they asked, 'Are not all these who are speaking Galileans? And how is it that we hear, each of us, in our own native language? Parthians, Medes, Elamites, and residents of Mesopotamia, Judea and Cappadocia, Pontus and Asia, Phrygia and Pamphylia, Egypt and the parts of Libya belonging to Cyrene, and visitors from Rome, both Jews and proselytes, Cretans and Arabs – in our own languages we hear them speaking about God's deeds of power.'

Acts 2.1-11

QUESTION

I wonder how it feels to be filled with the Holy Spirit?

PRAYER

We praise you and we bless you, our risen Lord Jesus, King of glory,
for you promised that your disciples would be baptized with the Holy Spirit
and now we see the fulfilment of your promise.
Fill us afresh with your Spirit today,
revive your Church,
and renew the face of the earth.
To you, Lord Jesus,
giving to your people the greatest gift of all,
be honour and glory, now and for ever.
Amen.

[T&S 465]

STATION 19: JESUS APPEARS TO SAUL

READING

Saul, still breathing threats and murder against the disciples of the Lord, went to the high priest and asked him for letters to the synagogues at Damascus, so that if he found any who belonged to the Way, men or women, he might bring them bound to Jerusalem. Now as he was going along and approaching Damascus, suddenly a light from heaven flashed around him. He fell to the ground and heard a voice saying to him, 'Saul, Saul, why do you persecute me?' He asked, 'Who are you, Lord?' The reply came, 'I am Jesus, whom you are persecuting. But get up and enter the city, and you will be told what you are to do.' The men who were travelling with him stood speechless because they heard the voice but saw no one. Saul got up from the ground, and though his eyes were open, he could see nothing; so they led him by the hand and brought him into Damascus. For three days he was without sight, and neither ate nor drank. Now there was a disciple in Damascus named Ananias. The Lord said to him in a vision, 'Ananias.' He answered, 'Here I am, Lord.' The Lord said to him, 'Get up and go to the street called Straight, and at the house of Judas look for a man of Tarsus named Saul. At this moment he is praying, and he has seen in a vision a man named Ananias come in and lay his hands on him so that he might regain his sight.' But Ananias answered, 'Lord, I have heard from many about this man, how much evil he has done to your saints in Jerusalem; and here he has authority from the chief priests to bind all who invoke your name.' But the Lord said to him, 'Go, for he is an instrument whom I have chosen to bring my name before Gentiles and kings and before the people of Israel; I myself will show him how much he must suffer for the sake of my name.' So Ananias went and entered the house. He laid his hands on Saul and said, 'Brother Saul, the Lord Jesus, who appeared to you on your way here, has sent me so that you may regain your sight and be filled with the Holy Spirit.' And immediately something like scales fell from his eyes, and his sight was restored. Then he got up and was baptized.

Acts 9.1-19

QUESTION

How would Saul have felt being led by the hand and unable to see?

PRAYER

We praise you and we bless you, our risen Lord Jesus, King of glory,
for you transformed the murderous Saul into the great apostle, Paul.
As you revealed yourself to him on the road to Damascus,
reveal yourself afresh to your people journeying through this life.
To you, Lord Jesus,
who can fill even the emptiest of lives,
be honour and glory, now and for ever
Amen.

[T&S 466–7]

Adults

As the Stations of the Resurrection in *Times and Seasons* are a relatively new way of celebrating, which many people will not have encountered before, it is worth taking some time to explore them during Eastertide.

Week 1

In the first week, follow the service as it is provided in *Times and Seasons*. Use it as an act of worship together. If you do not have any pictures available, just use the words. You can do this in a home sitting in a circle if you wish, with a leader to read the prayers and different people to read each of the Bible readings. You might like to use the time of reflection suggested within each station.

Week 2

In the second week you might decide how you would like to provide illustrations for these different stations. If you are a group that includes people who are artistically creative, that might be one way forward, but you could also use artefacts to create the stations. Some people might prefer to prepare a written account decorated in some way: you could use simple collage using photographs or pressed flowers and other items. Some might prefer to research already existing pictures using art books and the Internet. You will need to decide whether to go for diversity or coherence.

Start your time together with the opening prayers of the Stations Service, and end with the closing prayers.

Week 3

Start your time together with the opening prayers of the Stations Service, and end with the closing prayers.

Spend the time together working on the visual presentation of your stations.

Week 4

Install the stations in your chosen venue this week. Admire and criticize one another's work and make any necessary adjustments. Conclude by using the service again, moving from station to station.

Week 5

Invite guests and your congregation to attend and view your installation. Invite them to talk to the people who have prepared each station. You might also like to write something that your visitors can take home with them. Conclude with the service.

Week 6

By this time you will be very familiar with these texts. As the end of Eastertide approaches, concentrate on the later texts. You might like to gather together in the place where your stations are installed and spend your time each writing or responding to the later scenes: Ascension, Pentecost and the appearance of Jesus to Saul. Share your thoughts and conclude with prayers from the service in *Times and Seasons*.

The Stations at home

You might like to continue the notebook you began using for the Stations of the Cross. Or you might prefer to start a new notebook. Put the heading of each of the Stations of the Resurrection across a double-page spread as you did before (for the list, see p. 228). You can print the Bible text to go with it if you like. It might be harder to find newspaper cuttings for some of these stories: there are all sorts of conclusions to be drawn from this, and thinking about these is a work in itself. Maybe you would like to write about this. However, you can also use pictures, photographs and your own written thoughts and ideas to accompany the biblical texts.

The Stations in outreach

Consider ways in which you might bring the resurrection to your churchyard, graveyard or the area around your church, depending on your circumstances. Consider whom this might touch. If you are a city centre church with no substantial surrounding land, you may be speaking to shoppers, clubbers and passers-by. If you are a church with an extensive graveyard, then you will have the opportunity to speak of the resurrection to those who come to tend graves, in many stages of their bereavement. If your church does not have a graveyard, but has land around it, this may be a place where people come to seek quiet, space or just a place to eat their lunch.

You might like to team up with a group using the material for adults in this pathway, and consider whether immediately, or in years to come, an outside installation of the Resurrection Stations would be a possibility. A quick fix solution, for one year, would be to find pictures on the Internet and download these onto A3 sheets (if necessary you can tile them) and then get these laminated. Hang them by the entrance to your churchyard or space and prepare simple leaflets to accompany them. Then just leave them there – and trust God to speak through them.

Notes

How to use this book
1. *New Patterns for Worship*, Church House Publishing, 2002.
2. Alan Luff, Alan Dunstan, Paul Ferguson, Christopher Idle and Charles Stewart, *Sing God's Glory: Hymns for Sundays and Holy Days, Years A, B and C*, Canterbury Press, 2001.

Continuing to help the liturgy live
1. *Together for a Season: All-age seasonal resources for Advent, Christmas and Epiphany*, Church House Publishing, 2006, p. 1.
2. *Eucharistic Presidency*, Church House Publishing, 1997, section 4.45.
3. Howard Gardner, *Frames of Mind: The theory of multiple intelligences*, Basic Books, 1983; 1993.

Lent, Holy Week and Easter: Mapping the journey
1. See Eucharistic Prayer F (*Common Worship*, Church House Publishing, 2000, pp. 198–200).
2. See Eucharistic Prayer F.
3. A grace note is an extra note that adds an embellishment in a piece of music.
4. From the hymn 'Crown him with many crowns', Matthew Bridges 1800–1894 © Compilation The English Hymnal Company Ltd.

Lent
1. Prayers after Communion, *Common Worship*, p. 182.
2. Augustine of Hippo
3. From the hymn 'Crown him with many crowns' (see note 4 above).
4. An annual Christian Arts Festival that takes place in Cheltenham.
5. See Dennis Linn, Sheila Fabricant Linn, Matthew Linn, *Sleeping with Bread*, Paulist Press, 1995.
6. G. K. Chesterton, *Orthodoxy*, John Lane Co., 1908, reprinted 1995, Ignatius Press, San Francisco.

7. Benedicta Ward, *In Company with Christ: Through Lent, Palm Sunday, Good Friday and Easter to Pentecost*, SPCK, 2005.

Holy Week
1. J. S. Bach, 'At the Sepulchre' from *St John Passion*, Novello, p. 161 (libretto in a translation by T. A. Lacey).
2. Eamon Duffy, *The Stripping of the Altars*, Yale University Press, 1992.
3. From the hymn 'Ride on, ride on in majesty', H. H. Milman (1791–1868).
4. Philip Pullman, *The Amber Spyglass*, Scholastic, 2001.
5. C. S. Lewis's *The Lion, the Witch and the Wardrobe* was first published in 1950 and is available in various editions today, either on its own or as part of *The Chronicles of Narnia*.
6. W. H. Auden's 'Funeral Blues' ('Song IX' from *Two Songs for Hedli Anderson*) was first published in 1936.

Easter
1. Michael Perham, *The Sorrowful Way: the mind of Christ, the path of discipleship and the Christian year*, SPCK, 1998, p. 1011.
2. John Milton *Paradise Lost*, Book 1.
3. Eucharistic Prayer F, *Common Worship*, p. 199.
4. William Temple, *Readings in St John's Gospel*, Macmillan and Co. Ltd, 1955.
5. *Readings in St John's Gospel*, p. 307.
6. Shirley Erena Murray's hymn 'Because you live, O Christ' (1987) appears in the *New Century Hymnal*, Pilgrim, 1995.

Resources

Liturgical resources

Common Worship: Additional Collects, Church House Publishing, 2004

Common Worship: Daily Prayer, Church House Publishing, 2005

Common Worship: Christian Initiation, Church House Publishing, 2006

Common Worship: Times and Seasons, Church House Publishing, 2006

New Patterns for Worship, Church House Publishing, 2002

General resources

William Barclay, *The New Daily Study Bible*, available in separate volumes or as a complete set. See www.chbookshop.co.uk for further details

David Barton and Jo Fageant, *The Life of Jesus through the Eyes of an Artist*, Bible Reading Fellowship, 2004

David Barton and Jo Fageant, *The Life of Jesus through the Eyes of an Artist: Teacher's guide*, Bible Reading Fellowship, 2004

Jerome W. Berryman, *The Complete Guide to Godly Play* (5 volumes), Living the Good News, 2002

Frances Hodgson Burnett, *The Secret Garden*, Kingfisher, 2002

e. e. cummings, 'I thank you God for most this amazing', available in *One Hundred Selected Poems*, Grove, 1989

Trevor Dennis, *The Book of Books*, Lion, 2003

Eamon Duffy, *The Stripping of the Altars*, Yale, 1992

Eucharistic Presidency: A theological statement by the House of Bishops of the General Synod, Church House Publishing, 1997

Caroline Fairless, *Children at Worship: Congregations in bloom*, Church Publishing Inc., 2000

Good News Bible: The Bible in Today's English Version, American Bible Society, 1976, revised with inclusive language in 1992

Benjamin Gordon-Taylor and Simon Jones, *Celebrating the Eucharist*, The Alcuin Club/SPCK, 2005

Bob Hartman, *Telling the Bible: Stories and readings for sharing aloud*, Lion, 2004

Bob Hartman, *The Storyteller Bible*, Lion, 1995

David R. Holeton (ed.), *Renewing the Anglican Eucharist: Findings of the Fifth International Anglican Liturgical Consultation* (Dublin 1995), Grove, 1996

Gerard Manley Hopkins, 'God's grandeur' in *Poems and Prose*, W. H. Gardner (ed.), Penguin, 1974

Laurie Lee, 'April rise', available at www.poemhunter.com

C. S. Lewis *The Lion, the Witch and the Wardrobe*, HarperCollins, 2005

Dennis Linn, Sheila Fabricant Linn, Matthew Linn, *Sleeping with Bread*, Paulist Press, 1995

Eugene Peterson, *The Message*, NavPress, 2006

Philip Pullman, *The Amber Spyglass*, Scholastic, 2001

Richard Schechner, *Performance Theory*, Routledge, 1998

Nicola Slee, *Easter Garden*, Zondervan, 1990

Dean Lambert Smith, *The Lenten Tree: Devotions for children and adults to prepare for Christ's death and his resurrection*, Abingdon Press, 2004

William Temple, *Readings in St John's Gospel*, Macmillan, 1955

Michael Perry (ed.), *The Dramatised Bible*, Marshall Pickering, 1997

Benedicta Ward, *In Company with Christ: Through Lent, Palm Sunday, Good Friday and Easter to Pentecost*, SPCK, 2005

Murray Watts, *The Miracle Maker*, Hodder and Stoughton, 2000

Tom Wright, *Paul for Everyone: Romans*, SPCK, 2004

Tom Wright, *Paul for Everyone: The prison letters*, (second ed.), SPCK, 2004

Small group resources

The *Alpha* course (various volumes); more details from www.alpha.org

The *Emmaus* course (various volumes) published by
Church House Publishing; see www.e-mmaus.org.uk

Music resources

John L. Bell/Graham Maule, 'Darkness is gone' in
God Never Sleeps. More details of the CD and song
sheets from www.ionabooks.com

34 Songs for All Occasions, details available at
www.johnhardwick.org.uk

Jump Up if You're Wearing Red, Church House
Publishing, 1996

Junior Praise, Collins, 2004

Kidsource 1, Kevin Mayhew, 1999

Kidsource 2, Kevin Mayhew, 2002

Many and Great, Wild Goose Publications, 1990

Mission Praise, Marshall Pickering, 2005

Music for Common Worship 1, RSCM, 2000

Music for Common Worship 2, Music for the
President, RSCM, 2000

*Sing God's Glory: Hymns for Sundays and Holy
Days*, Canterbury Press, 2001

Songs and Prayers from Taizé, Continuum, 2002

Recorded music

Peter Gabriel, *Passion: Music For 'The Last
Temptation Of Christ'*, Geffen Records, 1989

'St Patrick's breastplate' (widely available on CD
hymn compilations)

Nina Simone 'Feeling good'/'It's a new dawn' on
Feeling Good, Mercury, 1998

'Ubi caritas et amor' on *Ubi Caritas*, Taizé, 2003

Vaughan Williams, *The Lark Ascending* is available
on several CDs, including Vaughan Williams, *The
Lark Ascending*; Walton, *Viola Concerto*; *Violin
Concerto*, EMI, 2004

Films

Babette's Feast, World Films 1988

Chocolat, Buena Vista 2000

Jesus of Nazareth, Incorporated Television Company/
Sir Lew Grade Productions 1977

The Easter Story Keepers, Authentic Video and DVD
2005

The Gospel according to St Matthew, Titanus
Produzione 1964

The Miracle Maker, directed by Derek W. Hayes and
Stanislav Sokolov 2000, available on DVD

The Passion of the Christ, Icon Productions/
Newmarket Films 2004

The Selfish Giant, Reader's Digest Association 1972

The Shawshank Redemption, Columbia Pictures 1994

Images

Michelangelo's *The Creation of Adam* (detail: God's
hand and the hand of Adam) can be found by typing
the artist and title into the images section of an
Internet search engine

Rembrandt's *The Return of the Prodigal Son* can be
seen at www.hermitagemuseum.org

Rublev's icon of *The Holy Trinity*: full details are at
www.wellsprings.org.uk/rublevs_icon/rublev.htm

*The Christ We Share: See Jesus through the eyes of
Christian artists from Africa, Asia and Latin America*
(includes free CD-ROM), CMS, USPG and The
Methodist Church

Web sites

www.biblia.com/mary: source of pictures of St Mary
the Virgin

www.domestic-church.com: an excellent source of
many religious symbols and ideas for their use in
activities at home

www.embody.co.uk

www.godlyplay.org and www.godlyplay.org.uk:
further information on Godly Play

www.labyrinth-enterprises.com

www.textweek.com

Other resources mentioned in the text

Caroline Fournier's scheme of readings can be found at:
www.domestic-church.com/CONTENT.
DCC/19990301/FRIDGE/readings.htm
for the 40 days of Lent

Holding cross: these are available from
www.spckonline.com in the gifts and cards section.

Instruments of the Passion: for more details see:

crown of thorns: www.en.wikipedia.org/wiki/
Crown_of_Thorns

cross: www.en.wikipedia.org/wiki/Christian_Cross

title: www.en.wikipedia.org/wiki/INRI

nails: www.en.wikipedia.org/wiki/Nail_
%28relic%29

five wounds: www.en.wikipedia.org/wiki/Five_
Wounds

Using the CD-ROM

Running the CD-ROM

Windows PC users:

The CD-ROM should start automatically. If you need to start the application manually, click on Start and select Run, then type d:\tfas.exe (where d is the letter of your CD-ROM drive) and click on OK.

The menu that appears gives you access to all the resources on the CD. No software is installed on to your computer.

Mac users:

The CD-ROM should start automatically. If you need to start the application manually, click on the CD icon on your desktop.

Viruses

We have checked the CD-ROM for viruses throughout its creation. However, you are advised to run your own virus-checking software over the CD-ROM before using it. Church House Publishing and The Archbishops' Council accepts no responsibility for damage or loss of data on your systems, however caused.

Copyright

The material on the CD-ROM is copyright © The Archbishops' Council 2007, unless otherwise specified. All industry trademarks are acknowledged. You are free to use this material within your own church or group, but the material must not be further distributed in any form without written permission from Church House Publishing. When using images or resources from the CD-ROM please include the appropriate copyright notice.

Outline services

The written resources require Adobe Acrobat Reader for display and printing. If Acrobat Reader is already installed on your computer, it will be loaded automatically whenever required. If you do not have it, you can install Acrobat Reader by downloading the Reader from www.adobe.com.

Graphics

The cartoons and images can be loaded into your own image editing software for resizing and printing. The files are within a folder called images on the CD. The CD includes both high and low resolution images; the low resolution images will be more suitable for older computer systems.

The hi-res images are in the TIFF format and are suitable for printing, projection and OHP acetates. The low-res images are in the JPEG format and are more suitable for web pages and other applications where high quality definition is not essential.

You can edit the JPEG and TIFF files with most image software. Remember that the image on the CD is 'read only'. If you want to edit the image, you should first copy it to your computer and remove its read-only attribute.

On the CD are two image browsers called IrfanView (for PC users) and Goldberg (for Mac users). These are free for non-commercial use and can be used to view the images and perform basic editing tasks such as resizing. IrfanView runs under most versions of windows (www.irfanview.com). The version of Goldberg supplied is compatible with Mac OSX 10.2 or later. Please note that Church House Publishing accepts no responsibility for the use of third-party software nor can we provide support for its use.

Error messages

You may receive the error message, 'There is no application associated with the given file name extension.' If you are trying to read one of the handouts, you should install the Adobe Acrobat Reader and try again. If you are opening one of the image files, your system does not have any software registered for use with JPEG or TIFF files. PC users should install the free copy of IrfanView and during its installation make sure you associate .TIF and .JPG extensions with IrfanView. For Mac users, the files should open in Preview and for editing functions install Goldberg.

If you do not have PowerPoint, install the free viewer from the same folder.

Links

The links to web sites require an active Internet connection. Please ensure you can browse the web before selecting an external web site.

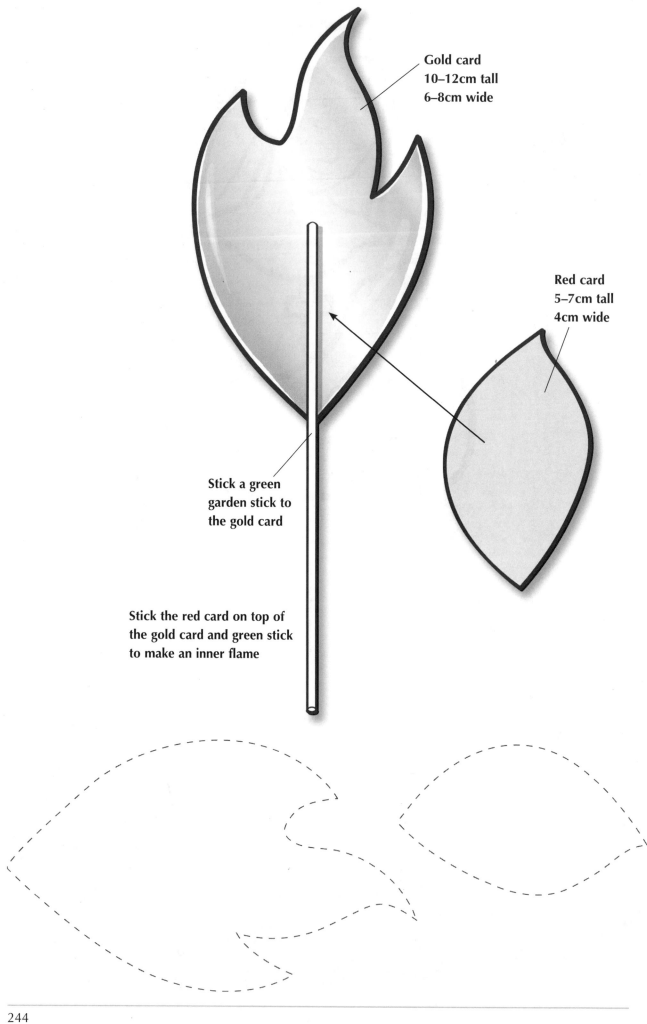

Gold card
10–12cm tall
6–8cm wide

Red card
5–7cm tall
4cm wide

Stick a green
garden stick to
the gold card

Stick the red card on top of
the gold card and green stick
to make an inner flame